T0114123

Between Mothers and Sons

Women Writers Talk About
Having Sons and Raising Men

Edited by
Patricia Stevens

A TOUCHSTONE BOOK
PUBLISHED BY SIMON & SCHUSTER
NEW YORK   LONDON   TORONTO   SYDNEY   SINGAPORE

FOR MY SONS

TOUCHSTONE
Rockefeller Center
1230 Avenue of the Americas
New York, NY 10020

Copyright © 1999 by Patricia Stevens

All rights reserved, including the right of reproduction
in whole or in part in any form

First TOUCHSTONE Edition 2001

TOUCHSTONE and colophon are registered
trademarks of Simon & Schuster, Inc.

Designed by Brooke Zimmer
Text set in Goudy
Manufactured in the United States of America

1   3   5   7   9   10   8   6   4   2

Permissions are on page 251.

The Library of Congress has cataloged the Scribner edition as follows:
Between mothers and sons: women writers talk about having
sons and raising men/[compiled] by Patricia Stevens.
p. cm.
1. Mothers and sons. 2. Women authors—Family
relationships.
I. Stevens, Patricia, 1944–   .
HQ755.85.B49 1999
306.874'3—dc21   98-44022
CIP
ISBN 978-0-6848-5072-6
0-684-85072-9 (Pbk)

CONTENTS

Between
Mothers and Sons

PATRICIA STEVENS

❦

Sons as Teachers: An Introduction

IT IS THE LATE 1980s, an unseasonably hot Saturday afternoon in May, with only a few weeks left in the school year. A water war is about to erupt in my backyard. Six boys ranging in age from ten to thirteen are dividing into two opposing groups. My sons, one on each side, will use their own personal rivalry to keep the battles escalating.

Before the first shot is fired, however, the boys sit in a shady spot on the grass and draw up the rules of conduct. They choose weapons. Each side has access to two battery-powered plastic Uzi's that can shoot a stream of water for a distance of twenty feet or more. They have a few ordinary water pistols and these, they decide, are acceptable weapons, though for a conflict of this magnitude, nearly obsolete.

Sitting at the dining room table near the open window that faces the backyard, I can hear their entire operating plan as I write out checks to pay the bills. Soon, my older son appears inside the house and begins rooting around in both of our junk drawers. "Do we have any balloons?" he asks. But before I can answer, he has opened the hall closet and is rummaging through a box on the floor.

"No balloons in there," I say.

"*Advertiser* bags," he says excitedly. Though his younger brother no longer delivers the free weekly paper filled with classifieds to every house in the neighborhood, we still have a large cache of the very thin clear plastic bags that had been an essential part of the paper route. My son runs into the bathroom, half fills one of the bags, and ties off the open end. *Yes!* It holds water but is thin enough to break on contact. Once he is outside again, another arms control agreement is carefully negotiated. Each side is limited to a specific number of preloaded *Advertiser* water bombs, but all combatants can refill their Uzi's and water pistols from strategically placed buckets at any time. There are also boundaries: our entire front and back yard; another boy's yard, which is two doors down; the unpaved alley that runs behind the houses on our side of the street.

After the boys fill the buckets and all their weapons from the hose in the backyard, they go off to their separate bases of operation, where they spend another fifteen minutes planning strategy. Then the war begins—the shouting, running, hiding, shrieking, and the splattering of water bombs—and soon all six boys are wearing soppy shorts, clinging T-shirts, and dripping hair. By this time I am at the window taking in as much of the war as I can. I feel the joy of seeing them completely delighted and absorbed by child's play on this perfect day, but I also feel more than just a physical distance as I stand back and watch this world of boys. A water war was something that I had clearly missed as a child. If my older brother's friends had tried to organize such a match, I would have either been excluded from it or quickly overpowered. If there were battles in our girl world, my friends and I fought them either with words or calculated silence. If we squabbled too long or if someone ended up in tears, my mother would use her dictatorial powers to call off the war and send the other girls home. It never occurred to my friends and me that we might fight for fun, that we would admit to a battle of any kind.

• • •

That day in May marked the first of several backyard water wars, but it was also the first time I had consciously envied my sons' obvious "otherness." Although before that time I had certainly admired what I saw as their boyness—both sons at two and three fearlessly racing their Big Wheels down our steep driveway; Jeremy at nine building a tree fort completely without adult interference; Jordan spending hours each day after school fishing for crawdads in the creek—I had little experience with, or interest in, any of these activities myself. Although I am certain there were girls from my generation who enjoyed digging in the mud, racing their bicycles, or collecting slimy, fat night crawlers to skewer on the end of a fishing hook, I was not one of them. Content with my girl world of jump rope and jacks, paper dolls and playing house, I saw no need to cross a gender boundary and had little reason to believe I might be missing something on the "other side." As an adult, however, this particular inexperience often left me puzzled over the habits of my sons and their friends, particularly their methods for satisfying a need for physical contact. Why, when more than two boys were together in my living room, did they have to spend so much time wrestling and rolling around on the floor? This behavior always left me in a state of agitation: *Can't you stop that for just one minute?*

My sons were born during the 1970s, a time when a large part of my self-image was in the process of being torn down and reconstructed under the light of the feminist movement. For a time I belonged to a consciousness-raising group, and the members of this association all believed in the same basic tenet: with regard to nature versus nurture, the scales tipped substantially on the side of nurture. As we sat around one another's living rooms on Wednesday nights (after cooking dinner, doing dishes, and getting the kids into their pajamas), we talked about two issues: our bodies and how to take care of them, and our men and how to get them to be more like us. There were six of us; we were close in age, from twenty-nine to thirty-five; and each of us had at least one young son, a toddler or preschooler, whom we were raising in our own image. It was the adult men who were the "other"—or so we wanted to believe.

Despite the obvious physical differences between them and us, when our sons were small, we believed that everything was environment. After all, we were in the middle of a revolution; we were finally asserting our power; and as we fought out the gender war, we were seizing control—blazing the trail for ourselves, our sons, and the future women in our sons' lives. The boys we were parenting would be cooks, housekeepers, caretakers, and good listeners; we would train them well—to be just like us. And even though most of us climbed into bed with one every night, an adult male was the enemy, and we would do whatever it took to stop our little boys from ever straying into the enemy camp.

At the co-op nursery school my sons attended, parents were required to work three hours a week. Except for the last year I was there, those parents were all women who thought of themselves as "enlightened" moms: We were raising our preschoolers by the unisex method. The girls (by God) would be doctors, astronauts, chemical engineers, *and* gourmet cooks; the boys would be gourmet cooks *and* doctors, astronauts, and chemical engineers. There was only one problem with this ideology: at the co-op nursery school, most of the boys stayed clear of the play kitchen, and most of the girls avoided the Tonka trucks. After much discussion among the parents, Barbara, the school's director, decided that each child should be encouraged at "free time" to become engaged in an activity that she or he did not ordinarily participate in. Parent helpers would usher the girls, who spent most of their time at the dress-up corner pretending to be princesses and brides, over to the Legos and send the boys, who always gravitated to digging outside in the sand, over to the dollhouse. This plan failed miserably, of course, as the three- and four-year-olds could not be persuaded to alter their daily routines, but no mother would dare to suggest that the cause of the failure might be some inherent gender . . . *differences*.

•   •   •

As time passed, and I could see that my sons, despite me, were developing a number of stereotypical masculine interests, my rigid ideology gave way. Getting older, getting divorced, and acquiring more life experience helped in this process, but I credit my sons with moving me toward a more humanistic view. Each of my sons, in his own way, made me see that by trying to create a dream child in my own image, I was also creating mile-high hurdles and asking him to jump over them. It took many years and a great deal of painful conflict to learn to be aware of, to respect, and to honor my sons' unique and separate identities. The challenge for mothers of sons is to realize that because we do not share a sexual identity, that because we have not grown up in a male body, we cannot presume to understand everything there is to know about our sons' world. There is as much to learn from the experience of raising young men as there is to teach young men about what it is to be female.

The idea for this anthology came to me one quiet Sunday afternoon when, with both of my sons in college, I decided to tackle a project I'd been avoiding for years. From a dusty storage room, I brought two large cardboard cartons filled to overflowing with the boys' old schoolwork down to my living room and began sorting. I planned to end up with two much smaller boxes, one for each son, that would be representative of his school years. I saved only a small portion of the worksheets and timed math tests (the ones with the perfect scores, of course), but I lingered over each piece of art and writing: my older son's second-grade journal, illustrated to show that his father no longer lived with us; a bound collection of fifth-grade empathy cards expressing concern over the accident in the school yard that resulted in my younger son's broken arm; cartoon drawings of warplanes dropping their bombs on a company of stick figures below; construction-paper Mother's Day cards, complete with white-paste-encrusted paper doilies.

Behind each item was a story, and in the days and weeks after I had finished this project, I began to think more and more about how my life over a period of twenty years (thirteen of those as a single parent) had been shaped by these two male children. While they were at home and I was completely occupied getting through each food-shopping cycle, each soccer or baseball season, each school year, I did not have time to step back and see what these boys had taught me. My focus was always on how much I had to prepare, advise, and instruct *them*. As I sent each son off to college, I lamented, *If only I could have one more year, I could get through all the lessons I didn't have time for*.

But when I finally had the house to myself and had accepted the reality that there were some lessons that would never be taught, I began to see how much my children had influenced me. The best times for the three of us together, I recalled, were extended car trips where we drove halfway across the country and camped along the way. I remembered that even when they were thirteen and fifteen, before either of them had a license to drive, I felt in many ways protected by these budding young men, who by then had already begun to tower over me. They taught me to be more adventurous (*Let's see where this unpaved road leads us*), to face fear head-on (*Bears are as afraid of people as people are of them*), to be less uptight when things don't go as planned (*So what if we've forgotten the tarp that goes over the tent roof and the rain is coming in through the net ceiling*). They taught me to respect and admire differences, showed me that I can marvel at the intensity of their interest in fly-fishing or rebuilding car engines when I have no inclination to take up either of those myself. Or, as Deborah Galyan says in "Watching *Star Trek* with Dylan," "I want to honor all that he is, without denying his essential architecture, the structures and circuitry that shape his dreams." I also learned from my sons that it was not necessary to compromise their maleness when promoting my feminist leanings. In "Soldier Son," Janet Burroway puts it this way: "I'm forced to be aware of my own contradictions in his presence: a feminist often charmed by his machismo."

·   ·   ·

When I began this anthology, I wanted to put together the book that I had so often looked for when my sons were growing up. Throughout the child-rearing years, I craved the stories I heard from other mothers, particularly mothers of sons. Although there seemed to be an extensive literature on mother-daughter relationships and another growing body of work on fathers and daughters, I could find few printed stories about the mother-son relationship—the very foundation of all female-male connections.

This silence, I discovered, could be broken. In response to my letter inviting the writers in this anthology to contribute an essay, I received only the most enthusiastic responses. I had asked these writers to commit to the collection by sending me only a brief description of their proposed essays. The proposals came back to me quickly, the writers thanking me for giving them the opportunity to write about their sons.

This anthology, I believe, questions the current mythology about mothers of sons as controlling, meddling, overly protective, smothering, punitive, or emotionally distant. By diffusing these cultural myths, the narratives in this collection also create new metaphors for this intense attachment. These are personal stories by mothers who have all come to acknowledge and celebrate their sons' individuality. They have also acknowledged the struggle they face in coming to understand their sons' "otherness." (*Who is this male child who came out of my female body?*) My hope is that this book will break the silence surrounding this powerful relationship.

Patricia Stevens
Iowa City, Iowa
March 1999

SALLIE TISDALE

𝄢

Scars;
In Four Parts

I

wound (*woond*) n. [OE. *wund*] an injury in which
the skin or other tissue is broken, cut, torn, etc.

Four years ago he was born and everything changed. Daily we
leave jobs, friends, lovers, but the child always comes along.
When the going gets rough, my son and I can't call it quits and
cut our losses. I can't pack a bag, make a break for it, find a more
compatible child. The contract cannot be broken.

We are strangely entangled. When I wake from a bad dream
without a sound, he wakes in the next room and cries for me.
Between us there is no shame, no holding back. I take risks with
him I wouldn't dare take with anyone else. I treat him with
rough impatience, with all the bile I hide from friends and lovers
for fear of losing them. I am less tolerant of deviation, more
injured by separation. We fight, and then make up with a tentative, weary kiss. I demand so much: loyalty, obedience, faith.
And he gives me all I demand, and more—he thinks me beautiful; he wants to grow up to be just like me. And I am bound to
fail him, and bound to lose him. Strangers' hands will stroke
where I stroke now, and already I'm jealous of this secret future
apart from me.

I quail at the mistakes I'm bound to make, what I'll saddle him with, what the price for each of us will finally be. For nothing is free. Daily the gap between us grows, in tiny steps. He is not mindful of it—but I am. Oh, I am. I'll give the world a son, heavy with the grief of giving him at all. Then and after, he'll drift in and out of my view, keeping secrets, neglecting me, while I watch from a distance, unrequited.

My mother shows up, startling me, when I speak to my son. I repeat what she told me, the phrases and platitudes, in the same tone of voice and inflection I heard as a child. She is my forebear; I am his inheritance, and will prevail despite his efforts. Years from now I'll show up, a sudden surprise.

Could my own mother have felt this fierce love for me? I treat her so casually. If she ever felt this way it seems she should be grieved—bereft by my distance. Can it be that she misses me? We don't speak of such things: our closest contacts are narrowly averted, sudden swerves from danger. Will it be the same for my son and me, the boy who now crawls like a spoiled child-prince across my lap?

"When I grow up," he tells me, "you'll be my baby."

2

dehiscence (de-his' ens) n. [L. *dihiscere, to gape*] A
bursting open, as of . . . a wound . . .

He's tall now, and lean: when he comes running toward me, breathless from some grand injustice or new idea, I see his ribs pressing against the skin, light and shadow. He takes deep, thoughtless breaths, free of blemish, taut and promising. He has my brother's face, a handsome face, and he wears his lucky muscles with negligence and not a whit of gratitude. He is eight years old.

Sudden sufficiency. What binds us is less visible, as though we'd been cloven in two. I would not have thought it possible to feel so halved. I can wonder now what it is like to be him—wonder, and know I'll never know. What does he think in a privacy

I can hardly bear, a privacy that seems entirely unfair? I am still the dictator of this tiny country; he is still my subject, but he dreams of revolution.

I may not kiss him in front of others anymore. He holds the car door for me, calls me "ma'am," with a giggle. He has great white teeth, dark circles below his eyes, a scratch on his cheek, dirt in the lines of his neck. He wants his hair cut "like Elvis Presley," he wants it cut "like Michael Jackson," he wants a Mohawk. He sings commercial jingles for hamburgers and jeans and toothpaste while he builds elaborate block constructions; he strews his room with Viewmasters and action figures ("They're not *dolls*, Mom," he says in irritation) and books and dirty socks and sheets. He is, above all, busy; I am tired. "You are," he tells me, "more beautiful than the women in *Playboy*," and he's out the door before I can ask where he saw *Playboy*.

How does he know the exact inflection? He has the same disgust and injured dignity I felt all those years ago, dying a thousand deaths in the face of my mother's twittering concerns. He comes into his own and it is my turn to be out-of-date, to be shocked, to drone on long after he ceases to hear me. I am, he tells me, so *old*.

The neighbor boys tease him and he runs home in a paroxysm of despair. "No one likes me," he sobs, and lends to his crying a thorough attention. What courage children have. I lead him to the dentist and he climbs shakily into the great chair, looks at me and asks me to spare him this. I won't; seeing my refusal, he turns away. He wants me to keep him a baby; he doesn't know that I would if I could. Already *I* am separate. He looks at me and sees—only me.

He is an infant again, arms around my thighs, moaning with love, whining for cereal, a story, my lap. But he's too lanky, too long for my lap; his elbows get in the way of the book. Then he longs for the mysterious pleasures of adulthood: freedom, mobility, explanations. But his brow furrows when he calculates the cost.

At night he is drenched in protest. He licks his teeth clean, stumbles out of the bathroom in a dirty T-shirt and yesterday's underwear, crawls over the mess on the floor of his room, and hides his stuffed bunny shamefully under the covers. I wait. And when he falls into the humid sleep of children, that greenhouse dark, I slip stealthily in beside him and stroke his honey hair. He sprawls out, clutching the bunny; I balance on the edge, listening to the ruffled quiver of his breaths. I stroke the fear, my fear, of his life, his death. When I contemplate the space he takes up, how vast its emptiness would be, my heart shakes like a rabbit in the jaws of the wolf. I watch his face turned soft with sleep, the smile that skips across his face as he turns smug and safe, and I can see that he's dreaming. He dreams without me now; we dream different dreams.

The balance is shifting. I withdraw sometimes; I want to read my book or be alone when he craves my attention. He will always live with me, he says, or perhaps next door. A transparent gift of beauty is evolving in his bones and skin, beauty made of equal parts grace and pain; I see that he will have a face of triumphant perfection if he wants. And I see the bruises rising under his skin from life's blows. I know he won't live next door, and I'm glad. I don't think I can bear to watch. Right now, I can't remember life without him—I can't remember *myself* without him, but the time will come.

I put my book aside and wander to his room to watch him play. I find him reading a book, curled in a corner.

"Would you mind leaving, Mom?" he says, hardly glancing up. "I feel like being alone."

3

inflammation (in' fle ma/shen) n. [<l. inflammation—
see inflame] redness, swelling, pain, tenderness, heat

I wait in the car in the grocery store parking lot, watching the bright automatic doors in my rearview mirror. It is almost ten o'clock at night, much later than usual for me to be out shopping. For fifteen years I've been confined to childish hours. But everything changes.

I see him walk out the middle set of doors, which slide silently apart and then close behind him. He is tall, several inches taller than me, slender, graceful, arrogant. He wears his thick hair in a high tuft, dyed boot-black, and his black leather, silver-studded jacket swings open with each long step.

I used to have crushes on boys like him.

We all have blows—we learn to expect a few, to roll in the force of life's fist. That awful job, that last paycheck, the broken heart, the broken nose. All the broken promises no one has even made yet—wounds that can't be helped. I don't have to fear failing him anymore—I already have. What's done is done.

But I hadn't expected this.

I hadn't expected to be knocked to my knees in grief when he marches out after I tell him to stay, when he slams the door and disappears, and I drive through dark streets seeking him, and find him smoking in the park with the silent, leggy girlfriend who won't speak to me at all. I draw myself up, demand *decency*, *respect*; they stare, and whisper to each other.

And I hadn't expected the sorry business of petty crime. He's been arrested for shoplifting—for stealing candy bars, for stealing cigarettes, for stealing condoms. I drive to juvenile hall again and face the disapproving eyes behind bulletproof glass, and sign the papers, and wait outside until I'm joined by a raggedy, rude, foul-mouthed boy I hardly know. We drive home in silence and as we walk in the door I tell him to wash the dishes and he says, "No," and I say it again and he refuses again and then he adds, mockingly, "And I don't want to have to say it again." And suddenly I'm soaked with white rage, a face-slapping high-dive, and I'm inches from his face brandishing the nearest object, yelling, "Don't you dare, don't you dare, don't you *dare* speak to me that way!"

When we're calm, I can see he thinks I miss the point, the urgent momentum of growing up. I seem to have no ground,

nothing to rely upon. He calls me a "disagreeable old hag" at the
dinner table and suddenly it makes me laugh. It's all so absurd. I
saw my parents' anguish in my own small crimes from a cool distance; I remember their stupefaction. I drew up painful words for
them deliberately like poison into a syringe. Children grow into
strangers who disappoint and perplex us, having long wakened
to disillusionment with us. They seem oblivious to our loss—
after all, they've lost nothing. We are only their parents. And
now it's my turn and I am so sorry now for what I did then.

He disappears for three days and I cannot find him. The fear is
horrible, sickening; the remorse and guilt meaningless, confused. Then his girlfriend's mother calls to tell me he's staying
there because we "kicked him out," and I try to tell her it's not
true, to send him home so he will work it out with me, and she
refuses. She believes him, his tales. I ask her not to shelter him
from this. "I'm going to take care of him," she tells me. "*I* like
him."

When he finally returns, we fight round after round, and
there's no bell. Every victory is a Pyrrhic victory. *Baby, I want to
say, baby love, I don't know what to do. Show me what to do.* Harsh
words again, the stomp of heavy boots up the stairs. From two
floors above me he lets loose a deep-throated cry, an animal cry,
and then the noise of something heavy thrown with what seems
an irrevocable, rending crash.

4

> *scar* (skar) *n.* [< MFr. < LL. < Gr. *eschara*, *orig. fire-
> place]* a mark left after a wound, burn, ulcer, etc. has
> healed

Like all the other scars, this one is slowly filling in, closing off.
Scars may be tender, or numb, but they are always there. Scars
change the shape of things—they wrinkle, tighten, shorten
things. I brought this person into the world and everything
turned upside down and all that's happened since has been in

some way connected to that event, his birth. The parent-child bond, I know, is truly bondage, and its end is in many ways a liberation, an enormous relief. Here he comes, hat in hand, to claim himself and go.

He is almost twenty-one, towering above me, his voice booming on the telephone. He is gorgeous. He is no virgin; he has learned to love love. He is kind to his little sister, worries about his carefree older brother. Every day, changes: he drops out of high school, grabs a quick diploma at the community college, makes plans, finds a job, is shockingly responsible. He gets a checking account and an 800 number and big ideas: conspiracy theories and politics, tales of hidden alien artifacts and government cabals. His union goes on strike and he walks the picket line with all the other workingmen. And then he finds a house, and moves out, miles away. He calls—righteous, indignant, a defender of the weak. I bite my lip not to laugh and cry at once; oh God, it's the way I was at that age, it's exactly the way I was.

He absents himself delicately from my life.

Visiting one day, he stops me in the hall without warning, dragging his foot and looking at the floor, and mumbles, "I'm sorry," and I ask him for what and he says, "Because I was so hard," and without meeting my eyes he reaches down from his height to hug me awkwardly and adds, "I love you, Mom," and dashes down the stairs and is gone, again.

ANNE LAMOTT

9)

Operating Instructions

September 12

Sam is two weeks old today. His umbilical cord fell off. I'm probably supposed to feel like the cord is very lovely and natural, but I must say I'm going to be able to live without it somehow. It's like something a longhaired cat would get stuck in her tail.

Sam is unbelievably pretty, with long, thin, Christ-like feet. I told my friend Carpenter this and he said, "It's an often difficult world out there, and it's good to have long, grippy feet." I've decided the reason Sam's so gorgeous is that God knew that I wouldn't have been able to fall in love with this shitting and colicky little bundle if he looked like one of those E.T./Don Rickles babies.

I'm crazy tired. I feel as stressed out by exhaustion as someone who spent time in Vietnam. Maybe mothers who have husbands or boyfriends do not get so savagely exhausted, but I doubt it. They probably end up with these eccentric babies *plus* Big Foot skulking around the house pissed off because the mom is too tired to balance his checkbook or give him a nice blow job.

This is strictly sour grapes. I wish I had a husband. I wish Sam had a dad. I hope God sends him one someday. It is a huge thing not to have. Some friends of mine are having a baby in a couple of months, and they already know it is a boy and that he has only one whole arm, which of course is also a huge thing not to have. They are also going to call their baby Sam. The other Sam's father and I were both teaching at a writing conference in Napa a month ago, right before I delivered. I was massively pregnant, looking and feeling like a skinny, ugly teenager with a giant baby in her tum. Even the oldest black people at my church had been laughing when they saw me the week before. The other Sam's father and I were floating around a swimming pool, and I was thinking about how sad I feel sometimes because my dad is dead and he won't ever get to know Sam, at least on this funny blue marble. Then I got sad because Sam wasn't going to have some Alan Alda/Hugh Beaumont dad hanging around, throwing him up into the air and teaching him how to do manly things, like how to pee standing up and how to fix the toaster oven. Thinking about the other Sam without much of a left arm and of course no left hand, my chest just ached. I pictured the two Sams at the fiction workshop the following year, hanging out together while we taught our classes, and my Sam studying the other Sam and saying, "So where's your arm?" and the other baby shrugging and saying, "I don't know; where's your dad?"

September 15

There are a couple of things I want to remember about Sam's earlier days, his youth, now that he's kind of an old guy with no umbilical cord. The first thing happened the day my friend Peg and I brought him home from the hospital, during what for me felt like the most harrowing ride a person could take through San Francisco. The first time we hit a pothole, I thought, Well, that's that, his neck just snapped; we broke him. He's a quadriplegic now. But we did get him home safely, and Pammy was there to greet us.

She and Peg are Sam's godmothers. Peg is big and athletic and deeply spiritual, sober in Alcoholics Anonymous for three years now. Toward the end of her drinking and using, she'd done

so much cocaine one night that she woke up in a motel in Monterey with her face glued to the pillow by all the blood that had
poured out of her nose while she slept. But she still didn't think
she had a real problem, and she didn't get clean for another few
months. I *like* that in a girl. That's pretty much how I was.
Whereas Pammy, with these two hideous falling-down-drunk
parents, has a couple of glasses of wine every few nights, and
maybe pours a third glass, and then leaves most of it. That used
to drive me crazy. It would seem like an act of aggression. I'd ask,
"Why don't you finish that wine?" and she'd say, "I just don't
really want it," and I'd ask why, and she'd say, "I'm already starting to *feel* it," and I'd look at her like I was going to have to take
her back to the asylum in the morning.

Anyway, being there with Sam and Pammy and Peg was a
dream come true, except that I was also having little blips of
fear. I had all these nightmare images, left over from the last few
months of my pregnancy, of what a petri dish my house was.
Largely because we live under the redwoods, everything ends up
breeding lots of mold and spores, and even though Peg had hired
her housekeeper to scour the place for me, I was worried. It's
such a drafty old house, rust red, a hundred years old, with three
stories. We're on the bottom floor, and you have to climb up fifty
stone steps to get to it. It's beautiful, everything is green when
you look out any of the windows, and there's a creek in the front
yard. Deer come through the yard nearly every day, and you hear
a million birds, and butterflies fly by, but my apartment is really
funky. It's got one big long living room with massive built-in
bookcases everywhere, and then a smallish kitchen, and then a
tiny little bedroom with an elevated platform for the mattress
and about five square feet of floor. Through its windows you see
so much green beauty that you don't mind how cramped it is.
There are little holes and gaps everywhere, and lots of spiders.
Of course, there was also the kitty, who I thought might be a
problem. She has been so spoiled for the last five years, like some
terrible feline Leona Helmsley, that I felt sure she would sneak

into Sam's crib late at night and put a little pillow over his face or at the very least suck his milky breath out of him, like in the old wives' tales.

Sam had a slight fever following his circumcision, and his pediatrician at Mount Zion had made me promise to take the baby's temperature when I got home to make sure the fever was going down. I was scared that there would be terrible complications from the circumcision and that I had, after all, made the wrong decision and now he would get a brain fever and need emergency surgery on his wienie. Although about half of my family and friends had made circumcision seem about as humane as nipple piercing, it had been a relatively easy decision to make at the time. To begin with, I had read that penile cancer occurs almost exclusively in uncircumcised males, that uncircumcised men have much more frequent urinary tract infections, and that their female lovers have a much higher rate of cervical cancer. So there were those medical reasons, but there was also the matter of keeping the damn thing clean—you would have to cleanse the foreskin daily with, one supposed, Q-Tips and 409. Who's got the time? One of my best friends had had her baby circumcised ten years ago against much protest from her family. It then turned out that her son was terribly uncoordinated as a young boy. She told me that circumcision was the best decision she ever made: "I had a terrible time teaching him to wash his hands," she said.

Then there was the matter of aesthetics. I mean to cast no aspersions on the presentability of anybody's wing-wang, and I certainly don't mean to imply that all uncut males look like they're from Enid, Oklahoma, but I've got to say that I prefer the look of the circumcised unit. The uncircumcised ones look sort of marsupial, or like little rodents stuck in garden hoses. And the feel of the uncut ones is a little disconcerting, with all that skin to peel back and then the worry that it won't stay, that it will swallow the missile head right back up. Women's nerves aren't bad enough as it is? So for any number of reasons, it seemed obvious to me that circumcision was a great invention—as my friend Donna put it, "It pretty much restores one's faith in Judaism, doesn't it?" And while I had not thrust my baby into the doctor's arms urging, "Cut! Cut!" I had with a trembling bottom lip handed him over.

So there we were, me and my feverish little baby, with Pammy and Peg puttering around the house putting things away. I put Sam facedown on my lap and took off his diaper and even his little T-shirt, so he looked very sweet and vulnerable, like a chicken. Right then the kitty ran into the house and straight through the living room into the kitchen, very deliberately keeping her eyes off Sam and me. I was putting petroleum jelly on the thermometer when she tore from the kitchen, back through the living room, and out the front door, still with her eyes averted, as if she had little blinders on. A minute later, I inserted the thermometer into Sam's rectum. I think it surprised him a little bit, and right at that exact second the kitty tore back into the house and ran up to the couch to check out the new arrival. In the next few seconds, with the kitty's eyes on us, shit began spouting volcanically out of the baby's bum, and I started calling for help. The shit just poured voluminously out of Sam while the kitty looked up at me with total horror and disgust, like "You have *got* to be kidding, Annie, this one's *broken*." Like she had put her trust in me to pick one up at the pound, and this was the best I could do.

For the next few hours, she avoided him, as though the image of the shit storm were too painful and disgusting for her to forget, but by that night, she was butting her head against his and licking his ears. We all slept together on the big queen-sized futon in the living room, where it's warmer.

September 18

Pammy came by for tea this afternoon, as she does almost every single day. We decided that giving Sam sponge baths makes him seem too much like an outpatient, so he had his first real bath today. He took it like a man. We still dress him almost exclusively in these baby bags, one-piece legless outfits with little rip cords at the bottom. It feels good to say "we," even if that means me and my best friend instead of me and a man. I could not have gone through with this, could not be doing it now, without Pammy. In the early evenings she returns to her husband, whom she adores, but she says she counts the time until she can be with Sam again. I'm never ready for her to leave. She's my partner. In twenty-five years of friendship we've never even kissed on the lips, but in certain ways it feels like she's my lover and she's helping me raise my baby.

After Pammy went home, Sam and I played with his key chain for a long time, and it seemed to mesmerize him. He fell asleep and I finally got to eat a Häagen-Dazs bar with toasted almonds that Emmy and Big Sam had brought me earlier in the day. It made me feel that I was on the road to some small sense of normalcy. Then I broke every rule in the book by picking him up when he was sound asleep so that I could rock him in the rocking chair, holding him and smelling his clean hair and skin. I could not take my eyes off him. He didn't wake.

His key chain is made of five big plastic keys on a cord with a heart-shaped key ring. I hold up each color key for him to study, and I always say the exact same thing: "The blue one is the key to the sky, the green one is the key to the lawn, the yellow one is the key to the mustard, the red one is the key to the car, and the pink one is the key to my heart."

September 19

Sam's three-week birthday is today. There's a big party scheduled for this afternoon, with Pammy, my brother Steve, Julie, who lives in the apartment upstairs, Sam, the kitty, and me. I'm sure a fabulous time will be had by all.

Sam's so beautiful and I feel such a desperate love and protectiveness that my chest tightens with it.

People kept trying to prepare me for how soft and mushy my stomach would be after I gave birth, but I secretly thought, Not this old buckerina. I think most people undergoing chemo secretly believe they won't lose their hair.

Oh, but my stomach, she is like a waterbed covered with flannel now. When I lie on my side in bed, my stomach lies politely beside me, like a puppy.

We watched Mr. Rogers this morning. He was in an ebullient mood. When he was changing from his street shoes into his sneakers, he tossed the first one into the air with a much wilder sort of jauntiness than usual, and then caught it, and then acted so pleased with himself that he actually looked crazy. Pammy says he must have gotten laid.

Sam and I sit around and stare at each other. I call it putting on the Sam channel. I talk to him constantly—I say, "A bunch of bigheads are coming over this afternoon to celebrate your birthday," and he looks up into my face like maybe my freckles are forming themselves into familiar letters.

He's so fine all day, so alert and beautiful and good, and then the colic kicks in. I'm okay for the first hour, more or less, not happy about things but basically okay, and then I start to lose it as the colic continues. I end up incredibly frustrated and sad and angry. I have had some terrible visions lately, like of holding him by the ankle and whacking him against the wall, the way you "cure" an octopus on the dock. I have gone so far as to ask him if he wants me to go get the stick with the nails, which is what my friend Kerry says to her dogs when they are being especially bad. I have never hurt him and don't believe I will, but I have had to leave the room he was in, go somewhere else, and just breathe for a while, or cry, clenching and unclenching my fists. I have four friends who had babies right around the time I did, all very eccentric and powerful women, and I do not believe that any of them are having these awful thoughts. Of course, I know they're not all being Donna Reed either, but one of the worst things about being a parent, for me, is the self-discovery, the being face-to-face with one's secret insanity and brokenness and rage. Someone without children, who thinks of me as being deeply spiritual, said the other day that motherhood gave me the opportunity to dance with my feelings of inadequacy and anger, and my automatic response was to think, Oh, go fuck yourself, you New Age Cosmica Rama dingdong head—go dance with *that* one.

I have always known, or at least believed, that way down deep, way past being kind and religious and trying to take care of everyone, I was seething. Now it's close to the surface. I feel it race from my center up into my arms and down into my hands, and it scares the shit out of me.

I hope that somehow I am and will be a wonderful mother for Sam. Perhaps I should stop asking him about the stick with the nails. I want him to grow up to have a lot of faith and to be a very gentle person, and also to be militantly on his own side, as I have come to be. I hope he grows up to be caring and amused and political, someone who does not give up on the ideals of peace and justice and mercy for everyone. Of course, on the other hand I am already actively and consciously poisoning his mind against Republicans.

He has the most beautiful hair, his dad's hair; I feel about this like the oldest women at my church, who cry out, "THANK ya, Jesus, THANK ya." I grew up feeling like E.T. with an Afro. It was too hard having this crazy hair. I still don't think I look like a white person—I look like a very pale person of color.

Sam's father has white-people's hair. He is very tall and nice-looking, although his character is a bit of a problem, in that he doesn't seem to have a great deal of it. This is probably not true—I think maybe I'm a little angry. Sometimes it feels awful, the fact that he has so entirely rejected both of us. We were friends. We slept together several times a week for several months. We talked on the phone four and five times a day, every single day. I was finishing up my book, the one that will be out in another month. We spent Christmas Eve together, Christmas morning. He gave me, ironically, a wonderful extra-large white T-shirt that has an airbrushed mama cow nuzzling her baby on it. Then two days later I found out I was pregnant, and we never spoke in a friendly way again. I don't really get it, how he can know that there is a child of his in the world and yet have absolutely nothing to do with him. Peg keeps reminding me of something that her alkie pals over in AA like to go around saying—more will be revealed.

He was so furious when I even considered keeping the baby that he temporarily lost his mind. He was calling six and seven times a day to tell me what a piece of shit I was, how unethical it was of me—and how I actually *couldn't* have the baby because he had supported Planned Parenthood all these years (which, the more I think about it, probably means that he had delivered dozens of girlfriends there for abortions). So for three or four days I was completely on the ward, just devastated, having decided that I couldn't survive any more abortions, having decided that I did in fact want this baby, and at the same time feeling it was impossible to have a baby when the father (who is six-foot-four and two hundred pounds) was so frantically and maybe violently opposed.

So I wrote down all my fears, and as I folded up the piece of paper, I said to God, "Look, I am trying to keep my sticky little fingers off the controls here; I am willing to have the baby if that is your will, if that is the right thing for us, and I am willing to have an abortion, if that would be best for the baby and me; so I am putting this in your in-box, and I'm just going to wait for my next operating instructions."

Then Sam's dad's best friend, Manning, appeared on my doorstep, and I thought he was there to browbeat me into the abortion—they've been best friends for twenty-five years (both are in their early fifties). He asked how I was doing, and I said terribly depressed, and he said, "*Why?* This is a great blessing!" What a gutsy thing for him to do. Then we drove around on his motorcycle for a while, me with this tiny pollywog in my belly.

For two weeks I vacillated between thinking I had no choice but to have the abortion, and thinking maybe there was a way for me to pull this whole thing off and that maybe God had something up his sleeve and I was going to come into some money or something. And two weeks after I found out I was pregnant, I went to bed with so much pain in my chest that I lay there breathing like a three-hundred-pound asthmatic, just lost in the ozone, wheezing, blinking back tears. Early that morning I dreamed that I was walking along the dock of the houseboat where I used to live, carrying my little baby boy, and I tripped, and he ended up falling into the bay, and I dove in but knew I had lost him. I kept swimming downward and downward, and I kept managing to just touch his body as it fell through the really freezing black water. Then I couldn't see him at all. Through a small miracle I felt my fingers on his body again, and I actually dug them into his flesh, like the psychic surgeons supposedly do, and my fingers went all the way into him, like he was the Pillsbury Doughboy, and I got hold of him and swam to the surface. When I broke through, holding him above my head like the Olympic flame, there were friends waiting there who rushed him to the hospital, and I knew he was okay.

I woke up from the dream smiling, shook my head with amazement, and said to myself, "Honey? Looks like we're going to have a baby."

JANET BURROWAY

♪

Soldier Son

I HAD BEEN to a couple of parties here before—a slightly stuffy, pleasantly scruffy London flat with worn leather on the chairs, Kurdish rugs on the floor, and etchings of worthy ruins on the walls. It looked like a grown-up version of Cambridge "digs," and most of us looked like middle-aged versions of the Cambridge undergraduates we had mostly been—now pundits and publishers, writers and actors, what the British call the "chattering classes." Both my sons were with me on this trip, sixteen-year-old Alex out with his guitar and the punks of Piccadilly Circus, nineteen-year-old Tim somewhere in the adjoining room in Harris tweed. I recognized the man crossing toward me glass-in-hand as somebody I vaguely knew—first name Jeff (or Geoff), last name lost. Slender, sandy, he looked too young to be the president of London PEN International, though I seemed to remember that's what he was. I remembered he was witty and articulate, an impassioned campaigner for free speech and the freeing of imprisoned writers; my kind of person. So I was glad to see him headed toward me.

He charged a little purposefully, though, his look a little heated. "I've been talking to your son," he said, and set his glass against his chin. "My God, how do you stand it!"

My stomach clenched around its undigested canapés, brain wrung like a sponge. Shame, defensiveness, and rage (*I am responsible for my son; I am not responsible for my son; who are you to insult my son?*) so filled my throat that I could not immediately speak. What I felt was that I, literally, closed down. The free-speech champion offered me the kind of face, sympathy and shock compounded, that one offers to the victim of mortal news.

"I manage," I managed presently, and turned on my heel.

I have never so far as I know run into Jeff or Geoff again, but I credit him with the defining moment, when choice is made at depth: the Mother Moment.

Let's be clear. I live in a knee-jerk land, impulses pacifist to liberal, religion somewhere between atheist and ecumenical, inclined to quibble and hairsplit with my friends, who, however, are all Democrats and Labour, ironists, believe that sexual orientation is nobody's business, that intolerance is the world's scourge, that corporate power is a global danger, that war is always cruel and almost always pointless, that guns kill people.

My son Tim, who describes himself as a fiscal conservative and social liberal, shares these attitudes of tolerance with regard to sex, race, and religion. His politics, however, emanate from a spirit of gravity rather than irony. Now thirty-three, he is a member of the Young Republicans, the National Rifle Association, and the United States Army Reserve, with which he spends as much time as he can wangle, most recently in Bosnia, Germany, and the Republic of Central Africa, all places where, he says, he felt that he was "making a difference," "doing something that mattered"—also, "on the tip of the spear."

I love this young man deeply, and deeply admire about three quarters of his qualities. For the rest—well, Jungian philosopher James Hillman has somewhere acknowledged those parts of every life that you can't fix, can't escape, and can't reconcile yourself to. How you manage those parts, he doesn't say. What Tim and I do is let slide, laugh, mark a boundary with the smallest frown or gesture, back off, embrace, or shrug. Certainly we deny. Often we are rueful. I don't think there is ever any doubt about the "we."

Most parents must sooner or later, more or less explicitly, face this paradox: If I had an IdentiKit to construct a child, is this the child I'd make? No, no way. Would I trade this child for that one? No, no way.

This week in Florida I receive in the mail a flyer from Teddy Kennedy that asks me to put my money where my mouth is, and my mouth is by fund-raising ventriloquism assumed to be saying, "Yes! I will stand up and be counted to help end the gun violence that plagues our country." I am considering a contribution when Tim drops by. Recently returned from nine months in Frankfurt with SOCEUR, this afternoon he is headed *back* to the gun show where he spent an earlier hour, thinking he will maybe indulge himself with a Ruger because it's a good price, has a lovely piece of cherry on the handle and fine scoring, and he's never *had* a cowboy-type gun. He's curious how it handles, heavy as it is. And a single-action will be new to him. Later still he comes back by to show it off. He fingers the wood grain and the metalwork, displays the bluing on the trigger mechanism— exactly as I would show off the weave of a Galway tweed, the draping quality of this crepe cut on the bias. He offers it on the palms of both hands and I weigh it on mine, gingerly. "It's neat," I admit. Grinning at my caution, he takes it back.

I used to say I don't know where he came from. I remember in the late sixties, when he was a toddler, standing in a gloriously sunlit kitchen and laughing to a friend: "I don't mind gay, and I think I could handle drugs, or even prison. Just please don't let him come home a priest!"—his father had had a teenage flirtation with the Catholic Church. In any event, Tim spent a few years as an Episcopalian, a mainly social interest, as he admitted at the time, then directed his allegiance toward other abstractions and institutions. But I must have forgotten that his grandfather was a Resistance fighter in Belgium in the Second World

War. I must have forgotten that my own father was an anti-labor Taft Republican—or that Dad taught me to shoot a rifle at tin cans on a cactus when I was less than ten.

No, the issue of "where he came from" is teasingly complex, and fraught with hindsight. I have a black-and-white snapshot of Tim and his little brother, both of them towheaded and long-lashed, squatting in an orchard full of daffodils. I also own a color photograph taken in the African savannah of my grown elder son kneeling over the carcass of a wild boar, surrounded by his wiry, smiling Cameroonian guides. (One image I hold in my head, of the convolutions of honor, is of Tim, White Hunter, being mocked by these guides because, rigorous about the rules of the sport, he was unwilling to poach on government land. They thought he was afraid.) Now, looking at the toddler in the daffodils, I can see the clear lineaments of the hunter's face. But squatting beside him I had no premonition of which planes, tilts, colors of that cherub head would survive. Looking back, I can see clearly that his passion for little plastic planes, the tank kits he painstakingly put together with glue on the point of a toothpick, the bags of khaki-colored soldiers on whose webbing belts he layered a patina with a one-hair brush, the history books of famous battles, the catalogs of insignias of rank—in all that, I can see that his direction was early set. But I was a first-time parent. I thought all boys played soldier. Alex liked little planes too, and it did not absolutely register that by the time he was ten Alex had given up soldier stuff and gone into other fantasies, to Dungeons and Dragons and from thence to the Society for Creative Anachronism—veering from the mainstream, satirical toward patriotism, cocky about his pacifism: *Hey, man, okay, I'm afraid of you. I'd a whole lot rather talk it out, okay?* (In such wise, my younger son faced and survived some serious dangers of his subversive lifestyle. Nevertheless, there was a period when he was grateful for his big brother's prowess on the playground. Alex *would* wear a diaper pin in his ear, and Tim would beat up the bully that called him fag.)

I have witnessed, in my younger son, the astonishing but quite usual transformation from radical-punk-anarchist to responsible-loving-husband-father. The journey with Tim has been otherwise: it is I who have come to understand that this is who he is, and has been consistently from babyhood.

As a child Tim was modest, intense, fiercely honorable, and had few but deep friendships. He lit with enthusiasm for his most demanding teachers, praising their strictness, their discipline. Once he wailed at me for mentioning pajamas in front of dinner guests, and once when a new puppy crapped on the doormat he informed me that I kept an unsanitary house (I handed him the soap and rag). At this distance I can see that the Spock upbringing I struggled to offer, and which suited his little brother, was anachronistic to Tim's Victorian or even chivalric character. He has admitted as much, saying that though he was glad of the freedom I gave him, nevertheless his own children will have their boundaries drawn tighter.

Tim was from the beginning a worrier after his own integrity, which he pursued with solemn doggedness, eyes popping. Once when we were living near a woods in Tallahassee, the boys discovered a cache of professional archery equipment, hidden in its original manufacturer's carton in a hollow log in a ravine. The label bore an address of a local sporting goods shop. Alex and I stretched the long bows, admired the glossy laminated woods, and wavered, tempted. But Tim was clear and adamant: we had to drive to the shop to return it *right now*. It turned out that the equipment had been delivered to, and stolen from, a city park recreation center. I was somewhat sheepish in the face of my son's virtue, and annoyed that neither the shop nor the city so much as acknowledged his honesty, for which, however, Tim seemed to need no reward.

As he came to puberty he developed no interest in sports but had a keen eye on world news. He read voraciously, mostly adventure novels, admired John Wayne's acting and his politics, and more than once to my despair quoted, "My country right or wrong." At eighteen he came home at three one morning, in tears because he could not go to defend England's honor in the Falklands. About that time I realized that both my boys, who had spent their early years in shoulder-length blond shag, had shaved their heads—Alex for a Mohawk and Tim for ROTC. Both wore combat boots, the one for busking around the Eros statue in London, the other for jumping out of airplanes at Fort Benning. At that point I added to my theory of "where he came from" that Tim was rebelling against sixties parents, the ones who had him out in the stroller at the sit-ins or confined to his playpen while we addressed envelopes for Mothers Against the Bomb. Alex, instead of rebelling against Mom (what's the point?—if she'll let you be a soldier, she'll let you be anything), rebelled against his big brother, the hero worship and the Top-Siders, all things button-down or flag-waving.

Much of the time it seemed funny, and much of the time I had to acknowledge that when we fought, my battles with Alex were the more bitter precisely because he and I were more alike. His impulses were generous, sloppy, and full of turmoil, whereas Tim would hold back and calmly stand his ground. Alex was a loud and messy liberal, like me. Tim said, "Yes, ma'am," ready to do a task right now, and I had to be grateful for military virtues in a son.

Nevertheless I knew that when I disagreed with Tim, there was a higher proportion of subtext to text. Our quarrels were less frequent and less personal, but they betrayed a deeper divide. In his late teens Tim went through a period in which he enjoyed goading my liberal friends with army swagger. He thought it was smart to interrupt them with tough talk. He had a bumper sticker that said, "This vehicle is protected by Smith and Wesson," and T-shirts with skulls and crossed rifles. Embarrassed, angry, and ashamed, I found no effective thing to say. I was grateful for the friend who told him, "You know, it isn't that we're shocked. All of us are familiar with the attitudes you have;

we've considered and rejected them." Tim took this in. He swallowed and said, "I didn't think of it that way."

Since then he has thought of it in several hundred ways, and so have I. He spent four years in the army, the happiest time of his life, and later still ran security forces in the Cameroons, guarding the embassies and the multinationals. He loved the army, deplores cruelty, fights bigotry—but disciplined his African troops in a way that *they* called fatherly. He is a self-described capitalist, but the only job he ever despised was as a financial consultant ("Those sleazeballs.") He is a swaggerer and an accomplished cook, a computer whiz with the soul of a Musketeer. I'm forced to be aware of my own contradictions in his presence: a feminist often charmed by his machismo, a pacifist with a temper, an ironist moved by his rhetoric. Tim can still set my teeth on edge speaking in acronyms or the metaphors of battle, then disarm me with a caustic reference to "evolving guidance" (behavior of an officer who doesn't know what he's doing) or the *snort* in Sierra Leone ("short-notice over-reaction team"). His rhetoric can be Hemingwayesque, his humor heavy-handed; he can be quick to bristle and on occasion hidden far back in himself. On the other hand, these faults unfold his virtues: you would trust him with a secret on which your life depended; neither will he betray you in trivial ways. He would, literally, lay down his life for a cause or a friend.

Tim doesn't expect a weapon for his birthday and I don't defend Jimmy Carter in his presence. But sometimes our ritual avoidances fail and we stumble into uneasy territory. I recall in particular an afternoon that I sat in my home office grappling with some inane, arcane university review, when Tim appeared in my doorway enthusiastically to opine, "The trouble with the university is that it ought to be run more like a business."

I blew up. "What the hell makes you think you know anything about running a university?" The stack of pointless paper on my desk was precisely the result of corporate-think in the administration. I flailed it in the air. "You and the idiot legislature."

He retreated coldly, withdrawing in more ways than one, and there were a couple of days of silence between us. Then I left a message on his machine, he left a reply on mine, we agreed to lunch on Monday, and talked it through. I explained the nature of faculty governance, and pointed out that industrial studies showed autonomy in the workforce increased, not decreased, productivity. He argued that although tenure protected academic freedom, it also protected instances of sloth. I used the word "productivity"; he said "academic freedom," which means that we found again the safe, familiar ground. But beyond this politesse we also came to acknowledge and agree that, mother and child, we not only don't share a worldview but *cannot respect each other's worldview.* Our task is to love each other in the absence of that respect.

It's a tall order. We agreed that we do pretty well at it. The very stating of the impasse seemed paradoxically to confirm our respect. And Tim is broad-minded enough to add this observation: "It's a good thing it's you who's the liberal, Mom. If I was the parent I wouldn't want to let you be you the way you've let me be me."

There are two things at work here: that motherhood is thicker than politics, and that a politics of certainty—the snap judgment, the closed mind, the blanket dismissal—cannot be what I mean by liberal. Tom Stoppard speaks in *Lord Malquist and Mr. Moon* of the "liberal cerebrum and conservative viscera." When I encountered that phrase I felt guiltily gratified, and in my most honest moments I acknowledge it again, because deeply to love where you deeply disagree creates a double vision that impinges daily in unexpected ways.

My grandfather was a small-town Republican banker. My parents were right-wingers of the working class—antismoking, teetotaling, antiunion Methodists. My mother did TV spots for

Goldwater in the fifties. When my first novel came out, my mother injudiciously showed me some letters she had received from friends, making it clear that she had written to them apologizing for the sex scenes I had written, curse words I had used. "Well, you know," I overheard her once say on the phone, "you have to put that in, or your books don't sell." My brother pointed out the ethical dilemmas my characters faced, their spiritual quests. "Mom, you keep defending her by saying she's sold out. Don't you understand what you've raised here is a Methodist moralist?"

But my parents were never able to see that though the forms in which I expressed myself were different and sometimes opposite from theirs, the underlying principles were the same. This half-blindness led to bitterness on their part and to lies on mine. I don't want to make the same mistake. Tim says, "Whatever you think of the warrior spirit, it isn't directed at self and it isn't devoted to money. It needs an extreme integrity." Rearrange the syntax a little, switch the nouns around, you might hear the rhythm of this sentence in my grandfather's mouth, my mother's, or my own.

The mail and the gun show were on Saturday. Sunday afternoon Tim is back to show me a double-cowhide holster he has cut, tooled, and stitched freehand. "It's a pretty fair copy of John Wayne's favorite; he called it his Rio Bravo."

"It's handsome," I say. I don't say that it's also delicate, with bursts of flowerets burned around the curve of the holster front and the loop that holds it to the leg.

"I need to make some kind of finger protection." Tim shows me deep cuts in his index fingers from pulling the beeswaxed linen thread through hand-punched holes. "You have the awl in one hand and the needles in both, you mark the seam line and punch through, then thread one needle from the blind side and the second from the front."

I recall for him how I had to rent industrial machines to get

through the leather when I costumed a play full of peasants in
jerkins.

"The leather needle is shaped like a three-bladed triangle
knife."

"So is the machine needle."

All those years while I taught my boys to iron and sew I
thought I was turning out little feminists. At Fort Benning Tim
was laughing-proud to be the only one in his barracks who could
put his military patches on his uniform with a sewing machine.
He can cuff his own pants and press a perfect sleeve. It never
occurred to me these skills would be put to use on cartridge belts
and camouflage. But why not? How many swashbuckling-hero
Halloween costumes did I sit and sew?

I must be confident of our accord today because it is I who ask
him what he thinks of the situation in Iraq. I'm not sure what I
think. Both of us have been following this week's particular crisis, he on CNN and I on NPR. Does he think Saddam Hussein
should have been tracked down at the end of the Gulf War?

"Sure, but it wasn't that easy. He had good doubles, and kept
moving. Our intelligence has always been heavy on the technology—radar, satellites, aerial photography. But we're a joke for
intelligence personnel. The British would be better at it."

Over the course of an hour our conversation ranges from Hussein to "deniability" to the general question of truth between
the military and the media, to free speech, to assumptions buried
in the English language, to our apparent helplessness in Bosnia,
to our sins of commission or omission in Africa, to the distinc-
tion between spirituality and belief. While he talks, in the
course of a few sentences I can wince; be convinced; be aware
that he knows much more than I do not just about matters military but also about history in general and current politics in the
other hemisphere; let pass what I hear as a faulty syllogism or
false logic; leap in to add a confirming point in some area of my
own knowledge; or feel that on some issue or other I must
protest. No doubt he goes through much the same range.

Because today I'm thinking in the double way; listening to us as we talk, I'm also aware that the points on which I find him most convincing, or perhaps on which we most readily agree, are those suggesting that there is little remedy, or no clear choice among options.

On Bosnia he says, "We have to decide either to get out and let them sort it, knowing that means they go back to war and they'll kill each other till they're sick of it. Or else we have to commit to a whole generation—military presence, education, political intervention, and oversight. I don't know which is right. But I know we have to do one thing or the other. And if we do get out, we wasted the ones who died there."

He has another gun to show me, one I've seen in various stages of its perfecting. I forget the name of this one, a semiautomatic from which, he carefully shows me, he has removed the clip. He has spent several hundred hours filing every edge inside and out so that all the parts fit with silken smoothness and the barrel blackly shines. This is the hammer and the seer, the housing, the clip well. This is the site he's got an idea how to improve. This is the handle he has crosshatched with several hundred hair's-width grooves to perfect the grip. Just so do I worry my lines across the page one at a time, take apart and refit the housing of the sentences, polish and shine. This is love of craft he's talking. This is a weapon that could kill a person I am holding in my hand. The conflict between conviction and maternal love stirs again, stressfully.

DEBORAH GALYAN

9)

Watching *Star Trek* with Dylan

UPSTAIRS ON the bridge my husband, the first officer, is at his station cooking up that brand of boxed macaroni and cheese inexplicably yet consistently preferred by the human young, and slicing bananas under the steady gaze of his commanding officer. The captain has friendly brown eyes and a deep dimple that appears like a Cracker Jack prize each time he smiles. He is guzzling a cup of apple juice and jiggling both feet. He is five and one half Earth years old. The captain is, in my opinion, exceedingly handsome in a big-cheeked, humanoid way. One sock on. One unaccounted for. He is Captain Dylan Walker, commander of our starship, whom I sometimes still think of as my son.

"More juice, Number One," he says to the first officer. (It is a tradition for the commander of a Starfleet vessel to address his first officer affectionately as "Number One.")

"One moment, sir," Number One says. "I'm receiving a macaroni signal."

Number One has earned his position between the cutting board and the range in this, the high command center of our ship. His macaroni-boil-over training has served him well. He performs the chemical bonding flawlessly, blending the secretions of lactating mammals with the garish orange powder our young perceives as cheese sauce. I slouch in the doorway between the bridge and Sector 1, waiting for my cue.

"What species are those bananas?" the captain inquires.

The first officer regards the sliced bananas with uncertainty. "Sir, I am inclined to say they are of Vulcan origin. I am uncertain of the species."

"If you don't know, ask Data," the captain prompts.

"Data!" my husband shouts. "What species are these bananas I'm slicing for the captain?"

I walk in stiffly, regard the bananas with androidlike curiosity, I hope. "Sir," I say. "These bananas are genus Overripus, species Chiquitum. A Romulan variety, grown only on the twin planets Norzac and Prozac."

Number One winces. "Now he won't touch them. Romulans are bad guys. And that makes these bad-guy bananas."

I'm prone to such mistakes. I feel miscast as Data, the opal-eyed android who is basically a super-computer in pants. I'm reduced to scatting gibberish spattered with malapropisms, changing the Ferengis into Ferraris, reaching for Cardassian but landing short on Cardamom.

We turn and face the captain, who scowls at us.

"Romulan bananas are against Starfleet regulations. I want Betazoid raisins with my lunch."

Number One hesitates. The evil Romulan bananas are already arranged in a pleasing spherical pattern on the rim of the captain's plate. But, wisely, he concedes.

"As you wish, Captain."

"Make it so," the captain says.

Dylan is having his first love affair with *Star Trek*. I am having my second. I watched the original series when it aired in 1966. I was eleven that year. I remember praying after each episode for NASA to somehow accelerate its timetable, so that I could have Lieutenant Uhura's job in real life, and hopefully her uniform and mod dangle earrings, the likes of which had never been seen before in the vast midwestern interior. Three decades later I haven't a clue what *Star Trek* meant to me back then, beyond the fact that it was immensely pleasing to spend an hour each week in a world where no person or alien life-form dressed or talked or behaved like my parents or teachers.

This time around, watching *Star Trek* is a more urgent experience. To watch it with Dylan is to watch someone in the throes of intense epiphany. I am not so much watching *Star Trek* myself as I am watching Dylan watch *Star Trek*, and I see in him a kind of deep recognition that suggests the presence of a paradigm encoded in the brain before birth. He sees something he recognizes, something he has been waiting to see for most of the two thousand days he has lived thus far on Earth. A world where life, as far as he is concerned, has recovered its one true objective, and therefore, its majesty and worth.

As every TV-acculturated American knows, *Star Trek* is a drama about people who navigate magnificent starships through our galaxy's outback, and possess cool technology and wear, as Dylan once put it, "excellent uniforms." In *Star Trek*, a person can be blasted with a laser and brought back to consciousness with another laser that looks eerily like the laser that blasted him in the first place. The crew go about their business with weird nonchalance, seemingly oblivious that they are hurtling through space at unfathomable speeds toward God knows what. The point is, after all, to go, and boldly, where no one has gone before, to explore new worlds, to discover new civilizations, perhaps—though this part is apparently too bold to include in the series's prologue—to map the shape of creation itself.

I hope I never forget the expression on Dylan's face the first time he saw the opening frames of *Star Trek: The Next Generation*. It was a late fall evening in 1996, toward the end of a busy work and school week. Tired, we had abandoned our dinnertime decorum for plates in our laps in front of the tube. Dylan, sensing acquiescence in his weakened elders, commandeered the forbidden remote and clicked it only once. And there it was, the good ship U.S.S. *Enterprise*, cruising majestically past an orange planet with lavender moons. Until that night, I had harbored a sort of high-minded idea of the countenance of rapture. I thought it must resemble a painting by Gustav Klimt or a poem by Rilke, but as it turns out, it looks like a little boy in baggy overalls, a half-eaten cheese sandwich in his fist, watching Captain Jean-Luc Picard command the bridge of the *Enterprise*.

That night I watched Dylan maneuver, in openmouthed awe, one limb at a time around the coffee table and across the floor, until he was in immediate danger of bumping his nose against the screen. If it were possible, he would have passed through it and taken his adventure inside, like Alice through her glass.

"What is this show?" he asked.

"*Star Trek*," I answered. "I'm not sure we should watch it."

"I need to watch it," he said.

My husband and I commenced secret communication, as all parents forced to negotiate in the presence of their children must, using a highly evolved series of shoulder shrugs and facial twitches. My twitches indicated that I wasn't sure what to do, since, technically, *Star Trek* qualifies as a "shooting show."

A shooting show is our private nomenclature for any television show in which people (morphed or otherwise), animals, robots, aliens, or mutant turtles engage in the use of weapons, no matter how poignant their reasons might be, or any show in which the accoutrements of violence or engagement therein is made to look awesome or cool. Shooting shows are not watched in our house, and the rule is so strictly observed that one need merely shout "shooting show!" once to justify a change of channel.

But that night, my husband's facial muscles argued, Oh, what the hell. Nobody is shooting right this minute. Let it go, at least for tonight.

So it was, on a night of lax parental discipline, that Dylan discovered the ultimate metaphor for his five-year-old boy life. What else had we deprived him of, I wondered, in our fevered efforts to make him a peaceable creature?

There is a great movement in contemporary parenting to prevent children from watching violence on television. This means
millions of parents must deny their children access to approxi-
mately half of all network programs and nearly all cable television programs, according to the National Television Violence
Study. There is something oddly omissive about this strategy, for
it amounts to withholding from our children an ugly truth about
their culture: that it equates violence with entertainment. I'm
not sure that this collective effort will save them from it, particularly the boys, who, in my observation, are plenty capable of
generating entertainment violence without the assistance of
television.

My son has, thus far, been sheltered from television violence
and seems no more or less aggressive than other boys his age.
Yet he thrives on rough-and-tumble engagement with other
boys, a karate contest or a round of sword fighting with sticks.
As a toddler he astonished us with his compulsion to hit, which
continued long after he developed the verbal skills to mediate
conflict, and now it's his demented genius for transforming the
most benign playthings into dangerous weapons. And so, we
remind him constantly that playing at fighting is a rehearsal for
the real thing. He listens and clearly understands and goes off
somberly to his room, where, we later discover, he has quietly
fashioned a laser gun from a fistful of Legos and is blasting
everything in sight. It's something buried deep in his bones. A
thing he must do.

As luck might have it, of all the action-adventure shows
Dylan might have fallen in love with, *Star Trek: The Next Generation* is the least likely to resort to entertainment violence.
Starfleet officers of the United Federation of Planets take great
pains to avoid war in intergalactic relations. There is a great deal
of talk about conflict resolution, many peace conferences, much
counseling of prudence. But every other episode or so, and much
to Dylan's delight, diplomacy breaks down, and the crew of the
Enterprise find themselves with no other recourse but to destroy

a Klingon Bird of Prey, or to blast away at some murderous crystalline entity or other. When that point of crisis finally comes, they make it look both awesome and cool with phasers, improvised warp weapons, and the ultimate: photon torpedoes. And to this day, on our particular starship, whoever engages the garbage disposal must first shout: "Firing photon torpedoes!" We have learned to wash dishes in the shadow of war.

I used to worry that our decision to let Dylan watch *Star Trek* would unravel everything he learned during his days at a Montessori preschool run by a goddess-worshiping, multiracial women's collective on Cape Cod. The school was a place of peace and wonder, a liberal parent's dream come true, where the children began their day sitting on a huge canvas floor cloth of Mother Earth, saying a pledge to protect and nurture Her and each other. The children baked whole wheat bread for their daily snack, made sculpture from recycled junk, composted with earthworms, and took turns feeding Sappho, the school guinea pig. Each child had a designated task of the week, one of which was peacemaker. And while Dylan benefited from these lessons and applied them where he could, he clearly loved the school less than I loved the idea of the school.

Something about it did not honor his boy soul. I think it was the absence of physical competition. Boys who clashed or tussled with each other were separated and counseled by the peacemaker. Sticks were confiscated and turned into tomato stakes in the school garden. And much to the dismay of their benevolent guardian-teachers, the boys worked out ingenious loopholes to bypass the ban on competition. They organized a daily tournament of extreme playground sports, including ant races and digging contests in the sand pit. It finally came to me that the school was a kind of utopia, based on a dream I harbored for Dylan. I wanted him sheltered from a competitive, narcissistic culture that teaches the wrong lessons to children, but more than that, I wanted to protect him from the dangerous excesses of his gender. I thought if I could keep him long enough in a place inhabited by a feminist guinea pig and a peacemaker, he would never develop the behaviors for which boys are often maligned and often guilty: excessive aggression and competitiveness and arrogance. And, until I saw him there, day after day, thigh-deep in wet sand, furiously digging a hole that would soon strike the water table, I didn't completely realize what I had done: I had sent him there to protect him from the very circuitry and compulsions and desires that make him what he is. I had sent him there to protect him from himself.

After much discussion, we all agreed that Dylan should attend public kindergarten the following fall, and I set about to answer certain questions. How could I be a good feminist, a good pacifist, and a good mother to a stick-wielding, weapon-generating boy? And, what, exactly, is a five-year-old boy?

A five-year-old boy, I learned from reading summaries of various neurological studies, is a thing that has a lot more wiring on the right side of the brain than on the left. This condition develops during a crucial stage of fetal brain growth, during which the brain is busy sending out nerve bundles that connect the right and left hemispheres. It turns out that girl fetuses get busy right away making lots of these connections, equipping themselves to access both right- and left-side functions equally well. For some mysterious reason, boy brains aren't quite up to speed when this process begins. When the nerves venture out from a boy's right brain hemisphere to connect with the left, they discover that there's not much there to hook up with, so they turn back and connect with one another on the right side of his brain. Upon learning this, I had to resist the temptation to suspect that the boy fetus is somehow already goofing off in utero, already not listening, not even to his own biological imperatives, while the girl fetus gets the job done and earns a star for neatness, too.

That boys have more elaborate neural networks on the right side of the brain accounts for their propensity for spatial relationships and problem solving. Girl brain functions are more generalized; boy brain functions, more specific. A boy's big, lopsided brain sends him one clear message: "Your job is to explore the world by Moving Objects Through Space." Of course, some of the neural fibers in a boy fetus do eventually cross over, connecting the right hemisphere with the left. This explains why boys are sometimes capable of answering a question or performing a simple task of personal hygiene before returning to their primary mission.

For a five-year-old boy, moving objects through space could mean playing with blocks, working puzzles, drawing pictures, playing soccer, mixing cookie dough, riding a bike, playing a computer game, making a bed. But because of that other biologically determined gender marker, testosterone, it also frequently means moving Power Ranger/Batman/Hercules/Masked Rider/Beetle Borg/Beast Wars/*Star Wars* and/or *Star Trek* action figures through space, or moving the self through space while performing excellent karate moves on parents and/or cringing siblings, or, even more gratifying, the combination platter: hurtling Power Ranger et al. action figures toward cringing siblings while performing excellent karate moves on parents.

This is what a boy is: he is a beautiful, fierce, testosterone-drenched, cerebrally asymmetrical humanoid carefully engineered to move objects through space, or at very least, to watch others do so.

Just to make sure the theory had depth, even in the most abstract of circumstances, I once asked my husband how the proclivities of right-brain dominance assert themselves in his not-exactly-action-packed life as an academic administrator. What could his job possibly have to do with the mission to move objects through space?

"I move degree programs through vast, uncharted stretches of bureaucracy," he said without a moment's hesitation. "And e-mail enables me to shoot dozens of information missiles through cyberspace each day."

So, what can I do to nurture my son, this practically alien being?

One thing I can do is let him watch *Star Trek,* for what he recognizes in it, I am now sure, is the plain truth about his destiny. Whether I let him watch it or not, he has already pledged himself to the mission. For these are biologically predetermined voyages not even a mother can halt.

A few weeks after Dylan watched his first *Star Trek,* we sat him down and told him that we would be moving in a month from our home on Cape Cod to Bloomington, Indiana. My husband had been offered a good job at Indiana University. The move meant a better work environment for him, one less fraught with political treachery, and more cultural opportunities for us all. Dylan took the news badly, looking glum at first, then stricken. To him, moving meant abandoning his two best friends: the fair, implacable Ardis, with whom he played a passable, if reluctant, John Smith to her emotionally commanding Pocahontas, and Robin, possessor of an extraordinary collection of Batman action figures, as well as interesting plastic weaponry, with which they joyously whaled away at each other at every opportunity.

"Why?" he wanted to know.

We explained. The new job is better, more opportunity, more money. We would have a new house in a lively college town, good schools, museums, closer to grandparents and cousins. We even went so far as to say that we would have a happier life.

"Okay," he said. "But do we have to?"

Every evening for the next three weeks, we sorted through piles of stuff, packed dozens of boxes, and made phone calls to Realtors and mortgage bankers. Dylan bounced around disconsolately amid the chaos of open boxes and empty cupboards. One night he approached me, wearing the missing packing tape like a Roman warrior's arm cuff, and threatened to bonk me with a cardboard mailing tube. "I'm not moving," he said. "So don't pack any of my stuff."

Each night we explained again why the move was necessary, and even a good idea, perhaps most of all for Dylan. Each night, our explanation sounded more like a big, fat indulgence cooked up by insensitive grown-ups. Each night for diversion, Dylan begged to watch the 7 P.M. rerun of *Star Trek: The Next Generation* and, each night, lacking a better idea, we consented.

One evening he traipsed into the dining room, which we had turned into a mini-warehouse for dish packs and huge, unwieldy clothing wardrobes, and said, "Dad, I know why you quit your job."

"You do?"

"Yeah. The people at your office are all Ferengis."

"What's a Ferengi?"

"Ferengis are opportunists with pointed teeth. They trick people."

"Opportunists?" My husband looked at me. We commenced twitching facial muscles.

"Yeah. That's what the people at your office are, right?"

"Right," his father said. "A bunch of Ferengis."

"You don't want to fight them, so you have to get another job, right?"

"That's exactly right."

"Let's pretend I'm Captain Picard, and I order you to transfer to a ship without Ferengis, okay?" Dylan said.

"Okay. But before I go, I have one final request."

"What?"

"I want you to transfer with me. You can be the commander of our new vessel."

Dylan's face opened itself up to wonder for the first time in weeks. Light shone in his eyes, his mouth was open in the throes of concentration. He had made the decision, finally, on his own terms. "Okay, I'll be the commander. But we can't go yet. I have to pack my equipment!"

Stunned, we listened to his sneakers pound on the wooden stairs.

"*Star Trek* is cool," my husband said.

A week later, Dylan and I are stuck in the Detroit airport, waiting for a connection to Indianapolis that does not seem to want to connect. Various parts of various planes, including ours and the one that should have departed before us, are being checked and replaced by freezing men in coveralls outside in the brittle, minus-three December evening. This I learn by listening to wisps of private conversation between tight-lipped gate agents who say, officially, only "delay, delay, delay." I try not to dwell on the combination of broken parts and impatient, freezing men as we sit on the cold floor near the drafty Jetway. Every last seat has been taken by members of a large youth orchestra and their instrument cases and various Mickey Mouse duffel bags. Their plane is even more delayed than ours. An hour passes, then two. We read every book, color every picture, and eat every snack contained in Dylan's travel pack. I think of my husband, somewhere out on the road in western Massachusetts or Connecticut by now, driving our little car toward Indiana through sheets of rain, while Dylan and I travel in comfort, or so we had planned.

"Why aren't we going?" Dylan asks once, twice, three times in twenty minutes.

I explain, explain, explain.

Suddenly Dylan stands up and looks around. "Data," he announces, "I want a full report from engineering." He points at two uniformed pilots who have paused to greet each other on the concourse. "Why aren't those men at their stations?" he demands.

I try to calm him, order him to stay put, but he is five and trapped like a rat in the Detroit airport. My command has been relinquished, and perhaps rightfully so. From *Star Trek*, Dylan has learned to know a crisis when he sees one, and to take command if no one else will.

He strides up to the check-in desk and locks eyes with the lone gate agent, who sits nervously amid the baleful hordes.

"You!" Dylan commands him. "I want you in the Transporter Room now!" He sweeps his arm in the direction of the sleepy youth orchestra, curled up in their coveted chairs with their little computer games and teen novels. "I want these people beamed out of here, and I want them beamed out now!"

The man grins at Dylan. "Yes, sir. At once, sir!"

The youth orchestra is giggling, punching one another and pointing. I slip up behind him and wink at the agent, who gives Dylan a set of plastic pilot wings before I haul him back to our spot on the floor. Dylan examines his wings. "This is not a Federation insignia," he mutters. "But I like it anyway."

Star Trek purports to be a lot of things. A voyage, a mission, a human drama, a myth about our future. The fact that it takes place far in the future is reassuring. It answers the question: With our destructive capabilities advancing faster than our consciousness, will we survive much longer? *Star Trek* assures us the answer is yes. The very idea of *Star Trek* invites us to imagine that humans have survived because they have somehow gotten better, that they might be capable of evolving beyond biology, beyond the culture of conflict and war. Yet the series never allows us to linger in that fantasy for long. A friend of ours teaches a course at the university on *Star Trek* entitled "The History of the Future," and I suspect his students discover in short order how much the history of the future resembles the history of the past. Like Earth in our time, the *Star Trek* galaxy is a dangerous place held together by fragile alliances that sometimes crumble into war. Individuals and entire species, human and otherwise, struggle with the ageless conflicts of territory and tribe. Hate, avarice, jealousy, love, narcissism, and compassion still prevail over logic, and the biology of species still rules the day. *Star Trek* reminds us who we are no matter where we are, in the midwestern corn belt or on the far edge of an unmapped galaxy. It doesn't deny our destructive qualities; it shows us how much can be accomplished when we opt to use our constructive ones instead. And it doesn't shelter us from the solemn consequences of our many inhumanities; these loom even larger against the backdrop of deep space.

If I ask Dylan why he loves *Star Trek*, he will not say: "Because it is an elaborate metaphor describing my biological mission to explore the universe by moving objects through space." He might say, "I like the uniforms" or "Captain Picard is cool." Typically, he will just shrug and roll his eyes, indicating what a dumb, parent question it is indeed, for how can a boy describe a love so elemental it dwells in the very shape of his brain?

Some might argue that, by reducing my son to his biological groundwork, I haven't understood him so much as diminished him. But that is not what I intend. I want to honor all that he is, without denying his essential architecture, the structures and circuitry that shape his dreams. He has already earned my deepest respect, having passed upon his birth through the gates of oblivion, down into the darkness of our arms. He is already on the voyage. At the age of five, he has already had to endure fear. He arrived mute, unable to speak the simplest of needs. He has survived thus far our well-intentioned ignorance. He has entrusted himself to us in the faith that we would turn out to be benevolent, even compassionate beings.

Having given up his celestial consciousness for Earth, his cord to the universe frayed, then severed, he soon set about the task of learning everything there is to learn. He has learned hunger, love, attachment, rage, disappointment, ambivalence, indulgence, and deprivation. He has learned trees. He has learned wet. He has learned ancient. He knows about Darwin. He can tell you about tectonic plates. He knows the power politics at his father's workplace. He can explain that his attachment to a stuffed lavender dog with a sparkling pink secret compartment that locks and unlocks with a key is a gender violation that he has chosen willfully to commit. He already knows that materialism is an addiction with a buzz to it like nothing else. He already knows the alphabet. He already knows that the alphabet he knows isn't the only alphabet. He can define "compassion." He knows that gamblers lose more than they win. He has already asked what are probably the most brilliant questions of his childhood.

He is five and goes to sleep each night clutching a stuffed

penguin, knowing all this, and, I suspect, feeling vulnerable about how much more he needs to know.

If you ask him what he wants to do, he'll say he wants to watch *Star Trek*.

He is already on the voyage. We go about our business as mother and son with weird nonchalance, mostly oblivious that we are hurtling through space at unfathomable speeds. I'm under orders to go with him, as far as I can.

KRIS VERVAECKE

⑨

Fourteen

SATURDAY morning. My feet are bare because I've been watering the flowers, and I look around for my thongs because it's time to pick up Eric, my youngest, two days fourteen, from a sleepover and get him ready for scholarship camp, but our puppy has taken off with them, and I don't want to be late, so I briefly squirt my feet with the hose, the smell of freshly turned soil and water filling my nostrils, and drive barefoot, which is probably illegal. It's early summer, and we're just emerging from a winter so dark and prolonged it aged even the children. Driving across town, I'm distracted by the unreasonable beauty of the flowers dipping and blowing along the roadside and have to remind myself to pay attention to what's in front of me.

I pull into the Meyers family driveway. There's a garage sale next door, and briefly I consider looking for shorts and pants for Eric, who has grown five inches since Christmas, but remembering that I am mud-splattered and barefoot and already self-conscious enough in the mother department, I shut off the car and wait. In the near distance, I hear girls' voices calling out a jump-roping chant, and its refrain rings in the quiet.

"A *butcher, a baker, a candlestick maker, a doctor, a lawyer, a football player!*"

Eric comes out of the house, sleepy and disheveled, black hair tousled, wearing his characteristic expression of engrossment and the T-shirt and shorts he slept in. By the time he was two and a half, it was clear that he had been cut from the same bolt of fabric as his mother, this dark-haired boy who falls into trances like her own. Last autumn, a friend who saw us walking together, my head tipped toward Eric's, engrossed by what he was saying, oblivious to the rest of the world, said she was envious of the intimacy between us, envious of Eric for having someone listen to him in that way. I think I listen to all three of my children with equal attention, yet I'm often startled to hear, from Eric, an echo of my most private self. Over the winter, as his body shed its childishness, the ease of our intimacy has fallen away. Suddenly he professes to be bored by books and art, is fascinated by weight lifting and martial arts movies, this child who carried a postcard of Leonardo da Vinci's *Ginevra de' Benci* in his back pocket to kindergarten. Although this is the third time I've lived through one of my children's adolescences, I was unprepared—although I shouldn't have been—for the violence with which he's been dismantling the old order of childhood. He tosses his backpack onto the backseat and gets in.

"I love you, Mom," he says, gazing ahead.

"I love you, too, sweetie," I say, patting his rather huge and hairy knee. "Did you have a good time?" I ask as I back out.

He says yeah, looking into the middle distance.

"How was the movie?"

"The plot was dumb, but the special effects were awesome. First the aliens kicked our butts, but then we kicked theirs . . ." Then interrupting himself, he says in a voice heavy with portent, "Tomorrow."

"Tomorrow," I say cheerfully, because this is my role: to refute the objections he'll make, because he's scared to go to the scholarship camp that begins the next day.

"I know it's going to suck! They'll treat us like babies, probably make us go to bed at ten o'clock!"

It will be the first time in his life he's been away from home for two weeks.

"Oh, I doubt it," I say. "They chose you based on your manuscripts and test scores, so they know you're not babies."

"Yeah," he says. "But I bet everybody will already know each other except for me."

"They come from all over the state, so I don't know how they'd already know each other."

"Yeah, well, I don't care," he says, sounding satisfied. "They're probably all a bunch of nerds, anyway."

"Probably."

Now he turns and looks at me with full attention. "You know Marvin?"

Because we are on the subject of nerds, in spite of my not wanting to think this way, I am momentarily put in mind of the wrong kid.

"That really irritating boy who was in Mock Trial with you?"

"No, that's Melvin Wilson. *Marvin*."

"Oh, Marvin," I say. "Oh, good. Is he going to be at the camp?" I picture Marvin doing his hilarious imitation of John Cleese returning the dead parrot and smile to myself. If Marvin's going too, I know Eric will be fine.

"No," Eric says. "Marvin died. Day before yesterday. Noo-Ry called Meyers's and said Marvin died."

"Died?" I see Marvin's sly smile turning into a laugh on his bright, wide face. "What do you mean he died? How?"

"They said accidental strangulation with a rope."

Fear tunnels a cold fist through my bowels, womb, stomach, and heart, and I fight not to swerve from the road. I concentrate on driving until I reach an intersection and come to a stop. Three sparrows take off from an apple tree and fly past our windshield.

"Eric," I say slowly, "how does someone accidentally strangle himself with a rope?" I'm struggling to remain calm against the panic and fury rising in me, irrational and cruel (*Who let a child die?*), along with a purely selfish impulse to refuse to accept such horrifying news on a perfect day.

"I don't know, Mom. All I know is that they found him hanging from a rope in his closet." Eric looks straight ahead at the street, empty of traffic, where we've stopped. The skin on his cheek above the emerging beard is smooth except for two faint scars from chicken pox. Part of my mind detaches from itself and remembers dabbing his pockmarks with calamine lotion on a Q-Tips.

"So how do you feel?" I ask in a low, careful voice.

"Really sad," Eric says. "Like if he needed to talk to someone, I wish I'd known. I wish he would have talked to me about it, talked to somebody."

"Yes," I say.

"Noo-Ry said there was so much pressure on him. His sister Clarissa got more awards than he did, but Marvin was really, really smart, too."

I remember his father's response when I told Marvin he'd done a good job at Mock Trial: "No," Mr. Chen had insisted. "No, it was Eric who did a good job. Marvin needs to learn from Eric." Do I put too much pressure on Eric? I ask myself.

"Well, nobody should jump to conclusions," I say defensively. "It's not right to blame his parents. He might have been trying that masturbation thing. Hypoxia. You know what I'm talking about, don't you? Remember when that university student died last year?" I try to sound matter-of-fact as I pull out onto the street.

"Yeah," Eric says. "That's so incredibly stupid and risky; I don't think Marvin would do anything that stupid."

"You know, maybe this isn't even true," I say. "Maybe there was a misunderstanding. I'm going to call Mrs. Meyers when we get home."

"NO! DON'T CALL MEYERS'S MOTHER! THAT IS SO EMBARRASSING!"

A true emergency: the embarrassment of his mother phoning another mother.

"Eric, I just can't believe it." But as I speak, I remember Eric telling me about Marvin's drawings that would be surreptitiously passed around the classroom, making everyone laugh: decapitated children sitting primly, hands folded at their desks, their respective pools of blood on the floor. And his fascination with the disembowelment scenes in *Shogun,* his delight in the macabre, his determination to overcome fear.

Puffs of cotton from the cottonwoods float past us.

"NO, DON'T CALL!"

When we get home, I go upstairs and call Mrs. Meyers. As I dial, I picture the framed cross-stitch she has in their entryway, "Jesus Loves Us," and hear Eric's mimicry of her ("Anybody for some caramel corn?"), a line from a movie he uses to characterize the sort of mother whose admonitions are so Pollyannaish they push teenaged boys into intense guilt and irritation. Speaking of guilt, I feel a twinge because Eric told me he's keeping Teddy Meyers's Smashing Pumpkins CD for him because his mom won't allow him to have it.

"Yes, it's in the paper today," she says. "The vigil service is tomorrow."

"It's so frightening, so sad," I say, shameful fear for myself coming before sadness for Marvin's parents.

"His parents don't believe he meant to kill himself," Mrs. Meyers tells me. "The coroner has ruled it a suicide, but he had wrapped a towel around his neck under the rope, and his parents think he was just experimenting, wanting to know what it would feel like to die."

We are quiet for a moment.

"Who found . . . ?"

She whispers, "His mother."

Sunday morning. While working out at the punching bag, Eric wants to talk, so I sit on his unmade bed and listen. That afternoon I'll take him to the orientation for the camp he'll be attending and pick him up afterward so that we can go to the late-afternoon vigil service for Marvin.

"Everybody says Marv didn't seem depressed," he says. "But why would he take a risk like that? It really pisses me off."

Bam! Kepow! Bam! He dances around the bag, punishing it, alive to an imaginary adversary. With some of his most powerful blows, the metal frame suspending the bag, even though it is anchored with weights, rocks dangerously close to the sliding glass door before tipping precariously back onto its base.

Reflexively I open and close my mouth, managing not to point out that he might break the glass. *Of course* he might break the glass. I'm still trying to sort out my own feelings, the anxiety and sorrow Marvin's death has aroused in me. I'm tired after having tossed and turned much of the night, wondering whether Eric might be vulnerable to whatever forces took Marvin's life. I'd half persuade myself that the towel around his neck suggested Marvin had been practicing hypoxia, when it simply went wrong, and I'd tell myself Eric isn't that sort of risk taker. But just when I'd conclude Eric was all right, I'd ask myself whether his sudden volatility was a sign of depression, or of being deprived of the daily presence of his father, and I'd be circling myself with fresh anxiety.

He punches the bag again, almost knocking the whole apparatus over. I watch the bag swing crazily on its chain.

"Do *you* think he meant to die?" I ask.

"I don't know," he says. "Probably not. There wasn't a note. Plus I can totally see him as somebody who'd want to overpower death, you know, establish such power over his body that he could come close to death and then walk away."

"Yeah," I say.

"And he had all these weird obsessions. He actually was really nice to his sister, but sometimes he liked to chop off her dolls' heads or hang them and stuff, and it would make her mad."

"Kind of like when you and Lucas tied Sarah's Barbie dolls to sticks and roasted them over the campfire?"

"Yeah," he says, "that's what I mean. It all seemed really normal, except that he did that kind of stuff a lot."

He removes his gloves and goes at the bag bare-handed.

"I know this camp is going to suck really bad," he says bitterly. "They'll keep us on a really short leash and feed us casseroles."

He'll be away two weeks. Losing my grip, I blurt out my question, even though I know it's all wrong. "Eric, do you ever feel, even remotely, like you could do anything like Marvin did?"

"What?" he says incredulously. "Christ, I cannot even believe you said that. Jeez! *Of course not*. What do you think?"

"But what if you felt horribly lonely or—"

"Mom," he says sternly. "Stop. I don't know what in the world you're talking about. *What in the world are you talking about?* You can be so irrational sometimes!"

I am thinking about the boys I grew up with who suddenly disappeared from our ranks, suicides no one had remotely anticipated. A boy who killed himself with carbon monoxide poisoning, in his parents' car, in the family garage. His mother found his body, his arms still wrapped around a stuffed animal his girlfriend had returned to him when they broke up. Another boy hung himself, leaving no note.

"Something had to go really, really wrong for Marvin," Eric says. "I found out his father had found *bruises* on his neck before."

Not that wrong, I think. *Not as wrong as you imagine. But I am so glad it's unimaginable to you.*

"There had to be a huge gap between how he felt to take a risk like that, and the way I feel," Eric continues.

I'd learned from talking to other parents that Marvin's father had consulted a child psychiatrist, who'd felt Marvin probably was okay. His father had elicited a promise from Marv, after he'd found the bruises, that he'd never to do anything like that again. Whatever "that" exactly had been.

"How do you feel?" I ask.

"Really lucky," he says, sounding annoyed. "When some of my friends talk about how they feel depressed and don't want to eat or something, I know I never feel like that. When I feel bad, I talk to you or somebody." He slams the bag. "Jesus! I mean it pisses me off you could even think that. What in the world were you thinking?"

As I try to explain myself, I have an unhelpful wave of emotion and have to fight an urge to cry. How can I air my fears to him? How could that possibly be fair? He interrupts.

"Don't you remember my telling you that thing? It's almost like a memory, I swear. Remember? It's like I remember being in heaven, or somewhere, before I was going to be born. And I got to sit there and think about everything and choose who was going to be my mother. And I chose you. I knew it for sure, that it was *you* I wanted as my mom. So *stop*. You know I'd tell you if something was wrong."

"Okay," I say.

"Don't make me tell you this again," he says, toiling at the bag.

"Fine," I say crisply, ready to be the adult again. "While you're at orientation, do you want me to buy you some dress slacks to wear to the vigil service?" The pants I bought him at Easter are three inches too short.

"No, I'd want to pick them out," he says. "I'll wear the shorts I'm wearing to orientation."

He showers; I drop him off at orientation and will pick him up at three-thirty to go to the funeral home.

When I pull up to the basketball court where we've agreed he'll be waiting, I don't see him among the crowd of boys. I wait a few minutes, then open the car door, squinting into the sun.

"Mom! Get in the car!" he says urgently, appearing from nowhere. "Jeez!"

He would be so much more comfortable if I could drive with my head tucked under the dashboard, completely out of sight.

"How was orientation?"

"It sucked. It was so *boring!* We're on such a short leash. WE HAVE TO GO TO BED AT TEN O'CLOCK! And the kids are all small-town Nebraska nerdy."

"That's too bad," I say.

"The kids are actually pretty cool, though. It might be pretty cool."

"That's good," I say.

"And there's this RA who's just *hilarious*."

"That's good," I say as we pull into the funeral home parking lot. I spot Teddy Meyers and his mother going up the sidewalk. Teddy Meyers is wearing khaki pants. Standing by the door are four junior high girls in pastel summer dresses and low heels, who turn and begin talking to Teddy as he approaches.

"STOP THE CAR!" Eric yells. "I CAN'T GO IN THERE IN SHORTS! TAKE ME HOME THIS MINUTE! I CAN'T BELIEVE YOU LET ME DOWN! WHY DIDN'T YOU GET ME SOME PANTS?"

"Eric, for heaven's sake, lower your voice," I say. He has startled me, and now dread and sadness make me shaky. "I can't believe you're getting so worked up over clothes."

"TAKE ME HOME SO I CAN CHANGE!"

Mrs. Meyers waves, and I roll down the window and smile weakly.

I drive to the back of the lot looking for a parking space with Eric yelling at me.

"TAKE ME HOME!" he demands again as I shut off the car. He is as angry as I have ever seen him. I glance at my watch; there isn't time to go home and change. Besides, change to what? His high-water khakis?

"Would you rather not go to this?" I ask quietly. "Maybe it would be better not to go."

"Of course I want to go! I JUST CAN'T WEAR THESE STUPID SHORTS!"

I know that the spectacle of junior high girls in summer dresses has influenced him, and of course he is angry because of Marvin's death—because of DEATH—and I can't rob him of his subterfuge. So I say I'm going on, because the service is about to begin, and if he wants to wait in the car, I'll understand.

I get out and begin walking toward the front door, my legs

trembling under me. Eric gets out, slams the door, catches up, and walks beside me, pointedly not speaking. I wish for perhaps the thousandth futile time, but never more than now, that Eric was flanked on the other side by his father. I want somebody to balance my weaknesses as a parent, a man he could turn to as he becomes one himself.

When we step inside and stand next to Mrs. Meyers and Teddy, the vestibule is so crowded with parents and kids that at first I don't understand we have cut into a line. I ask the woman behind me, with a son a little younger than Eric, if she minds. She shakes her head. She is slowly, steadily weeping. Eric, still punishing me, steps closer to Teddy, who is next to his mother, and now I'm standing alone. In front of us is the other kid from our town who, it turns out, is attending Eric's camp—wearing shorts.

The line seems not to move. I see Ellen Martinez, the pediatrician who was at Mercy Hospital when Marvin's body was brought in, her face smeared with weeping. What mercy could she offer a mother who'd found her child in his closet, hanging from a rope?

I slide closer to Eric. I can feel the warmth of his body apart from the heat generated by so many other distressed bodies. Almost imperceptibly, he leans closer to me.

Now we have progressed by inches around the corner into the next room, and all at once I see and then am momentarily blinded by the sight of Marvin's face and body, disappearing into the white satin of the casket. I had not imagined the casket would be open.

Eric and I reach for each other's hands and cling tightly to one another. Marvin's mother is sitting in a pew, staring vacantly, other family members silent beside her. Marvin's father, a slight, young-appearing man with glasses, whom I have stood next to countless times in school gymnasiums, classrooms, and court-rooms during Mock Trial, is receiving mourners a few steps away from his son's body. I hear his voice, pitched higher than usual, saying the same thing to each person, "Thank you for coming. Yes. Marvin tells very good jokes, right? He had a very good sense of humor, right?"

Eric and I, still clasping hands, have reached a bulletin board pinned with photos of Marvin as a baby, a toddler wearing funny hats and sunglasses, a grade schooler, a lawyer at Mock Trial, a cellist. Appearing with him in many of the photos is his sister, Clarissa, older than he by one year. In several of them she has her arm around Marvin and is smiling into his face, as though coaching him in the right way to face the camera. Or maybe she smiled most easily looking at him. He was always making her laugh, and so she'd end up forgiving him for subjecting her dolls to strange fates.

"He tells very good jokes," I hear Mr. Chen saying to Teddy ahead of us. "He had a very good sense of humor, right?"

Sadness tugs down on my womb like vertigo. Still clasping Eric's hand, I look over at him and find something like resolve on his face.

As we step forward, Eric straightens, grasps Mr. Chen's hand, looks into his eyes in a way that seems brave, and says he's sorry.

Mr. Chen cups his other hand over Eric's and looks back into his face. There is a long moment while Mr. Chen rests in his gaze. I see that Eric is completely there with him, and I am suspended in quiet surprise.

Finally Mr. Chen looks down. "I always think of how well you did at Mock Trial," he says. He turns slightly toward me and says, "Eric did so well."

"Oh, Marvin was tremendous," I say confusedly. "We're so very sorry."

Mr. Chen takes my hand, and, as I look into his face, his eyes seem far away. He turns and takes Eric's hand again. "Marvin tells very good jokes; he had a very good sense of humor, right?"

"He always cracked us up," Eric says. His voice falters, and Mr. Chen and I perceive at the same time the danger that he will cry in front of the other boys in his class, who, at this point, are somber but dry-eyed. Both of us incline slightly toward Eric, grateful to have reason to take care of him.

"We miss him," Mr. Chen says, "but we cannot be sad for him, because he is in heaven."

This is just opaque enough to release us. I step in front of Eric to shield him from the view of the casket, but he moves up to look. I cannot bring myself to step closer. Marvin's silky black hair is evenly combed straight over his forehead. His face, above his mouth, does not look too unusual: maybe those plump cheeks will come up above a smile, and the hoax—his best one ever—will be revealed. But over his lips his skin is a strange bluish-gray, and I despise myself for coming this close and being able to walk off, shaken but still in one piece, the equivalent, perhaps, of slipping off the noose at the last second.

Looking down at his friend's body, Eric is slightly trembling. At that moment, we're told to take our seats because the service is about to begin, and I lead Eric out of the room.

There is no place to sit. All four rooms are crowded. We stand with others in the hall, weeping, squinting to see the television monitor. The minister begins by saying a prayer. Because his native language is Cantonese, he must work to form the sounds of the phrases familiar to me, and I feel oddly comforted by the deliberate effort he must make to put his mouth around each word: *grace, God, eternal life, peace.* Still I hold back, because the emotion swooping around my heart and gut might settle, dishonestly, for anything.

The minister asks us questions, and we read from the bulletin our replies. I can feel the thinness of Eric's energy now; he's been robbed of his anger.

The minister announces that some of the children want to talk about Marvin.

The first girl pulls at her stockings, rocks back and forth on her heels, speaks in a singsong of forgettable phrases. The occasion might be any in which she gets to dress up and deliver a few lines. My back hurts from standing. My gaze wanders to the people next to us: it is the know-it-all, arrogant Melvin. Listening to him at a Mock Trial rehearsal, I'd found the way he attempted to intellectually humiliate the other kids so irritating I'd wondered at myself for feeling so much animus toward a child I didn't even know. I remember, though it seems sacrilegious, that my friend, waiting, too, to pick up her kid, had whispered to me that if he were her child she'd shoot him. Now I notice how his narrow shoulders, slightly rounded, make the vertebrae of his delicate spine poke out through his dress shirt. He is breathing rapidly; fawnlike, his nostrils flare. I look at his mother and am relieved to see she is watching him.

I check on Eric, who is still holding my hand. He whispers in my ear that the singsongy girl was always snotty to Marvin. He seems strengthened with indignation.

Two other kids speak in Ivory-soap platitudes. Finally a girl says that, ever since kindergarten, Marvin would make amazingly good drawings and pass them around when the teacher wasn't looking, and make all the kids laugh. There is a startled moment—who can forget their realistic, gory detail?—then everyone laughs. I love this girl, whoever she is, and find that I can breathe more deeply.

We finish the litany. I'm feeling weak in the knees when the priest tells us we will listen to a recording of Marvin playing the cello and Clarissa playing the piano.

There is a silence, then a series of clicks. Abruptly, Marvin's voice, teasing Clarissa. She giggles. A consultation between them while Marvin tunes the cello. They play a few bars. Too sharp, Marvin says. More tuning. The music begins again, ceases a few bars later. Clarissa giggles. Too fast, they agree. Again, slower.

Finally they are playing together, Fauré's *Sicilienne*, the music belying what all of us, weeping, see now on the video monitor: the soundless, unmoving body of the child. I close my eyes. The beauty of the composition belies the arbitrariness of this loss, whatever the explanation: a child daring death, or experimenting with something that felt rapturous, or momentarily rejecting life and its terms.

I open my eyes to see Melvin swaying on his feet. I step

toward him, but his mother grasps his elbows and steers him out the back door. Eric is crying steadily without embarrassment.

Now, over the piano and cello, we hear voices, cracked and high-pitched, saying something unintelligible into the microphone. My first, irrational thought is that some unauthorized persons, deranged by grief, have grabbed the microphone, and I wait for order to be restored. Then I realize the voices are those of Marvin's mother and father, talking to their son.

"We miss you," they say. "But we know you are in heaven, and now you can play the cello whenever you want."

Abruptly, the service is over, and those of us packed together in the hallway part uncertainly. As Eric and I walk to the car, he asks, "Mom, can we go someplace where we don't know anyone and talk?"

We drive and park along a side street, then roll down the windows. A breeze carries into the car the aroma of someone's barbecue and a fluttering scrap of laughter.

"It's really weird," Eric says. "I keep thinking of this time during Mock Trial." I remember Eric and Marvin and the other kids looking dressed up in borrowed suits, playacting at being grown-ups, abruptly earnest as they argued for justice and compassion, their sarcastic junior-high posturing momentarily forgotten.

"Marvin had just said something brilliant," Eric continues, "and it was obvious the district attorney was clueless about how to respond. Marv came and sat by me, and I whispered, 'Hey, Marv, you could cure cancer!' I wasn't, like, trying to flatter him, and he knew it. He said, 'I know,' in this totally calm way."

A moment passes, and, for some reason, an image from a photograph I have of Eric at eighteen months floats before my eyes. It's an overexposed, black-and-white photo, taken on a summer day. He's sitting on my lap in the grass, the two of us looking up at whoever is snapping the picture. Wisps of his hair and mine are lifted by a breeze, whiting out against the sky. We have half smiles on our faces, comfortable in the way we're nestled there together, but looking oddly too as though we're present in only a fleeting way. One day when he was in grade school, he happened to see this photo and began to cry. He wanted me to put it away where he wouldn't see it again. He said, "I look like I'm already in heaven."

Now, next to me on the seat, he's crying hard, sounding like a child, sounding like a man. As he allows me to hold him, I remember some of our many long walks during his childhood, when we speculated about eternal life and reincarnation and other ways life might be said to continue after death. Neither of us was willing to claim as certain what is not; neither of us was willing to set aside our longing. Holding my son, I think that if the soul is part longing and part memory of God, then every version is crucial.

I stroke his hair, thinking too of the way he comforted Marvin's father, and I know that whatever Eric has done without, he's done all right.

He's quieting now, and I move slightly away to spare us the embarrassment of his having to shrug me off.

Tomorrow he'll return to scholarship camp, where he'll be so busy making best friends with those small-town Nebraska kids and hanging with that hilarious RA that he'll forget to call home for days on end.

Next winter, during parent-teacher conferences, in the crowded school cafeteria that smells of steam trays and a Nebraska version of Spanish rice, I will hear a voice from the din in the hallway, where the kids are stampeding into the locker room after soccer practice. I'll look up, smiling, expecting to see Marvin. What is more real than someone that alive?

But tonight, the evening lies before us, and all the days ahead. We drive home together through the yellow evening air, which bends with the smell of freshly cut grass and the pulse and throb of insects.

JEWELL PARKER RHODES

9

Evan

Fingers curled about my thumb, eyes closed, rainbow bubbles bordering your mouth, you sigh and there is a slight tremor which moves through your body, then mine. Your head tilts toward my breast, your legs bow open, your spine arches and relaxes (you are a brown dough boy, softened and warm beneath yellow wool). Your fingers still clasp mine, you breathe dreamily as the bubbles from your saliva, my milk, stretch in the sunlight, glitter, and burst.

My lovely biracial boy.

I was warned not to have you. My body, past its prime for bearing babies, balked at getting pregnant, balked at carrying a load. "Don't press your luck, you have a healthy child."

But I didn't have you.

Already a mother to a daughter, I wasn't yearning for a son. Wasn't yearning for a child who favored me or my husband or had "new and improved" qualities from my first child. I simply yearned for the lush joy of my body, my blood, helping life thrive, helping the myriad cells from my egg and my husband's sperm root and multiply into a unique being.

Evan—warrior, independent. Khalil—lover, sensitive.

Your name is your charm. A mother's wish that you be strong enough to withstand this world; vulnerable enough to experience this world. *Evan Khalil.*

You were eager to be born. A month early you were lifted out of me and after your persistent kicks to leave the womb, you slept like a mewing kitten, not needing a pacifier. You slept, wires spiraling, monitoring your heart. You slept beneath heated lamps and I, in a wheelchair, peered at you through plastic glass. You slept only one night away from me. Your lungs were strong enough to exhale, inhale. After months of anxiety, our family was blessed with you—a healthy boy.

My one-year-old. You like tiny things, pieces, parts not the whole. The "under-three" Legos do not inspire you. You want the tiniest of Legos and you wail when I dislodge them from your fingers. We go outdoors instead and you learn about sand; you spend hours in the turtle-shaped box, letting the particles cascade through your fingers. From sand we move on to dirt, touching, spraying dirt, and making mud. But it is the insects that amaze you—beetle bugs, centipedes, spiders—the smaller the better. You teach me to look down not up, you squat like a mini-sumo warrior, for hours, watching ants trail between sidewalk cracks. Black eyes, lashes long like butterfly wings, black curls, an irresistible smile. Everyone says how handsome you are.

I am lucky to have time at home with you. You introduce me to worlds that had previously been invisible. There is laughter watching water ripple in a wading pool, intensity as your finger points at tiny mites crawling up the stucco wall, and joy as you string multicolored beads.

My two-year-old. The only grandson. You are only interested in trains. Thomas the Tank Engine trains, Brio trains, electric trains, plastic trains that squirt water, monorail trains.

Books about trains. Clackety-clack. You care less about Santa and more about the Polar Express moving, groaning, journeying on. Hiss. Smoke curling around the bend. Coals, glowing heart-red. Clackety-clack. The Steam Engine Stuck in the Tree. "Oh, no." The Little Engine That Could. "Choo-choo. I think I can, I think I can." Your face pressed against the floor, your hand holding a train, manipulating it like a god, I wonder: Where are you going? is it the wheels' motion? imagining people behind tiny windows? the power of the engine? where do you go?

I pride myself we live in multicultural Los Angeles—there is no better place to live. The Lab School at the university is a mini-UN. Multilingual, multiethnic, multieverything. Surely room enough for you. You are a California boy—raised far from the oppressive South, the stifling segration tucked in the hills of Pittsburgh. You are a brown boy who has made it to the promised land.

My three-year-old, loving numbers. You play tricks with numbers. You count from one to ten, then by fives, by tens. You spin the abacus balls: green, yellow, red, and count down the rows. You lift pudgy fingers: "Two fingers plus three fingers equal five," you squeal. At dinner, you group peas, corn, slices of chicken. You ask, "How many numbers?" I don't understand. "How many?" Your face puckers and pinks. "How many numbers?"

"They go on forever," your father answers.

Nodding, you look at all your fingers. "Forever," I say. You smile, then giggle and glimpse a universe filled with numbers. Devouring systematically, group by group, you eat your dinner.

Rodney King is alive on my television—writhing, turning, crawling on his knees. Seeing three policemen kicking King, shooting a Taser gun, fracturing his skull while twenty-three other officers watch. I am horrified.

Seeing King brutalized, I remember all the more vividly photographs I lingered over as a girl—images captured by *Ebony* and *Jet* of trees bearing mutilated, often naked bodies, of men tarred, feathered, and roped to a car as hooded men solemnly stood by. I've seen fourteen-year-old Emmett Till's lifeless, battered face— his penalty for saying "Hey, baby" to a white woman in Mississippi. My father sometimes stated succinctly, "Americans don't like colored boys."

My four-year-old, you like growing things. In prekinder-garten, you grow grass, a marigold, a carrot. We buy impatiens to plant in the front yard. Dark and light purple petals are your favorites. Soon there is an ivy plant in your room, trailing across your gerbil's cage. You rescue a lily that has sickened and almost died on me. "I'll have it. For my room." It blooms for you. During an Easter egg hunt, you announce, "I want to live in the country." Your imagination has razed buildings, concrete, bridges, and utility poles; you draw endless pictures of sun, sky, earth, and trees. Your class creates a town. Milk boxes and cardboard make land and buildings. Construction paper makes fences, garages, and, for some, oblong swimming pools. I recognize your house instantly. It is very small. Tiny. Your yard is covered with trees. With a yellow marker, you made daisies.

The police who beat Rodney King are acquitted. There is rioting in L.A. We all bundle into the car and drive, and drive, out of L.A. County. Not because we fear being harmed but because we fear the "thing" that set men beating Rodney King, the "thing" that allowed officers to be acquitted in Simi Valley, a community just over the hill from where we live. We drive out of L.A. County, we drive eight hours to Monterey. We hadn't intended to travel so far but we couldn't find a room to sleep, to rest, eat, to hug or cry—hotels, motels, inns are filled with flee-ing Angelenos. We drive because I—black, brown-haired, and brown-eyed—and my husband—white, brown-haired, and blue-eyed—have had dreams of ethnic harmony shattered. Once "one drop of black blood" was enough for a child to be a slave. Generations later, we are still struggling with physical and cultural differences. There is only one race—gloriously and foolishly human. Some people will extend privileges to my husband that they will not extend to his darker-pigmented son.

My five-year-old has discovered rhythm—sweet, maddening rhythms. You walk far slower than anyone else and when we complain, "Hurry up, Evan," you good-naturedly skip, skip some more, then slow to your natural amble. Even through Disneyland, you stroll contentedly and it doesn't matter if we never ride. You take your own good time—slow and easy. But when you dance, you dance fast, listening to the rhythms of "Deep Forest" or "Cats" or "Splish, Splash, I Was Taking a Bath." You prefer jazz to gymnastics and you leap across the living room, creating dances with your sister. You have discovered, too, your voice and, like your walking, you love slow, sweet songs which beguile. You sing like an angel. You sing all the time—in the car, in the bathroom, in your bedroom, I hear your voice rising and falling, "Who will buy this wonderful morning?"

I wonder what the world will think of my son. I worry more that the world will not think but instead react to hateful, lingering images that were once powerful enough for men to traverse seas and oceans to capture Africans.

The infant becomes the boy becomes the adolescent, the man.

"Evan."

You turn and, at six, you smile. A front tooth gone and another one dangling, and you stretch your arms wide, inviting me in. *I stoop, embracing, but it is clearly you who is giving the comfort. Your thin arms, hands that barely emcompass my back are so strong.*

"You are the best mom."

My son is wiser than I. He doesn't worry—just lives. His vision is unclouded by prejudice. When innocence gives way to a more complicated learning, I hope he'll grip fast to joy and, clear-eyed, view the world with compassion.

You are seven. We build a cave of pillows, sheets, and huddle close. You are spinning stories. Telling me how beetles lay eggs, how knights move diagonally, how Lyle purrs, resting on the small of your back. You sigh, a soft explosion of air. You practice giving me butterfly kisses.

I dream of birthdays to come. Of celebrating your birth anew. Celebrating when you became separate, distinct from me, my body—became part of this world.

Evan at eight, nine, thirteen. At eighteen, twenty-five, thirty-two.

Keep loving yourself, even when the world forgets to love you.

And the world will forget sometimes. Then, remember to wrap your arms about yourself as you did about your mother.

"You are the best son."

EILEEN POLLACK

❾

Syllogisms

All scientists are men.
I am a scientist.
Therefore I must be . . .

In 1974, when I was eighteen years old, a gynecologist at the Yale student health service explained that I excelled in science and math because I was actually a man.

I had scheduled an appointment with this gynecologist because I hadn't gotten my period since arriving on campus six months before. I knew I wasn't pregnant—promiscuous to a point, I found it harder to lose my virginity than other girls, who majored in English or art. Something in the intricate tangles and tubes of my reproductive system had gotten, well, stuck. In seventh grade I had bought a sanitary napkin from a vending machine. By eleventh grade, when I needed it, the wrapping had decayed, the cotton padding inside was brittle and ink-stained from lying in the bottom of my various purses, the safety pins with which I was supposed to attach the napkin to my underpants flaked to rust in my hand.

My period, even then, wasn't very periodical. It came, disappeared, came again three months later, then vanished like some puppy let out to do its business, too young and confused to find its way home. And so, when my parents dropped me off at college that first afternoon, I wasn't surprised that my period didn't stay. Such a recent companion, it wasn't yet loyal. It couldn't pick out my scent among all those male odors—centuries of pipe smoke, shaving cream, and sweat suffusing musty halls in which women had lived for only four years. I tried not to fret. A theory then current dictated that a girl's period would eventually fall into sync with the periods of the other women she lived with— something about the effects of shared schedules of feeding and light, so many seedlings in a greenhouse, an odd theory since no two women in that dorm kept the same schedule, and, as far as I could tell, the lights were on all the time. But I subscribed to that theory. The other women got their periods on some cue from the moon, and, half a beat behind, mine would catch up. In the meantime, I was thrilled to be away from home, studying the first challenging courses I had been allowed to study—physics, advanced calculus, chemistry, and chem lab. Still, six months was six months. I hadn't gotten my period, and even the most scatterbrained pup should have found me by now.

I went to see that gynecologist. I remember his name but I won't write it here; a women's group on campus eventually got rid of him, but he's still practicing *somewhere*, and I haven't got the money or the time to be sued.

I peed in a Dixie cup. A nurse siphoned blood from my arm. That was the extent of the physical exam. I sat across from that doctor in my baggy shirt and jeans, which only goes to prove that a gynecologist doesn't need to get your heels in his stirrups if he means to abuse you.

He intended, he said, to send away my blood and urine to be tested. But even in this office, without the results, he could diagnose what was wrong.

"Yes?" I said. "The diagnosis?" I was precisely that age when a woman suspects one freakish flaw prevents her from resembling other women.

The doctor leaned across his desk, hands steepled at the fingertips. "Do you mind if I ask a few questions?" he said. "Do you enjoy athletics? Are you proud of your abilities as an athlete?"

"Why, yes," I said modestly. In elementary school, I'd been so juiced with excitement at being alive you could have hooked me to a generator and powered my town. If I hadn't worked off that extra energy—beating boys at races, cracking balls across the fence—I would have sparked and blown up. In junior high I learned that beating boys at races wouldn't get you asked out, so I made myself over, joined the tennis team, skied—a girl could play tennis and ski and not be called butch. I looked like a girl. I acted like a girl—I wore hot pants to dances, knotted threads around my wrist in the cabalistic hope some older boy I loved would rip this bracelet off at midnight and so grant my wish that my love be returned. I necked behind the bakery with a certain kind of boy—not the most popular, but the smarter boys, the boys who overlooked my grades in favor of my reputation for being, well, a girl who would neck behind the bakery. But on hot afternoons, boiling with eagerness to escape my hometown, I wriggled through the fence around the track behind the high school and ran lap after lap, jumped hurdle after hurdle. This was still the early seventies. Girls didn't jump hurdles. At least girls in my town didn't. Even at Yale, it took me months to meet the Amazons who rowed crew or played rugby, so well lunged and well muscled I couldn't call myself an athlete if that's what *they* were. But I hadn't yet encountered them, and I therefore admitted what the doctor surmised.

He nodded—*I thought so*—then reached across his desk and stroked my cheek, near the jaw. The gesture could have been a lover's caress, but the way he rubbed his finger with his thumb he seemed more like a detective dusting some surface for cocaine. "And this?" he said. "Have you noticed that you have excessive amounts of fuzz on your cheeks?"

How could I deny this? I prided myself on not having a mustache, like the friends who had started bleaching their upper lips in eighth grade, but that didn't mitigate the evidence that I had fuzz on my cheeks.

"You're a science major, aren't you? You're good at science? And math?"

I flushed with the fame I was sure had preceded me: I was the first female undergraduate to major in physics since Yale went coed.

"I'm certain that the tests will confirm this," he said. "You've got too much male hormone. I wouldn't be surprised if you were sterile as well. You can take the pill in this envelope—a morning-after pill, it's called. It's a strong dose of female hormone. It might jolt your system into giving you a period, but it probably won't work. When we get the results of your lab tests we'll give you a call and you can come back to start your treatment."

I thanked him and left, relieved because the mystery of my strangeness was solved. I wasn't like the other girls because I was something better. A boy.

That night on the phone I told my mother I was sterile. I couldn't figure out why she seemed so upset. I didn't want kids anyway. I had gotten such a late start studying physics that I would have to spend the rest of my life catching up with the boys.

My mother recalls none of this. Announcing my sterility was only one of a host of unsettling revelations I issued that year. She must have guessed the gynecologist's diagnosis was nonsense. The women in our family were all "late developers." At some level I knew this. I took the pill the doctor gave me. My period bloomed the next day. The lab never called. The following month I got my period, and the months after that, with increasing regularity, until finally, one month, after I was married, it failed to show up: I was so fertile, it turned out, I could get pregnant from a single sperm sneaking through a pinhole prick in my diaphragm and surviving a toxic-waste dump of spermicide to fertilize an egg. Later, in my mid-thirties, when my husband and I conceived a child on purpose, we needed only two tries.

> *Girls never finish programs in science and math.*
> *I am a girl.*
> *Therefore I won't . . .*

I wasn't born loving science. The youngest child, I performed. I told stories. I lied. In first grade, to keep me busy, Mrs. Prettyman said I ought to "write down a story." I thought she meant I should copy some version of *Sleeping Beauty* I had heard somewhere else and I didn't see the point. Only when she urged me to *make up* my own story did I become crazed with this activity. I was clumsy with clay. I couldn't reproduce a tune, let alone invent one. My Lego inventions collapsed beneath the weight of impossible dreams. But I could *make up* a story, set it out on creamy paper with dotted blue lines so my classmates could read it, and immediately another story would pop up to take its place, an endless supply, like tissues from a tissue box. I was annoyed when my teachers conveyed their satisfaction that I would grow up to be a writer. Writing was a nice, acceptable hobby a woman could pursue while she raised children and cooked. But what else was worth studying? In math class we learned one new concept each fall, then spent the winter and spring reviewing it. Science class consisted of propping celery stalks in inkwells and watching black-and-white movies about tornadoes and rocks.

In junior high the principal corralled us in the gym and administered a test. Since our school was too poor to provide college-prep courses in science and math, the administration decided to skip ahead those few students who scored highest on the test; when they reached eleventh grade, these students would be bused to the community college to take advanced courses there. The boy who had scored first was jumped ahead one year. I had scored second on the test, but I wasn't selected. The boys who had scored third and fourth, like so many checkers being jumped above my head, were skipped ahead, too. When I sent my mother to protest, the chairman of the math department informed her that girls never finish programs in science and math, so what would be the point in advancing me now? Besides, skipping a girl would ruin her chances for a social life.

Since my older sister was studying for a bachelor's degree in math, I couldn't see that the first argument carried much weight. I had no social life to speak of, so what could be ruined? But my parents were the sort who took a teacher's word about what was best for their child, and the math teacher stood firm.

And the firmer he stood, the more clearly he conveyed his impression that I wasn't as smart as I believed, that I was too aggressive for a girl, and the more rebellious I grew. I handed in my homework on the backs of used envelopes, skipped class or came late, tossed out challenges to stump him, leaned my chair against the wall and cracked vulgar jokes he could hear. And then, junior year, I stopped coming to class. I stopped coming to *school*. I drove to the library at the community college and tackled the shelf of science books there. I taught myself calculus from a textbook I had found with the answers in back. At the stationery store on Main Street, I tried to buy some paperbacks about astronomy and physics by men like Isaac Asimov. The proprietor refused. "Oh, I can't let you spend your money on these! You'll never understand them." She pointed to a rack of Harlequin romances. "The girls books are back there."

Whatever my motives, I came to love what I read. What was time? What was space? How did life come to be? In texts written in the thirties by well-mannered Brits with "Sir" before their names, I thrilled to descriptions of Schrödinger's cat, uncertain Mr. Heisenberg, the reasons that prevented any being in the universe—even a girl as clever as me—from traveling faster than light. I forced the principal to let me take the advanced placement exams with the boys who had been skipped. I got a five in every subject, including English literature.

But none of this prepared me to keep up with the boys in my classes at Yale. Most of them had studied two years of college physics and college calc at their prep schools. The male students, I learned later, formed study groups in their dorms and divvied up the problems while I labored through pages of calculations alone. Every time I asked a question I could hear the boys think: *Sure, the dumb girl is slowing down the class.* Though later they admitted that pride kept them from revealing how befuddled they were, that they were always relieved when I demanded the professor slow down and explain how he had derived some result.

I was hopeless in lab. I hadn't grown up rebuilding cars with my dad, nailing birdhouses in shop. My hands shook with anxiety, knowing as I did that all the male students were watching me and waiting for *the girl* to fuck up. On the first day of chem lab I spilled hydrochloric acid; my nylon stockings dissolved into reddish-brown rivulets I took to be blood, my skin sizzled and smoked until the teaching assistant dumped baking soda on the nylon to neutralize the acid, and everyone stared at my mottled, red-and-white legs. I vowed never to wear a dress or skirt on campus. I would chop my hair short, speak gruffly or not at all, and try to pass as a man. A few weeks later the gynecologist informed me that my blood was brimming with testosterone. Everything fit.

Except my desire, which was always for men. Physicists and mathematicians have reputations as geeks, but Michael Z., who taught the three-term introductory physics sequence, was graceful, broad shouldered, with a dark curly beard, eyes blue as swimming pools, and the most illuminating smile I had ever seen in a man. I got a 17 on my first physics exam—I had never seen lower than a 95 in high school—and went sadly to Mike's office to drop the course and switch majors.

"The other students . . ." I complained. "They all have better backgrounds."

"No, no." He smiled knowingly. "The problem is that you're looking at the guys in the other lanes."

Other lanes?

Sure. At Stanford, he had always come in second in his swim meets. *Mike,* the coach said, *you keep looking over your shoulder to see how the other guys are doing. That's the reason you lose.*

This was good advice, I knew. But the reason I didn't drop introductory physics was that I wanted Mike to like me. I devoted twenty hours to each week's homework for his course. I went in for extra help. And yes, I came in fourth out of one hundred students on the final exam.

After three terms with Mike, I took another three-term sequence, this time in quantum mechanics, from a lanky Hungarian I'll call Peter N. A menace in labs, unable to assemble the most basic apparatus, I found I had a talent for imagining things that couldn't be imagined—electrons whose locations were clouds of probabilities, particles that could move backward and forward in time. I took courses in higher math from a brilliant mathematician who had earned tenure in his twenties. Handsome in a distracted, otherworldly way, this professor, Roger H., would cup his palms like the insurance agent cradling that house in the State Farm commercial and stare at the n-dimensional solid only he saw. He wore a Mexican poncho; when he pulled it off in class, his shirt lifted from his jeans, and the sight of that gap, and the gap between his teeth, which he revealed when he smiled, led me to consider impossible realms. *What if*, he always said, introducing a problem. *What if, what if . . .*

I kept these crushes to myself. Desire seemed small and out of place on Science Hill, a puny topic compared with the curvature of space, quasars, black holes. I continued to wear my jeans and baggy sweatshirts. But once, in Roger's office, as we studied some text about the propagation of waves, the wind slammed his door shut. He stopped in midsentence, got up, crossed the room, reopened the door, then resumed our discussion. Despite my disguise, he seemed to know I was a woman. Which I wanted. And didn't.

We've all heard the tale: in terror of disgrace I overshot the mark and completed my major with nearly all A's. I imagined I had achieved this honor not through talent, but stubborn brute force. I thought I couldn't think, although, looking back, I only lacked confidence. If I had gone on to grad school—and I could have gotten in, as my classmates reminded me, because grad schools needed women—I would have learned how to think.

But I didn't go to grad school. At least, not in physics. I asked Peter N. if he would write me a recommendation, and he surprised me by saying he would write this letter only if we went to lunch first.

"This way I can find out more about you," he said in that thick Hungarian accent that made me so aware of his tongue and his lips. Introducing a new principle, he would stand beside the board with one leg folded flat behind him, jerk his head so the shank of brown hair between his eyes would fly up. "All right then!" he would say. "Let's devil up the math!" or rather, as I realized with disappointment much later, "Let's *develop* the math."

We took the elevator to the cafeteria on the top floor of the Kline Science Tower and found seats among the men eating lunch.

"So, tell me what you like to do besides physics," Peter asked.

Do? Besides physics?

He motioned me to start the tuna fish sandwich I was too giddy to eat. "All these years I think this Eileen must be interesting person, she asks such interesting questions, only woman in class, and now I find out she's as boring as rest." As for him, he loved music. He and his wife went to concerts all the time.

But when did he find time to go to concerts? I asked. Wasn't he worried he would fall behind in his research?

He flapped his bony hands. "My classmates said the same thing."

And? I said.

"And!" He laughed a goofy laugh, then flapped his hands to indicate the scientists around us. "I'm still here! I'm at Yale. How far behind can I be?" He finished off his sandwich. "So?" he said. "What is some hobby you like?"

Hobby? I thought desperately. "I used to like writing."

"Writing!" He smiled. He would furnish a recommendation—provided I signed up for a writing seminar first.

All right, I said. I promise.

"Good!" He slapped the table. "Someday you write novel and dedicate to me!"

When strangers ask why I threw away those years of brain-cracking toil and allowed my high-school math teacher the right to say, "See? Girls never finish programs in science or math," I give various replies. I wasn't brilliant enough to be a theoretical physicist. I was too clumsy and proud to spend my life working in a solid-state lab, where failed theoreticians tend to end up. I was exhausted by the struggle to overcome my slow start. I lacked confidence in my own ability to think, to set myself a problem and *devil up* an experiment to pursue some result. On the other hand, stories flowered in my head. I played with content and form with the bravado of someone who has been writing for years.

These reasons are true. But the truest reason is this: I took that first writing class, then a second, and a third, and I found myself discussing longing and love with attractive young men who complimented my stories but never expressed a longing for me, and beautiful young women with pre-Raphaelite hair whom the male writers *did* sleep with, and I knew that I couldn't spend the rest of my life pretending that desire was a weaker force than gravity, electromagnetism, or radioactive decay.

> *All writers are women.*
> *I am a writer.*
> *Therefore I must be . . .*

I studied literature in England, worked as a journalist in New Hampshire, enrolled for two years in the writers' workshop at Iowa. I grew my hair long, bought myself a wardrobe of dresses and skirts—first with long hemlines, then with much shorter. Men no longer edged away when I mentioned what I did. But I missed the respect, the sense that most people, when they heard I studied physics, assumed I was smart. What do you need to

know to be a writer? How people kiss? Whenever I taught freshman comp, I sneaked in a reference to my physics degree and so
gained the grudging regard of the engineering majors, who were
taking a writing class under duress. I married a scientist in part
because I loved him, and in part because I considered scientists
to be smarter and more serious than businessmen or artists. I
wrote passionless stories heavy on themes that would demonstrate my brilliance, avoiding any subject such as marriage or sex
that might cause a male editor to dismiss my work as "women's
fiction."

And then I gave birth. I nursed my son, marveling how I
could have lived thirty-five years on this earth without reading a
description of the throat-clotting tenderness a nursing mother
can feel. I came to think that nothing in life was more important
than a parent's love for her child, came to see that it was as difficult to write something beautiful, moving, and profound as to
devil up a theorem about space-time or genes.

> *All scientists are men.*
> *All writers are women.*
> *My son is a man.*
> *Therefore my son must grow up to be a . . .*

We hold an infant and decide if his almond-shaped eyes came
from Mom's side or Dad's, and then, when he is older, if his pro-
clivity for science was passed along with those eyes. We map
variables of character along axes we have been taught to see as
orthogonal. We tie our children to these crosses and graph their
silhouettes: this much art, that much science, this much female,
that much male. We raise them by the "logic" implanted in our
brains from our earliest years. Busy as we are with parenthood
and work, who has the clarity of mind to examine all the cocka-
mamy syllogisms that govern our lives? Or we wreak some opposite harm by inverting those theorems, not stopping to consider
that an illogical theorem standing on its head is no less absurd

than such a theorem standing upright. Which would be worse, if I pressured my son to be a scientist, or pressured him to write? God knows what I might have pressured a daughter to do.

I tell myself I'm not pushing Noah to be a scientist. At a year he would sit with a plastic toy called Mr. Twisty, unscrewing the hat, the head, the left arm, the right arm, the body (even older children tried to tug apart the pieces rather than untwist them), then he would screw the parts together, one by one, unscrew them, until strangers, unbidden, came over to say that they had never seen a baby who could concentrate so long on such a hard task. At the video store he insisted on renting "yellow movies"— not pornography, but *National Geographic* specials, an hour long each. At three, he stunned my mother by naming dozens of fish at the New England Aquarium, including the Humu-humu-nuku-nuku-apuaa (she thought he was talking baby talk until I pointed out the triggerfish swimming by his face). In the bath, he grew furious at my unsatisfactory explanations of how the universe started, what lay beyond its edge, how millions of species of animals evolved from those first simple cells. He discovered how to multiply while sitting on the toilet, staring at the ceramic tiles on our wall, then spooked his teachers at preschool by asking them to give him "times problems" to do. Four times three? Six times four? "I see pictures in my brain and count the answer," he said. It wasn't a parlor trick; he could think in abstract terms. "Mom," he said one evening, "did you know if you add 'finity and 'finity, you still get one 'finity?" And he laughed at how ridiculous infinity was.

If a talent for thinking in scientific terms can be inherited, my son received a double dose of that gene. He also has two parents who encourage him to think as a scientist thinks. His favorite bedtime reading consists of a series of books his father ordered: *Cell Wars, Amazing Schemes Within Your Genes, DNA Is Here to Stay.* Just yesterday I found Noah staring at the sink. The light from the window shone in such a way as to isolate the drops in the thin stream trickling from the faucet. "Why's it doing that?" he said. "You can see bubbles in the water. Is water made of bubbles?" We talked about how hard it is to predict the exact instant that a succession of drips switches to a flow, how the equations that govern the behavior of water are so complicated that scientists haven't ever solved them. Noah stared a while longer. "It's like these photographs," he said. "They use a strobo . . . strobo-something." "A stroboscopic light?" He flapped his hands, as he does when some new thought excites him. "They used a stroboscope light to take pictures of this drop splashing in a puddle. That's what's happening now, isn't it, Mommy? The light from the window is being like a stroboscope and slowing down the water so we can see the drips." I never could have thought such a thought at his age. Then again, my own parents would have snapped the faucet shut and said to stop wasting water. My son, unlike me, will never be behind. He'll have the head start I didn't.

But a head start at what? Why am I so anxious he grow up to be a scientist, undistracted by the detours that made me the insecure but many-sided person I am? Why don't I want my son to be a writer? He spoke at nine months, which is young for a boy. He loves making up stories. When I'm practicing the piano he likes to sit beside me and "play his emotions." The truth is, these days, I barely can be bothered to skim the garbled accounts of scientific discoveries in the popular press, let alone study the unintelligible journals like *Nature* and *Cell* to which my husband subscribes.

The years my husband spent working through the night, holidays and weekends to earn his Ph.D., and then his M.D., working as a post-doc to publish enough papers to earn his own lab, then staying late to work beside his own post-docs and technicians to produce enough *results* to guarantee his funding, the resentment with which I respond to his announcement of a new mutation he's found, the lowering of his lids as I persist in discussing some novel I've been reading, all this prevents me from seeing science as I used to—as a thrilling abstraction, a monu-

ment to human creativity and intellect. I see it now as a jugger-
naut that demands bone-crushing sacrifice. Do I really want my
son to serve such a god?

In my less self-critical moments I think Noah will be happier
as a scientist than as a writer. He'll be better paid and respected.
He won't need to work a shit job (while I was waitressing at
HoJo's or transcribing Dictaphone belts in the screwy insurance
office where I earned money for school, my husband was already
a teenage technician in a pharmaceuticals lab). If my son
becomes a scientist he won't find himself correcting *it's* and *its* at
age forty. Scientists may bicker about who left the wad of paper
towels in the sink, whose name gets listed first on a paper, but
the communal give-and-take of a lab is healthier than the soli-
tude of a morning spent alone hacking at a paragraph, not a single exchange with anyone except the telephone solicitor who
calls to persuade you that your chimney needs cleaning.

The frustration is the same—the months of failed experi-
ments, the heavy chunk of manuscript thudding in the trash—
but scientists waste less time questioning that their work will
help humankind. Most scientists are optimists. They find comfort in the way everything *fits*. The Invisible Hand performs its
deft trick and supply meets demand. One universal constant
governs the conversion of energy to matter. Every coil of DNA
codes for some protein, enzymes bond with substrates in a lock-
and-key fit, each gland secretes a hormone, blood flows in, then
ebbs out, billions of reactions loop and interact within the neat
package of our skin. Conservative scientists believe Nature will
eventually straighten out our problems (so what if evolution
moves on a scale geologically slow?), while liberals keep faith
that human beings whose minds mastered calculus and quarks
will come up with solutions to poverty and war.

Writers, on the other hand, meditate obsessively about conflict and despair, desires rarely met, the suffering and loss that
mark most human lives. A student of mine, a handsome young
man so gifted and kind it is impossible to imagine that any man

or woman could refuse him, produced technically proficient but slick stories for my class. "He might become a great writer," remarked a colleague, "if some girl breaks his heart." No one would say such a thing about a physicist. There's something boyish about most scientists, as if they've spent their lives enjoying some delightfully complex, if mind-taunting game. Scientists think of love and sex as recreation, what you do to relax after hours in the lab. Sure, they've been hurt, but rather than pursue an irrational passion or succumb to despair, they shrug sadly, give up, and devote even longer hours to their work.

Perhaps, like any mother, I want to spare my son heartache. A running jump in science will propel him to success. He'll never get sidetracked by the spirit-stealing jobs and impossible passions like the ones that distracted me. Established in his field, he'll look around and choose some nice female colleague with whom to settle down, build a house, and raise kids.

But is that really all I want, that my son have an easy, confident career? Do I want a son who doesn't know the sort of romantic desire that disrupts the neatly planned boundaries of your life?

To give my son the biggest head start, he ought to go to Greenhills, the private school in town. But a private school would mean he wouldn't come in contact with the sorts of students I knew—poor kids and mean kids, kids who couldn't grasp the concept of a cosine but played the violin so beautifully they drew the bow across your heart. Science labs are filled with Chinese and Russian immigrants, but if my son becomes a scientist the only native-born minorities he's likely to encounter will be the guys who empty the cans of radioactive waste and the women who wash the glassware. What if he comes to scorn anyone less gifted than he? One afternoon, Noah begged me to help with a computer-game puzzle. The gears and levers on the screen filled me with dread, but I feigned bravery, the way I pretend I'm not scared when he wakes me to kill a spider. But every way I tried to rearrange those gears, the machine jammed, the gears froze. My mind jammed and froze, too.

"Mommy, that's stupid!" he said. "Can't you do gears?"

Maybe the answer is to raise your child laissez-faire, as my parents raised me, their only concern that I be healthy and happy, well clothed and well fed. I might not have been so fired with ambition if someone else had been pushing me. I have no one to blame for my mistakes but myself.

But I can't accept that a parent can do nothing to give her child a head start. I can help my son acquire the ability to sit quietly and pay attention, with love; the capacity to enjoy the beauty of a detail; the talent for wonder; the confidence to ask a question worth answering.

Once a year, Noah's school sponsors something called an interest fair. Not a science fair, an *interest* fair. I helped Noah brainstorm, but my most inspired idea—papier-mâché sculptures of fish—didn't seem to, well, interest him.

Then his father suggested a project on bones. A classmate had recently pushed Noah off the monkey bars and he had broken his arm, though no one seemed to believe this. When I picked Noah up from school he seemed shaken and pale, but the nurse assured me several times the fall hadn't been serious. When an afternoon of cartoons didn't make Noah forget to cradle his arm, when he told me that his wrist just didn't feel right, I called my husband at the lab to see if I shouldn't take Noah to the hospital. He hinted that I might be overreacting and advised me to make an after-hours appointment at the pediatric clinic where we usually go. That evening, in the waiting room, I tried to comfort my child by promising him that someone would make his arm better soon. But the doctor dismissed my concern. She sent Noah into tears by pressing on his wrist, then took this as evidence that my son was a sissy ("He's not very stoic!") rather than a sign he was telling the truth. She wrapped a bandage around the arm and said, if I insisted, I could take him to the hospital for an X ray the next morning. *Are you sure?* I kept saying. *Shouldn't we take him to the ER to have it diagnosed now?* Even at 2 A.M., when Noah woke screaming for his mother to please, *please* stop the pain, his father and I argued about whether it was necessary to make a trip to the hospital in the middle of the night or to wait until dawn.

A month later, arm healed, Noah couldn't help but wonder about the nature of the skeleton he had once taken for granted. With his father's help, he put together his exhibit—the X rays of his fracture, the neon-orange cast the doctor sawed off, vials of bonemeal and chalk, a chicken bone soaked in vinegar to leach out the minerals and leave the bone bendy as a dog's rubber toy. As he and his father typed the captions to their specimens, I sat off to one side and tried not to resent this interest they shared, not to mention my own father's indifference to the science-fair project I had put together myself twenty-seven years earlier—a hydroponic garden of radishes, tomatoes, lima beans, and peas. Every evening after school I bounded up the stairs to observe each plant's growth, the naked white roots curling like a baby's toes around the chicken wire suspended across the mouths of huge tanks. With a tiny metal spatula from my brother's chemistry set I measured so many grams of magnesium or zinc—I loved handling the weights, those compact brass cylinders with the value inscribed in script on the bottom, this many grains of powder and the pans balanced just so. I can still recall the humid smell of vermiculite, the courage with which I bit that first radish, the salty flesh on my tongue, the paralyzing terror with which I watched myself tip an enamel vat of nutrients so it puddled on the floor, the panic as I raced down the stairs to the dining room and tried to blot the ceiling, only to see the plaster peel away on the towel in swaths.

On and on branched those memories: the smell of Magic Marker as I inked my display; the General Electric robot beaming by the door to the high school cafeteria, its lightbulb-shaped head swiveling *left right left right*, blinking us in; the nervousness and pride I felt setting up my project next to Randy Katz's display about African violets, the velvet feel of those leaves, how jealous Randy was that after all her hard work I still won first prize, how later that year she said I would never learn to dance because I *just didn't have soul,* a statement I believed for decades until I figured out that Randy Katz knew as much about dancing and soul as that gynecologist knew about women.

The night of Noah's interest fair two freckled boys in T-shirts and dotted bow ties stood beside the entrance playing violins with so much loopy passion, their arms bent at the elbows, flapping like wings; they reminded me of my old professor, Peter N. On the other side of the door a girl offered samples of the cakes she had prepared. My son grabbed my hand and pulled me through the maelstrom, pointing out the projects he especially liked—an Erector set robot, an exhibit of eggs painted to resemble a barnyard of creatures—pig, owl, moose. And there in the middle of that packed auditorium, we found ourselves stuck. All we could do was stand rooted in one spot and sniff the sharp odors of baking soda and vinegar from some child's volcano demonstration, the musty stench of frogs, hermit crabs, and hamsters displayed proudly as pets, the peanut-butter breath the children exhaled, the sweaty clothes their parents had been wearing at work, the diapers and moist zwieback of the siblings in tow. Standing there, immobile, listening to the kids exhorting their parents, *Look at this! Look at this!,* I came to think how meaningless phrases like "head start" and "catching up" really are—they brought to mind a driver who weaves between cars at ridiculous speeds, only to end up idling at the same red light as everyone else.

The most creative thinkers in any field use their imaginations to see beyond false dichotomies. Light is a wave and a particle, *both.* Inheritance *and* nurture determine our fate. Humbert Humbert is guilty and innocent, *both.*

What would Noah take away from his project? That a bone stewed in vinegar becomes rubbery and soft? That a kid, for no reason, might push him off the monkey bars? That even as he lay screaming in his bed in the middle of the night, his parents stood above him, arguing about whether his arm was really broken? If he grows up to discover the cure to some deformity, or to write a novel about how badly his parents bickered that year, the year he broke his arm, all that matters is this: he knows we both love him. He understands that he, like everyone else, is the miraculous creation of both science and art.

NAOMI SHIHAB NYE

9

Little Nomad

There are no bad towns.
LIONEL GARCIA

HE HAD A hundred beds.

His indigo traveling coat was stitched together with bright swatches of Guatemalan fabric.

He stood by the window of a plane reciting the alphabet, turning the necklace of letters on his tongue, when he was one. At two he chanted Bruce Springsteen with wild, fist-raising fervor.

He considered pretzels. Debated their shapes. Spoke to strangers easily and we encouraged it. Once a raucous drunk man on a plane asked him how old he was and he said, "Three," but continued, "You're acting younger than me." The surrounding passengers clapped.

He got mad if I answered for him, if the flight attendant said, "What would he like?" and I pretended to know.

Where did we go? We went everywhere, almost. When he was seven he said, "Are you and I just like specks of dust compared to the whole world? Well, you—you're bigger. You might be a spot in the carpet."

The first sentence Madison ever wrote was "One day a boy went to Mexico." He was three years old and scrawled it perfectly at the foot of a linen page. I was peeling mangoes and I dropped the knife.

Other than his own name, I hadn't realized he could write yet. He rode on my shoulders through the flamboyant vegetable markets of Chiapas before the uprising. He didn't like markets: too many rich, conflicting smells, too many people crowded close together. We were living in the ancient San Cristobal de las Casas house, once inhabited by monks and later by the poet W. S. Merwin, where Madison had taken his first steps on crooked paving stones two years earlier. Every morning his father went off into the streets to photograph and Madison and I did errands, fed pigeons, visited friends. It took us half a morning to haul a sack of laundry across town by foot.

At night a blazing fireplace kept us warm. Madison learned to throw by pitching balled-up Mexican newspapers into the flames.

Before he was ten we drove across the United States more than once, never regretting it. We camped at Miracle Beach, Vancouver Island, among the smooth, black stones, lived six months in Hawaii, draping our drying leis from nails in the wall, landed on the shortest jet-length runway in the Western Hemisphere (the Aleutian Islands), managed to be in Cairo for the worst sandstorm of the twentieth century, and in Jordan for the worst blizzard of the twentieth century. Soon it would be the twenty-first century and nobody could make such sweeping claims for a while.

Madison went bowling in Amman and sledding in Vermont. He ordered cocoa in Montreal. He had his own file of frequent-flyer cards. He touched the craggy cheeks of his Palestinian great-grandmother in the West Bank during the *Intifada*. She was 105 and he was five. I tried to picture one hundred years standing between them. It was impossible.

What did it do to our lives to go so many places?

He never once said, "I want to go home."

At home, if we hauled our suitcases to the attic, they had only a short rest. Sometimes we just left them openmouthed beside our beds.

Once, when we had been restored to our downtown San Antonio cottage, circa 1906, with its high ceilings, wraparound front porch, and purple porch swing, for about three days, Madison asked, *How long do we have to stay in this old house?*

He wanted to pack twenty-seven flashlights. He always needed batteries. Though other children must be steered firmly past candy displays at grocery stores, it was batteries that would set him off. *Double A! Oh Mom, Mom, I need a Double A battery DESPERATELY and you JUST WON'T BUY IT FOR ME!*

That's right, I won't. *Didn't you get a battery-charger for Christmas?* Keep moving.

But what if ALL THE LIGHTS GO OUT IN IDAHO?

Move.

His pocket-sized organizer needed a battery. His two weather radios. His hand-me-down laptop computer, his shortwave radio, which he purchased with Christmas money from grandparents, all battery-eating beasts. For a brief period he insisted batteries needed mothers, and that's why he always wanted extra ones. Once, passing through Presidio, Texas, in the blistering heat of July, he asked if we could please cross the border into Ojinaga, Mexico, to price the batteries over there.

The worst thing is, we did it.

They weren't a bargain.

No one is encouraging when you announce you are taking off on a far journey with a child. They say, *What if he gets diarrhea?*

No one says, *You will have a marvelous time and we will think of you.* They say, *Don't sit in front of plate-glass windows in case anyone throws a bomb at the restaurant while you are eating. Sit in the back.*

Someone even told me I should carry Madison's own tin plate and spoon around with us in Mexico because travelers most often took ill from water droplets clinging to recently washed restaurant plates. *Huh?* There are so many things we forget to worry about.

Okay, I did it. The waiters looked at me strangely. He never got diarrhea. He got a rash from flea bites in San Cristobal and vomited into the lap of a scuba diving instructor on a flight out of Dallas once, but diarrhea was never our problem.

His father had worse problems. His father fainted on the staircase on a double-decker transpacific jumbo jet out of Honolulu, toppled down from business class (they had upgraded us as a gift) into the startled coach division, and smashed his head on a drinks cart. He was out cold in the aisle when the flight attendant aroused me in urgent tones, *Quickly, come! Your husband has had an accident!*

On an airplane?

I pictured him flipping open an EXIT door and strolling out into the atmosphere.

Madison snoozed peacefully in his seat as I staggered downstairs to my horizontal husband surrounded by onlookers. A groggy doctor suggested he might have broken his neck. He pointed a finger into my face. "If he did, *YOUR LIFE* is changed." I could punch him even now, thinking of it.

Michael woke gradually, moaning that he was numb. The doctor tied him onto a plank of some kind that the attendant had produced from a closet. A whole bevy of beachcombers heaved him into first class.

The fancy passengers hated us. We kept turning on lights so the doctor could take his blood pressure. I realized I should go upstairs and reclaim our sleeping son, who would then ask his thousand questions in a high and chirping midnight tone. *What happened to Daddy? Why? Why is that America West blanket tied around his neck like a giant bow tie? Why is Daddy looking—so weird? Why did we have to change our seats? My seat is very big!*

At Phoenix the disgruntled passengers were instructed to remain on the plane while the local fire department came on board with a stretcher to collect my husband. *Where are they taking Daddy? Why can't we go with him now?*

We couldn't go with him because we had nine illicitly huge carry-on items, mostly my husband's camera equipment, to struggle off the plane with under the disgusted, good-riddance gazes of the flight attendants.

Michael's ambulance was long gone to the emergency room by the time we made it to the taxi stand.

We had not wanted to leave the islands. Madison had started kindergarten at a public school called Hokulani ("Reach for the Stars") with a beautiful teacher. He had learned to sing songs in Hawaiian. (Too wracked with sorrow over our precious baby growing older, I could not even accompany Madison and his daddy to school on the first day. Michael later reported that Madison, dressed by choice in a white shirt and bow tie, shrieked with sobs upon arrival and tore off running across a field.) Still we realized how lucky he was to begin his official education in a colorful classroom with a whole wide wall open to the outdoors.

I did not place socks on my feet for six full months. We lived in the same spartan one-room apartment Michael Ondaatje had lived in while writing *The English Patient*. Our windows stared out toward Diamond Head and glittering downtown Honolulu, then straight on to the sweet gigantic margin of the sea. We had one big bed, three bowls, three spoons, and a hot plate. At night the roaring trade winds kept us awake. I bought earplugs. Teaching creative writing at the university seemed very secondary simply to *being there*. Michael was photographing daily in a rain forest.

Each day after school Madison and I rode a bus down from our mountain to the beach to wander among towels and surfboards. I grew attached to the shoulders of young, skinny Japanese men. He slurped Hawaiian ice in fruity flavors. He ran and dipped and splashed. His first passport photo was taken in Honolulu—wavy hair down to his shoulders, a beachcomber's airy gaze.

Sometimes we strolled our hilly neighborhood in the evenings gathering succulent petals that litter the sidewalks so elegantly in Hawaii—magenta, pale pink, intoxicating fragrances. The sorrow I felt over dropped petals was impossible to understand. Was the romance with one's own child the single best gift of our lives? Profoundly elemental and excruciatingly fleeting at the same time, it bore an indelible scent. Once I had wondered something similar about *my* childhood, as I stood right in the center of it. Were the best, sweetest, deepest years flying away that very moment? I wondered this again while childhood skipped along beside us.

Madison called these nightly hikes his "potion walks." Carrying a small brown paper bag for collecting, he mixed up mysterious brews—sugar, water, stones, leaves, shampoo, petals—in a saucepan back at home. How could we bear to leave such a place? But my job in Hawaii was a finite one.

My husband, despite a stiff neck that lasted a week, was just fine. Obviously he had good, flexible bones and muscles. A few years later he would puff up like a blowfish on a flight to Anchorage, skin pocked with raging hives, an allergic reaction to a sulfa drug he'd been taking for a few days. He had trouble breathing and was whisked to an emergency room immediately upon landing again, where they pumped Adrenalin into his veins and told him he'd been fifteen minutes from *adieu*.

Do you want to fly with my husband?

Back in Texas, after a tempestuous pass-around bout of flu, we vowed to take another trip as soon as possible. My father, Aziz, agreed to cross the ocean with Madison and me for a month, though he'd just returned from his hometown of Jerusalem and barely read his accumulated mail. He was cranky about returning so soon. But I hounded him till he agreed. The possibility of a four-generation rendezvous with my Palestinian grandmother seemed too tantalizing to miss.

Since she was around 105, it didn't seem we should wait any longer. Madison had heard tales of his Arabic-speaking great-*Sitti* since he was born—her grinning photo hung near his bed. My father told us our Arab ancestors were nomads who "ran horses" across the vast deserts of southern Egypt before they came to Palestine and settled down. This was long, long ago. He said, "We don't know much else about them."

We met up with Aziz at Kennedy Airport and took off again. My father had requested "Muslim meals" for his flights and received picturesque platters of kebobs and rice. Madison was tantalized. "Kid meals," with cartoonish wrappings and boring bags of chips, had far less appeal.

From that first airborne meal together, eating would become a keynote element of our Middle Eastern wanderings, preferable to politics in any language—succulent Jericho oranges with thin skins, minty scrambled eggs, steaming stacks of pita, fried eggplant dipped in sumac, plump dates, stewed okra over steaming rice, and a thousand perfect dishes of hummus. Who needed politics? Obviously they hadn't done much good for anybody yet. We were met at the Tel Aviv airport by a thoughtful American diplomat with a box of Legos in his hands for Madison, to help him feel welcomed to Jerusalem. Every bed we slept in on our journey would now sprout a tall tower of primary yellows and reds.

Madison raced up and down the stairs of our ancient stone hotel in east Jerusalem. His voice bounced off the walls. The desk clerks seemed pleased to welcome such a young traveler. He investigated their clicking radiators. The clerks offered him bowls of fresh yogurt whenever he appeared in the lobby. He gobbled triangles of bread by the sixes and sevens.

The three of us wandered the sad, graffiti-ridden streets, visiting my father's friend, the shopkeeper at the Ritz Hotel, who pointed at Aziz and told me, *Your father was the most handsome* man in Jerusalem when he left . . . and your boy's not bad either, taking taxis to the village to see my grandmother, forcing her to have a four-generational photo made with us, though for some reason she would only stare at the ground this time.

Madison stroked her face and hands in a way that hypnotized her. I had never seen him do this to anyone before. They sat by a small portable heater cracking almonds into a big bowl. She liked his red boots and his bulky sweaters.

I gave a few talks and poetry readings in Palestinian universities ("*Please help the world hear our difficult story!*") and a few Israeli ones too, where students tried to engage me in hostile debates. What was the point of declaring there would never be peace? Better to work with whatever scraps of hope we could conjure together . . . A few shy Jewish students approached after such frustrating rounds to whisper, "We agree with you," not wanting their classmates to hear. One actually said, "I have always felt more like an oppressor than a pilgrim," and hugged me, tears clouding her eyes.

Madison, my father, and I got caught up in a few street crowds in Ramallah that scared me. Keyed-up Israeli soldiers skirted our peripheral vision, giant rifles at various angles of readiness.

The Arabs were striking during the afternoons at that time, all shops shuttered and silent. I admired the *Intifada*. I wanted it to do more. But I felt so edgy about the general scent when soldiers were around that I forced Madison to lie down on the backseat in the car between Ramallah and my grandmother's village, his head in my lap, in case anyone shot at our car. He was outraged. His head kept popping up. *I want to see out the windows! I am NOT TIRED!!! What is YOUR PROBLEM?*

Baby, it is a bigger problem than me. These people. That people. Our land. Their land. Everybody wants the same land. They have been fighting almost fifty years. It is very complicated and mean. A lot of people have died. A lot of Arab people including your grandfather and Sitti lost their houses and land. See that little town with the barbed wire around it? It's called a settlement. It's a town on stolen land.

SO WHY DON'T THEY ALL JUST SHARE?

Talking about it with a five-year-old almost made it feel solv-
able.

But we had our own troubles too.

A writer and producer for television took us to Wahat Al-
Salam/Neve Shalom, the "peace village" where he lives with his
wife and children. From their comfortable house on a high hill
we gazed down through olive orchards and neat terraces toward
a blue slice of Mediterranean in the distance. We walked to visit
the school. The population of this deliberate village is exactly
half Arab, half Jewish. It was nearly impossible to guess which
children were which. I loved seeing lessons on the blackboard in
Arabic and Hebrew, calmly side by side.

After a delicious dinner—stuffed grape leaves, fresh oranges—
with our hosts, Madison wanted to use their computer. They
showed him how to play a techno-game only slightly less hideous
than most, where a prince in baggy Aladdin pants kept leaping
from level to level and racing across the screen. *Where are these
characters going? Why are they always in such a rush?*

We grown-ups drank Arabic coffee till our cells were neon.
Then I told Madison we had to go. He was so absorbed by the
computer's beeps, bings, and whizzes that he gazed upon me with
primitive outrage. *Leave? No! No! No!* (I hated to have our son,
a generally good-natured lad, shouting in the peace village.)

So I leaned down to whisper, *Yes, we must,* whereupon he
scratched me mightily with his fingernails in three deep streaks
across my right cheek.

We were both horrified. The scratches puffed up and red-
dened. For the rest of our journey I would be dabbing at them
with flesh-toned cover-up. What a perfect metaphor for the
Middle East, I thought.

Two close people. A raw wound that takes ages to heal.

For some reason my father was carrying a fancy wristwatch
that had to be delivered to distant relatives outside Cairo. He
always gets into these things.

We were staying in the fabulous Marriott by the Nile, marble
floors and secluded gardens. The lobby clerks assumed my father

was my husband. "How is your husband today?" they would ask, when I came down early for coffee. "Fine," I'd say, thinking of Michael back home. "He's just fine."

Madison had a fetish for elevator buttons back then. He wanted to punch every floor even when elegant potentates in long robes were riding with us. We'd return to our room and find giant silver trays of sweets—baklava, *basboosa*—ordered up for us by the Mystery Relatives. They did this almost every day. We visited the Sphinx and the pyramids in a highly sugared condition.

I had harbored a delusion about climbing the Great Pyramid to the top when I was a child, but whenever I faced it in person, got dizzy just staring at it. Instead, we climbed into the pyramid's heart, discussing mummies and treasures. Later Madison stood in front of the Sphinx in the driving wind for a photograph, which would become my favorite picture, blown up back home. I called it "Old Stone, New Boy." We ate lentil soup at the Mena House hotel. Madison checked the gift shop for batteries.

That afternoon, what would quickly become known as "the worst sandstorm" erupted while I was working at a children's library with a translator and a bunch of schoolchildren, and Madison and my dad were at large somewhere in the vast swirlings of Cairo. I had suggested they visit the zoo. Later we heard the zoo was one of the most ravaged locations. Trees fell on top of cages. People were killed just walking around. Luckily my traveling team had decided to stay home at the Marriott and ride the elevator. Sand penetrated the cracks around our windows; an inch of reddish terrain etched finely across our beds.

Days later the relatives finally appeared to claim their watch, exclaiming over it mightily, and insisting we ride with them out into the farthest reaches of the city for a luncheon at their home. Madison had one motto that day, *I'm not hungry*. He grumbled, making weird faces in the backseat with me. We swerved past ten million people and buses and cluttered shopping districts. I pointed out vivid clotheslines on roofs, carts with donkeys. It made him mad. *Do you think I can't see? Don't show me anything!* He was in a stomping mood when we got there. He wore his blue velvet knickers and stomped around with a plunger from their bathroom.

The woman of the house carried so many platters of rich food to the table I sank into a swoon. Eggplant! Chicken! Cauliflower and rice! Roasted lamb! Arabs never understood it when they heard I didn't eat meat—how could there be such an *allergy?*— too much food in general gave me apoplexy. Then I had this child who wanted a single white cracker, please, and a slice of watermelon, thank you. My father was left to fend for himself. He kept rolling his eyes at me as new platters appeared from the kitchen. I hypnotized myself staring at a large burgundy trefoil on the Oriental carpet. They were talking in Arabic about three hundred relatives I'd never heard of before. I wanted to pick up the broom and dance with my son.

Back at the Marriott, after an extended tour of local factories and drainage ditches, all scented by auto exhaust, Madison collapsed in an elevator with me. *I'm starving,* he whimpered. *I want Mexican food. I need a taco desperately.* I placed my hand on his shoulder. *Baby, we're in Egypt. I'm sorry. See, you should have eaten something else at that house. They don't have Mexican food here.*

Whereupon a gigantic sheikh in flowing robes spoke from his corner of the elevator. *If you will excuse me, madam, but there is a fine Mexican restaurant in the basement of this hotel.* I couldn't believe it. Were we hallucinating? Our leader escorted us kindly to its door. We, who had seen every marble inch and cranny of the Cairo Marriott, had somehow missed its one Latino oasis?

Madison gobbled three bean and cheese tacos with such gusto the waiter wouldn't let us pay.

Picture this: a long-haired five-year-old boy in a belted trench coat marching through dignified Heathrow Airport, London, shouting, "I hate you!" at the top of his lungs.

What had gotten into him? We woke him up, that's what.

After the lengthy flight from Amman, we spoke into his ear. *Sorry, traveler. We're here.*

He wanted a doughnut. I said no. My father said, *Come on, let him have it.* My father paid for it. Madison took a bite and dropped it on the floor. He screamed. He wanted another doughnut. I said, *If you buy him another one I will be furious.* My father sighed the sigh of the long-suffering. I marched away from them, followed by the echo: *I hate you! I hate you!* (Actually, Madison utilized this phrase only for a few months. I would usually respond with "But I *love* you," which seemed powerless.)

Dizzily I stepped into the men's rest room by mistake, not even realizing it till I came face-to-face with a urinal and twelve unzipped Englishmen. *Holy!* What was a doughnut in the giant scheme of things? We had seen the world and we were fighting over a doughnut.

Here's an apple, here are peanuts. Trust me. I am your mother. I always have healthy food in my bag. He whirled in circles. *No!* His trench coat rose up like the skirts of a dervish. We rode a double-decker bus encased in sheaths of traveling gloom. He said soberly, *We have only been here ten minutes and already you are talking like an English person.*

What did so much traveling do to our lives? We grew wide. We were not scared of being unknown, alien, curious, side by side in any shape of elsewhere. Sometimes it was rocky, but wouldn't it have been rocky at home too? We quickly collected new words, town names, useful distances, tucking shops, and cafés we might need later into our brains.

There are people in my class, he said once, who have never been out of San Antonio. How is that possible?

We were used to the vivid sensation of being just-arrived.

"No small planes," I wrote in my contract when we traveled to Alaska. I had another offbeat writer-in-residence job in far-flung communities: Unalaska (aka Dutch Harbor), where we gathered for a full-community poetry reading at the roller rink smelling of stinky 1950s skates, and a man sang ninety-nine verses of "American Pie"; Bethel, four hundred miles from a paved road, with the entire sewer system placed above ground to beat the permafrost; the Fairbanks Public Library; and Nome. Madison couldn't understand my hesitation. Why *not* a small plane? He wanted the wild whir of crusty propellers. Why *not* dip and swoop all over the Arctic air?

I don't care for it. It's like a roller coaster.

I love roller coasters.

We flew in cargo jets instead, eighteen seats carved into a small space in the rear. We boarded after boxes and crates and cartons. We stared down on layers of glistening whiteness. One pilot who must have had a secret desire to be a tour guide loved to fly as startlingly close as he could to Denali peak. The flight attendant served us, oddly, ice cream bars once we reached our elevation. Madison, taking a Friday holiday from the public school he was now attending in Fairbanks, asked if he could have two or three.

In Nome we stayed with a man who said he was king of the Eskimos.

"And we ate king crabs," our son would report to his grandparents long distance. "Each one was as big as two telephones."

He didn't describe how we were taken to the crab fisherman's house, where huge crabs scuttled noisily across the floor after being pulled up through a hole in the ice. We were told, "Pick one," but stared at each other nervously with our wide, mostly vegetarian eyes. At dinnertime, the Eskimo king warned us about the crabs' mystery sac: if you eat it, you die. It expands in the esophagus and suffocates you quickly from the inside. He said this in a matter-of-fact voice, as someone else might say, "Did you bring in the newspaper?" We worried through our meal, examining each morsel, making busy mounds of shell on our plates.

Later Madison tugged at what appeared to be a stick poking up out of the snow. He wanted to etch his name into the ice of the Bering Strait. His daddy was over in Siberia photographing bakers and schoolteachers. He wanted to chip a hole clear through to the moving water deep down.

But our host said, "Stop! You are pulling up the only tree in Nome!" In that treeless region, even a knee-high barren spoke was valuable. The citizens planted their imported Christmas trees in the strait after the holiday season for the illusion of a little forest at the edge of town.

Our Eskimo friend taught Madison how to whip the furry, double-headed Eskimo yo-yo into a spiraling spin. It was harder than it looked. Madison followed me calmly around the local elementary school (where I had to visit nine or was it thirteen classes in a row?) swirling his new yo-yo into action. He read books and practiced computer skills. He stared out the window into what I would later recall as The Profound North, but he never once asked, "What are we doing here?"

When we were dropped off at the airport at midnight, that weirdly favorite Alaskan flying time, to catch a plane back to Anchorage, the tiny waiting room was packed—nursing mothers, men with fur tails on their hats. There was a blizzard farther up in the Arctic. The Kotzebue plane had been forced to land in Nome unexpectedly. Half these passengers were trying to get home to Kotzebue. They were upset to be grounded here. So our own plane, due to fly south, might try to "make a run for it" toward the north.

What? A sudden swell of panic thickened my throat. Flying into an Arctic blizzard, with extra passengers weighting the plane, after midnight—could anything be worse? I charged up to the flight desk, begging the ticket agent to give up the plan. I popped a Dramamine into my throat, gulping it without any water.

"Ma'am, we'll let the pilots make the decision," the agent told me.

But I couldn't leave her alone. I kept repeating, "Doesn't it sound like a BAD IDEA to you?" She gazed at me calmly. She wasn't going anywhere.

Madison, meanwhile, had comfortably claimed a corner of the mini-terminal, swirling his furry yo-yo in arcs and double passes. A crowd had gathered. Eskimo children sucked their thumbs and pointed. Even their uncles couldn't flip the yo-yo as well. He laughed and let them try it. He was always making friends.

I stared through the small square window into the velvet darkness over the runway. Why did we do these things? Why didn't we stay back in Texas where we belonged? South Texas never had blizzards. Why did I ever imagine I had anything to tell anybody about writing or reading? Why didn't I get *a normal job?*

My life passed before my eyes more than once in airports, late. But if I mentioned any anxieties to Madison, he'd ask, "Why do you worry so much?"

At 2 A.M., two hours late, they made us fly north to Kotzebue. They let the extra passengers sit in the aisle.

I tried not to think about it. We stared down on luminous banks of massive snow clouds, strangely blue-lit in that Arctic way. A doctor in the seat next to me read one of my children's books and criticized it. "I think you should have left this page out," he said. I was so tired I considered crying. Madison refused to fall asleep. Even the thought of falling asleep now was an insult to him. But he never complained about odd twists of schedule. Whatever the hour, he was fascinated by details: varieties of knobs, vent covers, seat-belt latches.

As the plane bobbled over the Kotzebue area, an announcement crackled through the loudspeaker. "There has been a mechanical failure—*crack, crack, crack*—on the ground. *Hissssssssssss.* . . . . The runway lights are—*crack crack*—out. Unfortunately—we will not be allowed to land. Those of you hoping to get to Kotzebue will, sorry to say—*hissssssssssss*—have to go back to Anchorage"—where they had started from, much earlier that evening. A loud groan filled the plane. But I whooped with pleasure. The plane turned heavily around in the Arctic sky.

Madison said later, *You shouldn't have made that happy sound. Did you see how everyone looked at you?*

• • •

Once he announced accusingly, "Do you realize we have never yet taken a *vacation?* We just go on a million TRIPS." "Trips" meant one or another of his parents had to do some work along the way. And he was starting to resent it. Not that we ever *left him* anywhere, at a baby-sitter's or day-care operation (except for one hour in Alpine, Texas, one day in his life)—no, no, he was always there, right with us, patiently, with his satchel of books, notepads, and traveling computer, unless some well-supervised basketball game for kids was going on right outside the window and they invited him to join them. Madison just got tired of us always thinking about our next responsibility. He wanted to see us traveling without papers or film.

So we drove eight hours west to the national park at Big Bend, Texas, the most breathtaking edge of our wide-open state. (It's true we stopped to see one photographer in Marathon, but stayed very briefly.)

We camped in the basin in a greenish dome tent that cost $19.95 at some junky store and didn't blow away. Exotic birds with fabulous, unfamiliar voices did mating dances around us at dawn. Roadrunners scooted across our path.

We walked the splendid "Lost Mine Trail" twice, gazing out over spectacular vistas of trees and slopes and horizons, never quite making it to the trail's end. Official victories didn't really interest us. Carefully taking note of the bear and mountain lion sightings on the list at the ranger's station, we hoped to encounter bears, at least—at a distance. Michael had never yet seen a bear in the wild, but Madison and I had thrilled to the ones we saw in Alaska, a whole snowy family of bears tumbling alongside a train and a solitary one spotted later as we hiked on a glacier. We wanted Michael to see one too.

Bear scat speckled our paths. The rangers said they might be watching us even when we couldn't see them. Lizards and foxes appeared with their quizzical gazes and scooted away. But the bears stayed hidden.

We visited the "Hall of Fame" museum belonging to Hallie Stillwell, the "Matriarch of Big Bend," who was months shy of turning one hundred. Now she lived in a nursing home in Alpine. I'd met her once in the early eighties at a writing retreat on a dusty ranch. She'd signed her book about Big Bend place names for me and we'd had a delightful conversation over dinner. At her museum, we stared at rifles, antique baby cradles, old photographs. Madison listened to a tape about Hallie's life. *Why do we always hope and pray our children will listen hard to our elders? While we dangle foolishly somewhere in between . . .*

One afternoon the boys wanted to hunt for fossils in the desert. It was so cool lying in the shade on top of the quilts I'd spread on the picnic table, I told them I'd stay back to tidy the campsite. What a joke—there was nothing to tidy. Oh, maybe a few blackened coals left by some previous camper to scoop into our fire pit for the evening's popcorn, or a shiny candy wrapper tucked into cenizo branches to discard, but that was it. My chores were over in no time. I lay back down to read Donna Tartt's book, *The Secret History,* which had been waiting on my bedside table unopened for the last three years. Now it sucked me in like a vacuum.

Did everybody have a secret history?

Cool breezes drifted through the trees. Birds trilled in rich circles, then vanished. The valley echoed its vast, clean note of quiet.

Why did anyone ever need more than this?

This listening, which cost nothing. This low tone which lay somewhere under the layers of *hub-hub* in cities. At stoplights. With the phone ringing and twenty messages still to be listened to. On the shrill playground at Madison's school. Even the book I was reading, in which people got pushed off cliffs and drank exorbitant amounts of alcohol, seemed to evolve from a deep silence of culture and time.

I drifted. The book made a tent on my chest.

"I like this trip best!" Madison's first words when he and

Michael returned, sunstreaked and sweaty, with empty canteens and fossil stories. "We found a bed of quartz! We saw worms shriveled in the sand! Dad touched one with his foot and it crumbled! We walked miles from the road! Nobody saw us!"

That night we returned to their secret desert spot with a bottle of wine and two coffee cups for us and some lemon drops for him. We sat on the side of a small hill to watch Michael's favorite dune (years ago he had photographed it) turn pink, then white, in the stunning moonlight. Extended families of worms had emerged from their desert holes to wriggle and carouse in the twilight. Cousins to centipedes, they gave me the creeps. I'd been stung by centipedes before and it is no picnic.

Madison scooted up and down over the rugged terrain, leaping like a gazelle, twirling in the cooling air, sliding down a slope on his bottom. He pitched a few large rocks to see them streak the sand and Michael and I called him on it.

"We're not here to rearrange the desert," I said, still in my tidying mood. "Travelers should leave things as they found them."

So Madison dramatically picked up the rocks he had thrown and tiptoed them home to their earlier resting spots—or reasonable facsimiles thereof. He was grinning widely. He stooped to smooth the ground. He stood up tall with both hands in the air.

"No one will ever know I've been here!" he announced and we laughed and tipped our heads back inside that giant view, hundreds of miles from any city.

What he said was not true.

JULENE BAIR

9

Nick's Door

I stand in our upstairs hallway, where the two doors with people behind them stand closed. One belongs to Aaron, the man who came to live with us two years ago, my lover and my son's acting father, the man who is due to leave us at the end of the month for an extended vacation. Behind the other door sleeps my son, Nick, and his best friend, Michael. It is not unusual for me to be positioned like this at Nick's end of the hall, watching over him, worrying about his future. Even when the detail at hand is apparently trivial.

I tap with my fingernails just above the Day-Glo *No Trespassing!* sign. "Nick, Michael, time to get up!"

"Mom, we're tired. Please, just let us sleep in."

During the past school year Nick earned a dollar for getting up on time and finishing his chores. But it's summer now and we all have differing views of how much sloth that entitles him to. Nick thinks he should be able to sleep as late as he likes, which would normally be well past noon. Although he doesn't make an issue of it, Aaron believes his own sleeping habits—to bed no later than nine regardless of the season, up no later than six—should be the model for the universe. I've settled on nine. I would like to cut Nick some slack this morning, since Michael is staying the week. But I can't today.

"You have diving, Nick. You need to get up and do all your stuff in time for that."

"Mom, please just let me skip diving. I'd go to sleep before I hit the water." He's trying hard to be nice. I must hand him that.

I lean against the wall and sigh. Nick and I moved to this Wyoming town four years ago, when I took a teaching job at the university here. It was perhaps a year later, after I'd painted his door white, that he rifled through his sticker sheets, given to him by our former housemates when I was going back to college in Iowa, and chose his favorites for the door. Which of the many women who had lived with us was he remembering as he applied the flying saucer, the alligator, the little felt ghost that hovers at the very top? Its round black mouth seems to be shrieking, more scared than scary, as if anguished by the approach of the jet airplane pointing up at him. I can imagine Nick, who seldom did anything at age eight without sound effects, imitating the engines as he smoothed the jet into place. Then, making his voice higher pitched and tiny, he would have mimicked the ghost. "Oh! Get me out of here. A jet is coming!"

My eyes land on a sunglasses ad that Nick traced and colored in his inimitable, electric style. The door has so much expression to it, while at the other end of the hall, Aaron's office door is typically blank, the sanctum behind it quiet except for an incessant rattling as his fingers speed over his computer keyboard.

I knock again. "Nick! Get up! You're only enrolled in diving for two weeks, four days a week. You miss one day, you miss a lot." As if he could follow that reasoning while still half asleep. "Nick? Did you hear me? Get up!"

"No! Go away! Leave us alone!" There he is, my morning child.

I run my hand over the swirled plaster in this upstairs hallway, which, like the dingy brown carpet, brown molding, and tan walls, recalls the former owners' seventies aesthetic. I consider all the interior work remaining to be done and wonder how much of it I'll manage this winter with Aaron gone. I chose this house because it reminded me of the Kansas farm home I grew up in, three hundred miles over the buffalo grass prairie southeast of here. I went overboard, buying a house twice the size we needed. As in Iowa, I thought I might rent out rooms, even if that practice had failed me before. Some of the women we lived with became dear friends, but they moved inevitably, leaving us bereft. Shortly after our move to Wyoming, when I was in the loneliest phase of getting settled in a new place, I began an e-mail romance with Aaron, a former boyfriend from my California days. After he visited us a few times, we began talking about his moving in. He could telecommute, doing his computer consulting work from home. Finally my son would have a father.

But with Aaron's door closed, as it almost always is, I am left alone with most of the parenting chores. I've tried to accept this, telling myself that, traditionally, fathers have always lived their main lives elsewhere. Even my father lived mostly for his work, in the fields. This didn't prevent our knowing he loved us, and my brothers and I competed to be the source of the light in his eyes. We repaid his love with demonstrations of our achievement, knowledge, and wit. Later, that love extended to Nick, who would kneel by his grandfather's easy chair on our visits. Dad would put his elbow on the cushioned armrest and capture Nick's hand. They would arm wrestle, Dad gritting his teeth the way he had with me when I was a child. "Oooh, ooh, ooh!" he would grunt as he pretended to lose. It was less of an act with Nick. My father's heart had been weakening for years, and Nick had been able to win easily ever since he was seven. Dad died two months ago, at age eighty-two. He hung on as long as he could, so I can't really add him to the list of men who let Nick down.

That list is long. First Nick's father, whom he's never met. He started calling recently, telling Nick he was a member of the Black Berets in Vietnam, not mentioning the dishonorable discharge that resulted when he brandished a knife at an officer. Then there were the two men from the Big Brothers organization—one who never wrote after we left Iowa, the other who failed in law school here and went back to live with his mother in Arizona. He didn't answer Nick's letters, this even though he knew that if Nick put anything willingly down on paper, all his heart was certain to be in it. One of my brothers died. My remaining brother is given to a sarcastic temperament. He only groaned last Christmas when Nick ran up to greet him. After that visit, I stifled tears as we began the long drive home, attempting to conceal from my son the hurt I felt on his behalf. It would take so little, I've often thought—an invitation for a walk and Nick would look to his uncle for his image of manhood. It would be a largely positive image. My brother has a sense of humor, loves life, and is decent toward his wife and children. But he only groaned, as if commenting through Nick on the dumb mistakes I've made. Ever since I left Kansas at age eighteen to live in San Francisco, my brother has considered me vacuous.

I stayed in California for twelve years, then returned from the western brink destitute, pregnant, and divorced. I have lived a hard-bitten life since then, trying to reconstruct community and family, first in Iowa and now here. I wanted someone else who would be constant, someone who would occupy a chair at the table like my father did. Every meal. Aaron has done that, and now he is leaving also—to Florida for the winter, we say.

"Nick, come on, get up." I tap on the door again. "Nick? You hear me? Now come on."

"Mom, just let us sleep in, okay? That diving teacher doesn't teach me anything anyway."

He's right. Diving is the only sport I could get him to sign up for this whole year. Sitting in the poolside bleachers, I've watched from behind glass, hopeful over another tenuous relationship between my son and a man. Nick flies two thirds of the way across the deep end, entering the water at an oblique angle. As with his baseball and soccer coaches when Nick was younger, this coach's back seems always to be turned when Nick performs. At first, he did watch, telling Nick to go for altitude rather than distance, but he's made no comment since, letting Nick dive incorrectly, reinforcing the error. I've wondered, is it pheromones, or a vibe that a boy raised by a woman emits, a manner that makes him seem hopeless to the jock mentality? After the lesson one day, I watched the coach talking to the father of one of his charges in the hallway. Nodding and proud, they each stood with one hand on the boy's shoulder. The boy was comely and mannerly and tough. Like all fathered jocks, he had submitted recently to a haircut. He wore Wranglers and a T-shirt that fit him, the typical Wyoming costume, whereas Nick . . . I imagine going up to that coach, arrogant college kid that he is, and commanding him to teach my son to dive, goddamn it.

On the left side of Nick's door is a label from a pair of jeans he got a year ago. "29 x 32 Relaxed Fit." Nick's quest for gangsta pants began with these, which seem conservative to me now, even though his waist was only twenty-five inches then, his inseam twenty-eight. Finally, the local Penney's store got with it and began selling the in brands—JNCO's Zonz, Home Boys. Nick can have big legs and a waist size that exposes the upper inches of his boxers without the pants falling off entirely. Which reminds me, I need to get in his room before he dresses and retrieve the current favorites for the wash. The bottoms have turned to rags from dragging on the sidewalk, but a least I can launder them. Embarrassed by his white legs, Nick won't wear shorts this summer. I keep trying to explain to him that his legs wouldn't be white for long if he got some sun.

Okay, I have to decide. Should I make him get up, or should I let him sleep in? It's just that I'm trying to teach him to meet his commitments. I envision him at eighteen in his dorm room, adrift in the detritus of his existence, hitting the off button on his radio alarm—if he has remembered to set it in the first place—and sleeping through the first college class of the day, then the next. Scattered around his door are several circular "I elect to read" stickers. If only. Yet lately Nick has acted in a couple of community plays. He also likes drawing and drumming. He doesn't practice like a young Olivier, Picasso, or Buddy Rich, but he does enjoy these outlets, which gives me hope.

What did I do during the summers at age twelve? Rode horses. I had that one active interest. And look what it led to. I rent a corral for my horse at the end of the street. This Sunday, I plan on riding around Crow Reservoir in the nearby mountains. That's what I wish for Nick—healthy interests and the will to pursue them. But the ghost of Nick's father hangs over me, like the little felt ghost over his door. I am haunted by that man's irresponsibility and by the anger and violence his drinking unleashed. For this reason, I sometimes affect a rigid stance in relation to Nick's behavior. *Get out of bed now. No ifs, ands, or buts. You signed up for it, so you see it through.* The fact is, I signed him up, and he consented to go only out of deference to my wishes.

I don't think Nick should have to work as hard as my brothers did. They were up early every morning and drove tractors all day. They lost their childhoods to the work, and greatly envied the town kids, who got to sleep in summer mornings and spend their afternoons at the municipal pool. My brothers did have a strong father figure, though, someone whose expectations they had no choice but to meet. Which is right? How do I instill manhood in a boy? Should I even try?

Aaron reassures me, saying Nick is a boy, so he'll be a man. I like this nonsexist attitude. But it's also passive, which is Aaron's style of child-rearing. Over and over, I see Nick turning, in the resulting void, to the negative influences penetrating the fragile bubble I've tried to create around him.

My eyes drift back to the door. On the right side of the middle panel, Nick defiantly pinned up the liner from the DRS CD I made him throw away. The quarrel was monstrous and he finally opted for a violent end to a violent CD. Staring angrily into my eyes, he broke the plastic to pieces between his fists. The song that put me over the edge was one called "Sickness," sung in the usual, street-cool voice of black rap. I had gone into Nick's room to put some clothes away while he was downstairs getting a snack. I froze, Nick's folded T-shirts resting in my arms. The rapper regretted the loss of his "fine bitch," whom he'd "had to hurt," the result being a blood-splattered ceiling and wall. It seemed the sickness referred to in the title was the habit of killing women and children and having sex with their corpses.

Nick loved the beat and the status of owning the parental-advisory CD, which Aaron, unaware of the coding system, had allowed him to buy. When I quoted the lyrics, Nick shouted, "It doesn't say that!"

"But it does," I insisted. "They are cynics Hon. They'll make a dollar any way they can."

"They are not! You don't even know them, Mom!"

"Don't use that tone with me."

"What tone? I didn't use any tone."

"That hateful, angry tone."

"It's not a tone, Mom. It's my voice. It's the way I talk."

And it's true. My son is growing into a man, and when he's angry, he sounds like an angry man. Which frightens me.

I knock louder this time, then open the door, or attempt to open it. It abuts against the futon Michael's sleeping on. Through the two-inch opening, I see a slice of life in the aftermath of a preteen sleepover. Nick is curled up between comforters on the floor. Both boys are shirtless, their naked arms and chests smooth and innocent, although the CD's, clothes, toys, spilled popcorn, and empty pop bottles scattered around them testify to the previous night's debauchery. Nick never thinks to pull his curtains shut, so sun pours past the giant spruce tree outside his east windows, warming the air in the room. Snowy images flick across the TV screen. I wouldn't install cable in Nick's room, but let him spend his savings on a used TV so he could play Nintendo games.

Somehow, a year or so ago, I got talked into letting Nick leave the TV on all night, the volume off. The reception was poor enough without cable that the practice seemed benign. Now the lit screen has become an essential link in his nighttime life support. Were I to pull the plug, he insists he would be enveloped by monsters. I make a mental note to end this practice once Michael goes home. Nick can have a night-light, but not endless, ghostly images of cops beating black boys into submission on real-life police dramas and of women being stalked by serial killers. It's a vicious cycle, the TV painting the fears behind his eyes and simultaneously dispelling them with a light he thinks is soothing, but which I find eerie and alienating, even immoral.

Jennifer, Nick's six-month-old beagle, stands, stretches, yawns, and scratches at the slit between the jamb and door. I can smell the dog pee in the carpet, which I've used all sorts of enzymatic concoctions trying to erase. Why does Nick always close his window at night, how have I failed to pass down a basic appreciation of fresh air? "Hey, guys!" I say. "Move the futon and open up! Jennifer needs out."

The torsos lie curled silently around their tenacious hold on sleep.

"Nick, come on, your dog needs out."

"Talk to Michael, not me," Nick says. "Why don't you ever blame him for anything?" They've been together two days and my only child is deep in the throes of sibling rivalry.

The jealousy is all the more intense because Michael likes to call me, supposedly in jest, Mom. His own mother deserted him when he was just a baby. It seems a far more heinous act when a mother does it. I even find myself using more sensational language. *She deserted him.* I have never used that phrase in reference to Nick's father, who left before Nick was born and never deigned to send him one birthday card or to call him until now, but I can testify that the yearning is the same in both children. From the time Nick was able to speak, he went on a quest in search of his father. "My daddy?" he would ask, pointing at strangers in cafés.

I admit that Michael's need has drawn me in. I often find

myself engaging in the fantasy that he is my son, that Nick and he are brothers. I remember the pangs of love, on Nick's birth, when my first conscious thought was *I can't have just one*. I confessed this feeling to my brother, who has two children of his own. "Yeah. Insurance," he said, summing up in one biting pronouncement the desperate dependency I would contend with the rest of my life.

"You need to move, okay, Michael? So the puppy can get out."

Michael stirs sleepily and pulls the top of the futon away from the door. "Sorry, Mom." I grab the dog and, with a long reach, am also able to snatch Nick's pants. Michael called me Mrs. Bair before he started calling me Mom, except I am not married to my father, a technicality I had a hard time explaining to him.

"You mean Bair isn't Aaron's last name, and you guys aren't married?"

"No. He's just my boyfriend." We live together in sin, I might have added, judging from Michael's widening eyes.

I cradle Jennifer, the lovable beagle, on my shoulder like a baby as I carry her down the hall past the door behind which Aaron works. He's on the phone now. I hear him explaining something work-related, his tone authoritative and confident, like the one he sometimes tries to apply to issues outside his field—politics or philosophy. I challenge his views as simplistic, and he allows himself to be defeated too easily, leaving me feeling like a bully. I suspect that his door remains shut so much of the time because, in his office, he can navigate the familiar ground of cybernetics, whereas the emotional realm of family life tends to baffle him. Meanwhile, he misses so much, this whole drama going on outside his door.

As I carry the dog down the stairs, she opens her jaws wide in a squeaky yawn. "Ew, your breath stinks," I tell her. Few kids come from standard families anymore, I reason. Michael should know this. His father raises him and his siblings alone and isn't able to give the kids anywhere near all the attention they need.

Michael doesn't get his homework done, but he's a sweet boy, always obedient. Standing by during the vicious battle over the CD, he said to Nick, "Hey, dude, you ought to come stay with my dad awhile. He'd straighten you out like a log."

I stuff the beagle out the back door and stuff the pants into the washer, remembering this time to empty the pockets of change and Nick's billfold. I've twice washed his wallet along with the photo inside it of him sitting on my lap when he was a satisfied two-year-old and I a pre-graying thirty-seven. In the kitchen, I pour myself a second cup of coffee, calculating what it will mean in terms of irritability, but then I didn't sleep too well last night, having to get up several times to tell the kids to quiet down. I lean against the counter, recalling the conversation Nick and I had here a few nights ago. Our most intimate moments occur in the night kitchen. It bugs me that Aaron always goes to bed early, but his absence does restore Nick and me to our former lives together. The refrigerator hums, the walls peel yellow paint, the overhead fixture casts too stark a light, but our love functions on full.

"Does it bother you that I'm growing up?" Nick asked as he dropped bananas into the blender.

"Hmm . . . I don't know." I got the ice cream out of the freezer and the scoop out of the utensil drawer, closing it with my knee. "I'm of two minds about it, I guess—happy to see you maturing, becoming a man. Sad to lose my little boy."

Nick contemplated that, then said wistfully, "Sometimes I wish I was still little."

"That seems natural to me." I stood poised with my finger over the whip button. "It's time to shake, rattle, and roll. Ready?"

Nick cringed and looked up at the ceiling. "You sure it won't wake up Aaron?"

"I'll make it fast." Perturbed at the way we were always tiptoeing around the house in deference to Aaron's work or his sleep, I pressed the button and counted to a steely ten. "Voilà! Banana shakes."

We sat on the counter, sipping and complimenting each other on our creation. Nick said, "You know, when I'm sixteen, there'll be nights like this when I'm gone for a long time in my car, and sometimes I'll be out all night."

He seemed earnest, so I reacted earnestly. "No! Not at sixteen."

"And I'll come home and you'll ask, Which one was it, Patricia, Ticia, or Marisha?" Like his father, my son is a charmer. The girls have been throwing themselves at him since fourth grade. I'm sure they like him because he can and will talk. Is this also a product of his being raised by a single mother, a correlative to the vibes the jocks can't abide?

"And I'll say all three—Patricia, Ticia, *and* Marisha."

I laughed. "Oh, yeah? You promised you wouldn't have sex until at least seventeen."

But Nick's mind seemed to have wandered off our topic. He put his glass down and absently licked the foam from his upper lip.

I suspected he was thinking about how much lonelier these nights would seem when Aaron was no longer sleeping overhead. "Does it bother you that Aaron's going to Florida?" I asked.

"No. Not much." Nick turned and set his glass in the sink. "I mean, he's had that big dream all his life of sailing, and he hates the winters here, and he's earned it." Nick kept his back turned to me and stared into the sink.

I reached over and plucked at the seam of his inside-out T-shirt. "He's not going for good, you know, he'll be back next spring."

Nick ducked out from under my hand. He went and sat in the tall director's chair on the opposite side of the room. "According to you," he said bitterly.

"You know, I'm not sure what's going to happen either, Nick. I only want the best for him, for all of us. You know that, don't you?"

"I know that, Mom. It's just that I feel like this was my chance at having a dad, and now I'll probably never have one." Nick's

voice pinched down around imminent tears. "It's like you're getting a divorce, and it's my fault."

He may as well have dropped an anvil on me. For years, sad-
dened by Nick's yearning, I felt duty-bound to provide him with
a father. *Give Nick a father.* I'm not sure where I heard the phrase
or if I ever heard it in exactly those words. But they were writ
large on my heart, inscribed there by society, which views family
life narrowly, and which narrows families until they are just a
tiny unit, islanded in the midst of unneighborly neighborhoods
and noncommuning communities. After ten years of virtual
celibacy, of being too busy raising Nick alone while also working, studying, and writing, my heart devoured the sight of Nick
and Aaron together, having fun. They spent a lot of time
together at first—swimming at the university pool in the winter,
riding bikes in the summer, but lately Aaron has withdrawn, and
I've been coming to the sickening conclusion that I am more
lonely with Aaron than without him. I was the one who suggested Aaron go somewhere warm this winter. "Oh, God, honey.
I'm sorry. Believe me, it's not your fault."

"It's not?" Nick asked, clearly hopeful.

"If anyone's to blame, I am," I said.

"No! It's not your fault either, Mom. To tell you the truth, I'm
kind of glad he's going. I mean, it wasn't gonna work out anyway."

"Why not?" I asked, feeling both relieved by Nick's diminished pain and guilty for his disillusionment. Having spent so
many years alone together, Nick and I are inextricable emotionally—his love for Aaron first inspiring love in me, and now my
dissatisfaction infiltrating him, wounding his trust of the only
man, besides his grandfather, who ever loved him back.

"He's not the kind of guy that says, 'Hey, kid, want to toss
some balls?' "

"But, Nick, you never wanted to toss balls. I tried to get you
involved in baseball, and you couldn't stand it."

"I know, but it would have been different with a dad."

I hate it when my son's emotions verify the stereotype. I hate it when it looks as if sons do need fathers for all the reasons those schmaltzy father-son TV shows imply they do. I hate it when Nick's tears tell me that, alone, I can't give him all he needs.

What drives me even crazier are the perfect families. I know, I know. They supposedly don't exist. But I see them. The kids are so lined out, so content and well-adjusted. They play sports. Never mind that I didn't play sports. I can't imagine the perfect-family kids yelling, like Nick did at me the other day, "Motherfucker!" He shouted the epithet over and over as he cleaned up the trash he'd spilled when, already angry, he'd grabbed the can from me. The argument had escalated as I'd heaped on more and more chores in reaction to his refusal to clean his room cooperatively. I get trapped in showdowns with him. I think I have to make my point now, stick to my guns, end this once and for all—each phrase born of an authoritarian outlook that doesn't come naturally to me.

I put down my coffee cup and go to the back door, where the beagle has been scratching at the screen door. She tumbles in, weaving curlicues around my legs. She still hasn't learned to perform the trick I've been trying to teach her—to wipe her feet. At least she does her circles on the mat, which will be a boon come the long winter, when the backyard is snowed in. There will be fewer tracks all around this winter, because Aaron won't be coming across the yard from the lot behind the garage, where he normally parks his car. That's one nice thing, I guess. I bend down and pick Jennifer up, nuzzling her sun-warmed fur. I sit on the stairs with her, accepting her puppy kisses, marveling at the butterscotch color in her coat and ogling her velvety ears. Shadows of willow leaves undulate over my bare legs and the floor, reminding me of the way sun ripples across the bottom of Crow Reservoir. Aaron has been after me to move to a warmer climate ever since he came here, but how can he expect me to move again, after all the work I put in, sanding and painting the outside of the house creamy ivory, sanding and varnishing all the downstairs woodwork? Let the kids sleep in, I decide. Why get uptight over diving lessons? Why get uptight over anything? Summer is too short and too lovely to ruin with pointless lessons and rigid rules.

The kids get up at eleven, watch TV while they eat cold pizza, then leave the house to play. Immersed in my writing, I call to Nick, telling him to wear his watch and be back by three. When they don't return by three-thirty, I begin to fret. I have prepared for them, readying paintbrushes, ladders, and tarps so they can apply primer to the spots I've sanded on the remaining unfinished side of the house. Two hours per weekday, I decided at the beginning of the summer. It's not too much to expect, and I'll pay. So far, Nick has taken readily to the plan. It's been a means of saving toward new pairs of pants, his current fetish. And it makes me feel as if I'm succeeding—instilling a sense of responsibility in him, teaching him that self-esteem derives from doing a job well, not from being told he's great and can do no wrong.

The watch—did he take it? Breaking the *No Trespassing!* edict, I shove open Nick's door, which drags over the rug. I always meant to fix that before the door carved an arc in the new carpet, but I note now that it's too late. This was one of the first rooms we fixed up. Aaron was coming out on his vacations then, and together we painted the ceiling midnight blue and the walls white. We laid a plastic tarp on the floor and allowed Nick to splatter paint in three different colors. While I was at work, Aaron lacquered the trim in white enamel. Then, holding an astronomy book in one hand, and using Day-Glo stars, he put up all the major constellations, varying from the real sky only to spell out *N-I-C-K* directly over the bed.

Now look at the room. It's a garbage heap. A sewer. From the other end of the hall, I hear Aaron's office door squeak as he opens it. Apparently he's sensed that the house is too quiet for the hour.

"Just look at this mess!" I complain as he enters Nick's room, where I sit on the bed.

"Aren't they supposed to be home by now?"

"Yes," I say, feeling defeated, unable to adequately express the lonely frustration coursing through me. "And of course they aren't."

"Oh," Aaron says distractedly, trying to struggle out from whatever computer program he's been working on and reenter the emotional realm that I occupy. "Isn't he supposed to straighten it in the morning before he goes anywhere?"

"Yes, but somehow they slipped out without me checking on them." I refrain from saying, *I work, too, you know, why don't you check on them once in a while?*

I gesture at the mess on the floor. "I know I sound like a cliché, but how is he ever going to amount to anything? I cleaned my room when I was a kid without anyone telling me to." I pause, remembering that my brother Bruce's room always looked like the aftermath of a tornado. "But you say you didn't?" I ask Aaron hopefully.

"Sure, I cleaned my room."

"But you said it was always a mess."

"That was more when I got into high school, and I had books and stuff scattered all around. I never cleaned it then."

Of course not, I think. *You had better, more studious things to do.* But then I look up at the ceiling, at the one deviation Aaron allowed in the sky of the Northern Hemisphere. I remember the morning's second cup of coffee and remind myself to watch my temper.

"Still, they should have been back by now. They should be working. How am I ever going to teach him to honor his commitments?"

Aaron is certain the problem is part of a general slovenliness that derives from Nick's not going to bed and getting up on time. I agree that ever since Nick's been earning money doing summer work, the dollar in the morning hasn't been as much of an incentive. And as is typically the case when my maternal doubts reach near hysterical proportions, Aaron suggests an algorithmic solution. All problems can be solved through binary logic, and now Aaron proposes a new set of strictures. Each morning Nick gets up late, he should have to go to bed a half hour earlier that night. It is a simple worldview, really—tighten the fist of authority until you squeeze the vassals into submission, except Aaron is the kindest man alive. He would never enforce the rule, and it would be up to me to keep faith with an idea I don't agree with in the first place. I tell Aaron this.

"Well," he says, trying to be just, "it should work the other way too. Each morning he gets up on time, he could go to bed a half hour later that night."

I sigh. "I like it in theory. He would get up on time for a few days, then self-destruct, and he would have worked his bedtime back to eleven-thirty, so he'd have to go to bed at eleven then, which would still be too late. I'd spend all my time keeping track of time and arguing with him about it." What I don't say to Aaron is that I feel ridiculous spending all this energy figuring out how to get my kid out of bed on time. Dad stood at the bottom of the hall stairs. "Rise and shine," he shouted in a bright lilt. We all did, knowing that there was no opposing a force so certain of itself.

But of course I had siblings. We were competing, not just for Dad's approval, but to be the first at the table for Mom's bacon and eggs. A traditional family at a traditional breakfast. When was the last time I served anything hot for breakfast? I make a mental note to prepare the boys French toast tomorrow. "If we just enforced the rules we've already made," I said. "If we just kept it plain and simple. The thing is, he needs to get up in the morning and keep his life in order. If he doesn't, there should be consequences."

"Okay, then, what if he has to go to bed early, at nine, any day he isn't up and finished with his chores in time?" Aaron's doing his best to conceal it, but I can hear the triumph in his voice. He's been angling for nine all summer.

Yet the plan does make simple sense. "And if he's late for work, like now? There have to be consequences for that too."

"Make him work that much longer."

"Without pay?"

Aaron thinks, then breathes, "Yeah-ah!" as if it were a brilliant idea.

I go into my office and tap out the algorithm. Once finished, I try to concentrate on my writing, but keep looking out the window down at the long sidewalk beside our corner lot. Each time I look, it is empty of kids. Even though Aaron offered to go find them, I said it would be silly to run after them when I know they're just hanging out, oblivious of the time despite the watch I confirmed was absent from Nick's room. But lurid scenarios play inside my skull. I ask myself the questions all mothers ask. How long would it take before I found out? How would they even know who he was? I imagine a police officer or doctor or kidnapper fingering the crumpled portrait of me holding Nick in my lap.

Finally, I hear rumbling wheels on pavement. I look out the window to see Michael flying past the side gate on his skateboard. Nick follows behind him on foot, his board under one arm.

When they wander in the door, I stand at the top of the stairs, affecting calm and confident authority.

Nick glances up at me. "Hi, Mom," he says flatly. "We're home."

"That's good, but I need you both to come upstairs for a talk."

"What? Are we in trouble?"

"Just come upstairs and we'll sit down and talk about it." Behind me, Aaron's office door opens. Will he just watch me lay down the law, or will he help? I keep thinking—if he would only take part more, be more of a lively presence, then maybe my loneliness in his company would abate.

They come upstairs cooperatively enough. "Are we in trouble, Mrs. Bair?" Michael's voice hasn't changed yet, and this lends everything he says an innocence that has given way, in Nick's voice, to apparent cynicism.

"What'd we do?" Nick says, already combative. "We didn't do anything."

They sit down on my office couch, as I bid them to. Jennifer jumps up and darts back and forth between their laps, licking their faces and biting their hands when they try to pet her. She swims between my hands, paws batting the air as I put her down in the hall and close the door.

"Where's Aaron?" Nick asks. "I'm not talking until he's here. We can't have a family conference without him."

"Okay, Nick. He's coming. I just closed the door because of Jennifer." I open it and edge into the hallway, careful to keep Jennifer out. Aaron's door is closed. I knock and, entering, find him back in his office chair, apparently on the verge of reentering cyberspace. "Aren't you coming?"

"Coming?" he says absently. "Yes, I'm coming." He reaches onto his desk. "I was just getting my glasses."

With this valiant reinforcement, I return to my office, where the boys sit as if chained in a dungeon, surly looks on their faces, arms folded.

I present them with a copy of the rules, explaining that they mainly clarify what we've already agreed to—rising time and the chores that must be done to earn the dollar—with the one addition of consequences.

Nick reads resentfully, making a sarcastic show of his anger. "Oh, God, Mom! More rules? Who thought this up? Aaron, I bet. Ever since he came, that's all it's been. Rules for everything."

I decide not to stand up for Aaron. He needs to speak for himself, although I know that I've had better cooperation from Nick since Aaron has lived with us. Nick actually does want to be the model kid of the model family. But he's truly indignant now.

"Mom! Nine o'clock! The sun isn't even down yet."

As I explain that the rule only goes into effect if Nick doesn't keep his end of the bargain, he pulls strips of paper off the bottom of the sheet and stuffs them in his mouth. He chews, staring into my eyes while I talk. I consider taking issue with this, but some Greater Understanding, some magnanimous insight, tells me this is an act he must put on in order to save face. Michael,

quickly getting the hang of the kid's role in this liberal household, begins shaping his copy of the rules into an airplane.

"What about you?" Nick says to Aaron. "Aren't you going to
say anything?"

"Well . . ." Aaron's voice has that stubborn, indignant quality
I dislike. He will seldom instigate action, but he often affects
injury, as if Nick's behavior were a personal affront. "If you just
get up on time, you won't have to worry about going to bed so
early."

"But, Mom, please," Nick says. "Nine o'clock? That's the only
thing on here I don't agree with. Couldn't we make it nine-
thirty?" He is pleading now, and I know we're winning. What I
resent is that it's Aaron's concurrence that's overwhelmed Nick.
If I'd laid down this law by myself, the fighting would have gone
on endlessly.

"That would probably be okay." I look over at Aaron. "What
do you think, would nine-thirty be okay?"

Aaron pauses thoughtfully. "Sure, that sounds fair."

"Okay. Cross out nine and put nine-thirty."

What a coup! Nick is writing on the form. He is committing
his pen to it.

His defiance meets defeat not only in adult numbers, but in
brusque efficiency, in the upbeat tone I've affected throughout,
and in the swirl of activity I create now, opening the door to the
ecstatic beagle, and telling the boys to go pin up the rules on
Nick's bulletin board and to get their room straightened. It's
time for supper soon. They'll have to do the two hours of work
they missed today, plus the late time tomorrow along with that
day's regular two hours. This announcement elicits one more
passing swipe at the bottom of the rules from Nick, one more
mouthful of paper, but I stretch out a maternal arm and usher
him into the hall. This is the above-it-all, decisive mom I wish I
could always be.

Despite Aaron's mute help in the effort, I'm not even sure
he knows we have won. He returns to his office, shaking his

head. He's battle-scarred, but goddamn it, I do this all the time. *Would it really be the end of the world if he didn't come back from Florida?* I wonder, hating how I've been thinking the unthinkable more and more often lately. I see what I've done. I treated Aaron, Nick, and myself as if we were objects—dolls that could be jammed together into a traditional-seeming family. Our personalities weren't ready to be subsumed in that way, although we were all cooperative—out of various but equally intense yearnings.

In the hallway, I discover that Jennifer, the lovable beagle, has torn up a whole bag of Pampers that I used to bandage a leg wound my horse suffered when he got caught in barbed wire. "Nick!" I call. The bedroom door is closing behind them. "Clean up this mess, please."

"You do it! We have to clean our room," Nick says sarcastically.

"I've got to get supper, and she's your dog."

"Hey!" Michael says, as they plod back into the hall. "How come you guys have diapers?"

"It's for Mom's horse," Nick explains, pride in his voice over his being the son here, clued in on all the mysteries in the household.

"You put diapers on your *horse?*" Michael asks.

I burst out laughing, and so does Nick. He squats down and scoops up the torn remnants. "They're kind of small for a horse's butt, don't you think?" he asks.

At the other end of the hall, Aaron's door stands closed.

After supper, when I go up to check the room, I discover that it actually is tidy. Even more miraculous, the rules are pinned to the bulletin board. They flutter in the breeze of the open window, the printed letters intact. Nick ate only the blank paper on the bottom half of the sheet. This pleases me. After twelve years of child-rearing, I've learned to discern between blatant defiance and the mere expression of discontent.

Nick comes in the door behind me and grabs his and

Michael's skateboards. "You know what, Mom, I wish you'd obey the sign."

"What sign?"

He takes me by the arm, pulls me out into the hallway, and points to the middle of his door. "Read. It says *No. Tres. Pass. Ing.* Get it?"

"Got it."

"Good."

That little riff comes from the movie *Taxi Driver*, Nick knows. A former housemate in Iowa taught it to him. She was one of the many people we lived with and loved. One of the many who, besides an occasional letter or phone call, have become history. "Except I reserve the right of executive privilege."

"What does that mean?"

"It means I'm your mom and I'm not going to simply roll over and stop doing my motherly duty."

"I guess we're stuck, huh? You're always going to be the mom and I'm going to be the kid, even when I'm grown up."

"Well, I won't always be your boss like I am now, but there's still plenty of parenting that goes on after kids grow up."

"It's forever, huh?"

"Yep." I draw my fingers across the many stickers. "You know, hon, I was noticing your door this morning. I really like it. It's artful."

"Thanks!" There's surprise and appreciation in his voice.

"It's got that zing, that special way you have. You always put so much color and energy into everything, like this sunglasses sign."

Again, "Thanks!"

"I was wondering what you were thinking about when you put all this stuff up. I mean, was there a plan or anything?"

"Well, yeah. Sure. See, the bikes are together, and so are the motorcycles, and this shiny yin-yang card; when I look at that I think about some dude writing about when the center of the Earth breaks open and he made a picture of it. And these toothpaste people, they're singing 'Do the Sparkle Motion.'" Nick pauses to reflect a moment. "I got that when I was in Iowa. In Montessori school."

I shake my head and look at him in wonder. "You have an amazing memory."

"You always say that."

"Well, it's true."

Nick turns back to the door. "And see here how everything goes from left to right. It starts back in the old times with the Indians, and it was just butterflies and coyotes and things, but then we got policemen." Nick points to a poison-control sticker with a policeman on it, his hands folded over his mouth. His face is green. I hadn't even noticed it before, even though it includes an 800-number. If something had happened, I might have run all over the house, searching for a phone book, finally resorting to 911. Nick's finger trails across the panel to the opposite side of the door. "And then it went to where we had stuff like this all the time."

"Is that the label from the CD I made you get rid of?"

"Yes." There is a resentful curve in the one-word answer, but it also contains acceptance.

I look up at the ghost, who, with his shrouded arms extended, seems to reign over the entire scenario. "And why did you put him up there?"

"You know how stars glow in the dark? Well, that ghost glows and Grandpa's a ghost but he's also a star now."

I hug my son, who is almost as tall as me now. "Grandpa will always be the grandpa, won't he? At least some things remain constant."

Nick's chin moves up and down on my shoulder. I release him, and we both contemplate the ghost. He put the sticker up years ago, before my father died, so I know the meaning wasn't intentional. But when things happen is irrelevant to a kid. All bad things have been happening for a long time. All good things are over too soon.

JOY HARJO

9

Understanding the Weave:
Notes on Raising a Son

I HAVE A BROTHER who qualifies as a saint. He never complains despite a life of much suffering, and few apparent earthly gifts. As a child he battled life without a father, disappeared into sniffing glue and general truancy. Now he has two beautiful sons, one a musician and the other a record-breaking athlete. When I asked him recently for his secret (because we had a similar lack of training, similar poor models), he laughed and said, "All I do is feed and water them, and they grow."

I do not envy my brother his relationship with his sons; I revel in their connection, study it for clues. I know that "feeding and watering them" implies many levels of attention. And I know that I have failed.

Often as a parent raising children, especially a son, I have wished for a guidebook, a map to direct me through the labyrinth of the human emotional field, to cleanly and gracefully assist me in leading my children through the hills and valleys of achievements and failures. I have learned that the only guidebook of any effectiveness is the human heart. But even that can be difficult to read and negotiate, especially when the heart is clouded by fears and negative emotions.

•　　•　　•

When I began the road of parenthood I was sixteen years old, curled into a defensive ball of sheer potential. I was a student at Indian school when I became pregnant with my son. I didn't plan to get pregnant, but like many teenagers I felt invincible. I did take haphazard and naive measures for birth control, but they proved ineffectual. When I told my son's father of the pregnancy he urged abortion. He didn't want another child, he'd been down this road before, a father at seventeen years old, just three years before. He had kidnapped his daughter from that union, and she was now being raised by his mother in the Cherokee Nation in Oklahoma while he was a postgraduate student at school. Abortion, however, wasn't truly an option then. I didn't have the money or connections, but there was always self-abortion. I considered it very briefly, for the techniques were known and discussed among female friends, but I had already begun to feel a tenderness for the life stirring within me. I had no idea where I would live, how I would make a living for either of us.

Years later I am stunned at the thoughtlessness involved in the act of becoming pregnant. It makes no sense at all. But reason was obviously not involved, nor was I aware at sixteen of making a decision. I wasn't even aware I had the volition to make decisions, or that by not making conscious decisions I was making them nonetheless. I did not know who I was, didn't even have a realistic concept of selfhood. That same year we had an assignment in drama class to make a mask of ourselves, a natural-appearing mask that would mirror our features. I did not know what I looked like, could not make the mask in my likeness. I couldn't complete the assignment.

Of course I was not ready to be a parent, to take on all that parenthood entailed. I was still a child, battling childhood. I had no idea who I was nor did I have healthy role models of parenthood. I was not prepared for becoming a mother. I was disconnected, shy, head tipped toward the earth, my need to be loved spinning out of control. Yet I calmly walked through the storm from a house of violence into the house of yet another man who did not love me, even though I was just beginning to blossom after years of repression.

As an art, drama, and dance high school student at the Institute of American Indian Arts it was the first time in my life I felt validated for who I was, an Indian girl/woman who was on her way to becoming an artist with other student Indian artists. We were at the vanguard of a new wave in native arts. I had been picked (along with my son's father) to be part of a touring ensemble for a show that was exciting in its mix of traditional tribal elements of dance and drama with elements of Greek theater. Many from New York City theater and dance circles were flying into Santa Fe to watch us, see what we were doing. I was beginning to know that it was possible to have a creative life. It was also the first time in my life that I could awaken each morning and know that I would not be under the control of a stepfather who hated me, who abused me, despite taking on the responsibility of caring for me and my brothers and sister when he married our mother. I felt safe because I was several hundred miles away, far away from his brutality. Now my life was sane and for the first time there was talk of college, art school.

By becoming pregnant I appeared to destroy my future and I appeared destined, as were many of my friends and maternal relatives, to a string of children and poverty. Luckily I had been skipped from the eleventh to the twelfth grades so I graduated from high school, two months pregnant, then went on tour with our ensemble to the Pacific Northwest. There my drama teacher grew suspicious of my swelling belly, but when confronted one evening I denied a pregnancy. After the successful tour, where we even performed in a theater under the Space Needle in Seattle, I returned home to Oklahoma because I had no place else to go. My son's father was supposed to send me bus fare to Tahlequah, where he had returned to live with his mother, sister, and daughter. He didn't. I borrowed the money from my brother Allen, told my mother I was getting married, and had her drop me at the bus station with everything I owned in my army trunk bought for Indian school. When I got on the bus I had no idea what would happen. I had not heard back from my son's father. I had photographs of his daughter playing in front of a house there. If he didn't meet the bus my plan was to find the house in the photographs. If that didn't work I had no other plans. I was terrified but utterly calm as the bus pulled into Tahlequah. I was relieved to see him there. In my memory he is just as terrified as I. He would have preferred I disappeared, written to him to tell him he had a son. Distant knowledge would have suited him. I think now I must have surprised him. He had no idea that I would be that brave and stupid to get on a bus with nothing to nowhere. But, he did show up for the only time in our lives, and took me to stay with some friends until he broke the news to his mother.

When I was an infant my mother tells me I cried often. I was premature and fussy. She was afraid of me at first because I appeared so fragile and small and death was predicted in my early hours. She would walk me at night, rock me to quiet me, attempt to shield me from the temper of my father. Often he beat me in the crib out of frustration. When a child is inconsolable, interminable crying can be frustrating, especially when sleep is broken, but resorting to brutality does not solve the problem. An infant is a thinking and feeling being. As a child, especially before the acquisition of language, you believe you must be a terrible person to deserve such treatment, and with each punch you take in shame and grief. The knowing is then perched in the muscle, waiting to be acted out.

When I was sixteen I still believed I had done something to deserve the anger of my father, which translated into the anger and frustrations of the world in the guise of men who wished to control me because they felt out of control. I was only a small part of a pattern that began unfolding long before my birth and pregnancy. It is a pattern that involves families, tribes, the nation and continent, and there is a very human shape and smell to the thing.

Of course I did not see the pattern then, nor did I anticipate any problems with raising a son, despite my experience of violence from the men in my life, or my immersion in the pattern that was unwinding toward the end of the century, a time marked by the detonation of the atomic bomb. The age represented the gross separation of the head from the heart. Ideas of maleness and femaleness were fierce exaggerations hammered tightly into existence by manufacturers of buying and selling. The female represented the territory of the heart and the home and was given less value, the male the territory of the head and war and this denoted power. To make roads of understanding that crisscrossed the boundaries threatened the status quo. This paradigm is a gift of the Puritan mind that colonized these beautiful lands, separated the heart from the mind, the male from the female, human from nature, beauty in all things from everyday life. I did not see this construct inherent in most Indian communities, but communities that had lost touch with their original teachings mimicked the pattern.

I was raised in a household in which the males had free-ranging power. They assumed it. My Muscogee Creek father came and left as he pleased, with whom he wished, often staggering with drink and anger, an old anger larger than himself, encompassing the tribe, the nation, with the smell of women other than my mother lingering like the smoke from an enemy camp. The prized women were often white, attracted by my father's sensual dark beauty. Old angers if not approached and handled continue to rise up, generation after generation. My father's father beat him and sent him to Ponca City Military Institute to get rid of him as he raised a new family of children born to his new marriage, after my grandmother Naomi Harjo had died. My father in turn beat his children when we frustrated him with our mistakes, with our normal childish needs for patience and love. He also beat our mother. One of my first memories is trying to stop him from throwing my mother up against the wall by pounding him with my small fists. I remember feeling powerless as my blows evoked no response.

My mother allowed my brothers to roam as they wished. They had a freedom I coveted. My sister and I disliked the discrepancy. We were kept close to the house, and to the chores that needed to be done, including laundry, ironing, and cleaning. I also had to baby-sit while my mother worked. Sometimes she hired baby-sitters but as I grew older I was the one in charge. My brothers' only chores were emptying the trash and mowing the lawn, something I longed to do. I even asked once that the chores be rotated. I was flatly turned down. This is the way things were to be done. Something was wrong with the paradigm and I promised myself I would not repeat it when I was able to untangle myself from the oppression of unfairness.

Though this paradigm enslaved my mother she embraced it. It was what she knew, and to follow it without thinking kept her and many preceding generations from the pain of injustice simmering beneath the surface of the house. My mother's life was also marked by brutality, the brutality of unrelenting poverty. She could still hear the jeers of the other children who fought her because of her ragged clothes, pitiful housing, and bucket lunches of biscuits and lard. Her Cherokee mother was also caught in this cycle. She was orphaned and raised by people who did not value her, gave birth to child after child she could not adequately feed and care for. Instead of finding an ally in my mother, her only daughter in a family of six brothers, my grandmother turned against her, favored her sons. I imagine that my mother had the same role as I—the oldest female, the child with the responsibility for the house, all heavy chores, especially in her household with no running water or electricity. My mother's father loved her, doted on her, much to the consternation of her mother, who then vied with her daughter for her husband's affection. My mother gave birth to four children in quick succession. She loved us the best way she knew how, provided food, clothing, and shelter, but she was constantly overwhelmed with motherhood. As a child I often felt I was a burden that kept her locked in the cycle of work-exhaustion-sleep and felt guilty about it. She began to associate us with her suffering and detached from us. She probably felt guilty too.

When I was fifteen I overheard my mother and stepfather talking about sending me to a very rigid Christian school. I had quit church because of the judgment, faulty reasoning, and racism that appeared at the root of the church's doctrine. Often other children refused to sit near me because I was Indian and my parents were divorced.

My stepfather wanted me out of the house because I was beginning to question the injustices in our home. After overhearing their discussion I made plans to run away. Already my vulnerabilities had been spotted by those who ran drug and prostitution rings and I was slated to be chosen as their next victim. Then Indian school became a possibility and I was elated. I didn't like leaving my brothers and sister to the insanity but I hadn't been able to save any of us. My brothers were forced out of the house very soon after. My brother Allen was also in high school and had to finish on his own. My youngest brother, Boyd, was barely in his teens when he went to live with Allen, and spent some time with me. He also had a brief stint at Wyandotte Indian School, where he ran away with another boy because they were both being picked on, the other boy because he was fat, my brother because he was light-skinned. (He looks like many of my mother's relatives.) He landed with a preacher and his family, who took him in when he got involved with sniffing glue.

We had been forced out of the house because we caused turmoil, revealed the lack of sanity. We had tried to take our mother with us, but she wouldn't leave. My sister found a way to survive. She kept quiet, walked diligently through the mess.

My son took his first breath in the W. W. Hastings Indian Hospital, in Tahlequah, Oklahoma, the capital of the Cherokee Nation, after a long but normal labor. When I heard his cry I

trembled from the weight of life and the stream of drugs coursing through my seventeen-year-old body. My son and I were
poised together alone, there at his birth, with no relatives to
assist us, guide us, as the hospital staff kept at their jobs of
recording and weighing. I cried quietly, deeply moved at the
sacredness of this birth. I was also terrified. I was dependent on
his father, a man who could not keep a job, and for the first time
in my life I worried daily about meals and shelter. I had no skills
or training for anything but the arts. I didn't know how we were
going to make it.

I felt protective of him, this small, alert boy with big black
eyes who looked to me for nourishment, warmth, and happiness.
My heart was prepared to give him everything he needed for
security and a good life, to find a way despite the situation.
When I left the hospital on a late-winter morning with my small
bundle close to my heart, I knew I would do anything I could to
protect him. During those early years people often assumed he
was my little brother because of my young age. I was complimented often on my mothering skills. It was not hard to love
this tender and beautiful boy, and I expected our relationship to
be always as it was those first years together.

We reveled together in each of his accomplishments, each
step, each new word, each song, and he grew with the feeding
and watering of my attention and love. His father could not love
either of us and I soon left him after discovering a relationship
he had going with a baby-sitter I had hired to watch the children
(my son and his half-sister, Ratonia) while I worked in Santa Fe,
New Mexico, where we had moved, while he was supposed to be
looking for a job. He abandoned my son. Though my son was
awarded child support I was only able to talk his father out of ten
dollars once because I happened to be present when he was paid
for a job.

My son's Cherokee father was gifted with the ability to leap
beautifully through mythic stories told in dance, gifted with lyric
in drawing and painting, but he could not leap past the gulf of

the distant father who left him in early childhood, the Cherokee mother who wished him to take on the role of the father who deserted them. Once his mother took him to the house of some white people she considered rich (probably middle class), who had consented to adopt him. He refused to stay, left with his mother to take care of her. His father was alcoholic and distant, a Cherokee-German man who rarely spoke, buried himself alive in a watery grave, beat the only woman who ever loved him until he killed her in El Mirage, Arizona. When she died, he sold the small hotel she had left in the names of her grandchildren, and kept the money.

My son walked alongside me as I transformed from a girl to a woman, as we went from near-starvation poverty, living in a small house in the Cherokee Nation with in-laws who resented us, to living and studying without his father in New Mexico, in the university community where I began my career as a poet, activist, and musician. It is here the relationship between my son and I shifted, when the weight of history tilted and fell heavily on us.

I have dragged myself back and forth over this territory many times to understand what went wrong, to know my part in it so it doesn't happen again. The point of departure for the fine relationship between my son and me happened with the appearance of a man in my life, a stepfather to him. And as I write this I suddenly understand the connection to the pattern, something that appears glaringly obvious as I stand back with the perspective of years to take another look. There it is, glimmering in the weave. My son is three when this man comes into my life. It is here that our relationship is disrupted. My son begins misbehaving. He's suddenly hyperactive, difficult to handle. He was always active and maybe he's just being active now, but maybe I am perceiving him differently because the expectations of this new person take over the atmosphere and I act different. I become my mother and betray my child to make a relationship. This man is charismatic, talented, and alcoholic like my father. He is also violent and my son witnesses the violence. More than once I wake my son up in the middle of the night, bundle up him and his newborn sister and run to the neighbors. I remember blood in the snow. I know he does too, and that he is witness to my weakness shames me. I silence him because I don't want to see it, don't want to feel the pain of the fathers, the sons, the nephews, the pain of the mothers, daughters, and how it has appeared once again, and has come between my son and me.

I don't stay long in the relationship but the damage has been done. My son and I are caught in the back-and-forth of distrust because we are two children together, the hurt larger than both of us, and I don't know how to disengage from the traumatic pattern until years later. Like my mother I become distant, emotionally unreachable to hide the pain. He tries harder and harder to reach me by acting out his confusion in ways that often alienate. Sometimes it appears he wants to control me. I don't even know I'm being controlled by such a pattern until I turn around and take that lone and frightening walk through the field of the human heart, accept the shame of the human ability to hurt and maim. Fear engineers these acts, the inability to see with the heart open.

When my son was four years old I was convinced his soul came straight from the killing fields of Vietnam and that he hadn't taken the time he needed to make peace with the destruction. He has a fine gift of drawing, and he drew with perfect detail the machinery of war from that era, illustrated particular battles with a deliberate hand. I still believe he was influenced by that war, perhaps all children born into the U.S. in that age were and are, but I also understand he was drawing our conflicts and disappointments. I've kept these drawings, as I have kept everything he has ever written and given to me. I loved this boy even though I had difficulty loving myself those confused times when he was growing up. He needs to know, as I did through all of those different ages in the transformation from childhood to manhood, that though I failed at times, I loved him. He needs to know that when he was a child he didn't fail. When I couldn't always give him what he needed it was because I couldn't give myself what I needed. When I looked at him I saw myself, saw my same fierce need to know, the same wry sense of humor, the same weaknesses. Now I love him for those qualities.

Once when my son was five years old I asked him to sweep the floor. Saturday morning began the ritual of weekly house-cleaning. He refused, said it was women's work. The comment infuriated me and I blasted into a furious and long explanation as I forced him to sweep the floor. Now, as an adult I understand that he was trying to find a place for himself in a household that often did not have any good male role models, that he was picking up the same signals that were still in place from neighbors, school, other family members, television watched at friends' houses, a false frequency that said housework was for women only. I understand that I was often harder on him because of the terrible pressure I was under to go to school full-time and raise two children alone with few financial resources, and to try and change the world of injustices. Of course he should help sweep the floor and take care of the place he lives, wherever that place is, share duties with whomever he shares that place, but these days I carry to that memory tenderness and understanding, relieve the pressure with a little teasing. I bless the two of us as I walk back into the present.

We did make a major turn toward understanding each other through the years as we both grew into ourselves. We became closer, writing to each other when he lived far away, talking on the phone every week, sometimes twice a week, about our issues, our history, the general dramas and comedies of life. It was the kind of relationship I had imagined for my son and me. I valued it deeply. Then he became involved in an intimate relationship with a woman who was to bear him a daughter. Once again as I write, the pattern emerges so startlingly that I have to stop and take a deep breath at the terrible weave, and wonder if it's possible to change the weave in the middle of a design, or are we fated to continue the weave, generation after generation?

My son picked a woman who appeared to have no connection with his childhood, a non-Indian who had no interest in the arts, who wanted him to be the wage-earner while she stayed home to bear children whom she would raise to be "popular in school." During one of our conversations when he was in despair over their violent interactions, I asked what he had ever seen in her. He told me she wanted the same things as him, she was willing to stay home and let him be the head of the family, she wanted to be taken care of in the way she imagined from idealized families in television and movies. The idea comforted them both; it provided a structure, an ideal that was in contrast to how each of them had grown up. I imagine he thought she would mother him, take care of the small boy who was confused by the turn his world had taken, yet allow him to be the man. She represented everything I wasn't and she was intimidated by me and my achievements and worked to destroy my son and my relationship with him from within. She called into question my love, outlined my faults, and convinced him I should be their main monetary support. I also imagine that being in an intimate relationship with a woman brought to the surface in my son all the pain and anger that rightfully belonged to me. He began to call less and less, then not at all, except to blow up and blame me for everything that had ever happened to him, refusing to pay back loans that would have been forgiven had he made a few payments in good faith. I wanted him to know how to handle the responsibility of money. Instead, he allowed her to convince him that I owed him for my failings, for every difficult thing that had ever happened in his life, and that I must pay, one way or the other.

Their relationship eventually blew up. There was too much pressure from within, the same pressure building from generations of expectations, false definitions, fears and struggles. Perhaps we fly into these short, intense lives to understand the pattern, to know ourselves utterly against the backdrop of our intimate failures and achievements.

My son and I are finding our way again through the weave of history. We talk on the phone and make plans to see each other. I would prefer to have him closer and encourage him to take up art again, as a means to find delight in himself (but I don't tell him this part) and to develop a gift that will reveal to him the beauty of who he really is, and the legacy of where he comes from in a long line of artists extending from both sides of his family. He's as gifted as his father in the lyric of creative leaps. This story is for him and I add it to the complexity of the pattern held together by love, the glue to generations. I need him to understand his own part in this immense, ongoing story, to know his own power, realize we are woven together from a need to understand.

Consider then what would happen if you turn over the blanket created by this weave of generations, by the year after year of pain and struggle, look at the weave from the other side, in the light of compassion and forgiveness. Featured are the whimsical drawings of animals my son drew as a child, the drawings I covered the garage walls with as a child. They mingle together to make a story. The love that drew my parents together remains there as a pattern of stars in deep blue, as is the love that draws any of us together. I've seen it, beautiful with the understanding of pattern and form. Knowing and believing this, as well as food and water when needed, is how you raise a son.

SUSAN LESTER

9)

Belongings

At twenty, he has square feet and wide bones and thick coarse hair; a smile that, while slow, is generous. You want to pet him. From all the bulk and fur of him you wouldn't expect his hands, magician hands. Quick. He draws caricatures in charcoal, plays Bach on guitar, juggles beanbags, and folds colored papers into deer and mice, cuts perfect stars with scissors in one snip, hiding, always hiding the effort.

"Ancient Oriental secret," he tells you when you ask. Understand that he drills himself in skills, wrests them painfully from nothingness, trains his hands as if they are wild animals.

Maybe it was night and cold. (According to almanacs, it snows in Seoul.) Concealed by darkness she took him to the orphanage, laid him on a table cunningly designed to revolve, outside to in, accepting infants without revealing mothers. She walked home, still tender from the birthing.

He is seven months old when they send him to us on an airplane. We wait at the terminal to receive him, our son. Thirty babies are carried from the jumbo jet by men and women with dark hair, dark eyes. He is among them, asleep, full head of black

hair sticking straight up, skin warm as a fever, voice deep when
he murmurs. He doesn't cry. They pass him to me. I cry. I undress
him in the airport bathroom like a gift I can't wait to open. His
diaper is dry. My hands are shaking.

Maybe it was daylight and, unashamed, she strode to the
orphanage to deposit him. She had meant the conception to be
a tool with which she would pry open a distinguished place for
herself. Too late, she saw it was her censure. She wiped her
hands on her clothing going home.

His brother is inside my belly, a quick little fetus seven months
old, conceived on the day we decided to adopt. Magic decision.
He turns in my womb, taps at me from inside as if curious. I
laugh. The Korean men smile for politeness when I laugh, not
knowing the joke that is passing between my children.

Maybe she was charmed by a stranger, felt his love like the sun's
light and opened herself, morning flower that broke laws with its
tenderness. That night when she walked to the orphanage, there
were stars above her, stars whose light had begun many hundreds
of years before. She knew about stars, she understood that many
hundreds of years hence, this moment would be seen by the stars
she saw now. Pure light.

They hand him to me, asleep, then bow. Two men. I look at
them covertly. This is how my son will look someday, this tall,
this dark, this broad of face.

Bewildered, he opens his eyes, dark eyes, so dark I can't see
pupils in them. He comes to me nuzzling his forehead in my
neck, moving his head back and forth, back and forth, as if saying, "No, no, no, no, no." He lays his head against me then
sleeps again. Once more, the men bow. They don't know my
tongue. We smile. We compare the name bands on our wrists.
Mine. His. Theirs. Yes, they match. We smile.

• • •

Maybe this was the punishment she meted out to her lover: to dispose of the object created by his passion and thus make all his passion negligible. Maybe on the way home she ate chocolate.

He is five and in school. He hates school. He says he fears he will fall out of line. On his first day, he asks me to pray to God to see if God can change his eyes. A child told him God could.

I pray a curse on the child who inaugurated this hope in him. I rake leaves in the yard for a week, turn soil, prune branches, master anger. I brush aside pebbles and branches and sticks to discover an anthill from which emerge a thousands ants. Within seconds they have filed themselves into lines. I shift a stone to divert them. I uncover, with a start, a lemon-colored toy car in a square hole, a small pebbled driveway for its entrance, a pinecone roof. I kneel and look, intrigued, my heart opened like a flower to the sunlight.

Maybe she was a New Woman, one who stepped away from the governing social order in which, antlike, individuals served as cells of a greater organism. She was warned that when isolated, one died; when shamed, one lost her place. But she stood brave against it, loved a man despite it, bore a child because of it. In anger she conceived, in triumph gave birth; in hope she gave away her son to live where she believed he would be free.

He is a mewling infant with moist, soft skin, infected navel, self-containment. I do not know him yet. A foster family keeps him. Five sons. They carry him on their backs and feed him rice milk. They sleep with him on their heated floors and tease him so he moved his head back and forth, back and forth, as if saying, "No, no, no, no, no." Outdoors, the country smells of minerals and earth, inside, of boiled rice and tea and garlic.

Maybe she hid herself, magician girl, appeared always to be obedient, all the while breaking with the order that sustained her.

She bowed as if she obeyed, but broke, then feared the law. She hid the hot fetus within her, the fetus that would cut her, like a sword, from her mother and her father and her husband-to-be. Isolated, she would die. She crept, terrified, to the orphanage's turntable, hoping to abandon there fear. But fear went home with her, and with it, grief.

He hoards things. I call him a pack rat, though he knows I'm intrigued by the things he keeps. He refused to cut his thick horse-mane of hair. "Are you saving it for something?" I try to show reason.

"It's only peach fuzz," he answers. "Ancient Oriental peach fuzz."

His room is a labyrinth of beautiful things: guitar, girlfriend's pillow, drawing board, the *I Ching*, broken clock parts, Holy Bible, plastic jars, blue glass bits, stuffed dogs, burnt-edge corks, wooden boxes, rolls of tape, his baby blanket.

I kneel and look. This, I say, is because, at seven months, he knew that a person could lose everything, his people, his belongings, the smell of his ground, the hot floor where he sleeps, the white robes of ceremony, even the sound of his language. He does not know he remembers these things, or remember that he lost them. I do not remind him, but I let him hoard; I let him explain.

"What happened to your real mother?" asks Clark, blond four-year-old living next door.

"She died," he says.

"So," I say. And maybe she did. I would have.

MARY GORDON

9

Mother and Son

WE WERE one of a minority of couples—one in ten, is it? one in a hundred?—who were hoping for a girl. The delivery room nurses, knowing my passionate wish, let out a joyous shout when they saw that the baby was a daughter. It took her twenty-two hours to be born, a difficult birth, she wanted to come into the world chin up, and she's kept it that way for thirteen years. Anna looked at us, and at the world, with a gimlet eye; as soon as she could focus, she understood her job description: separating the sheep from the goats.

She so delighted us that three years later, we decided to try again. This time, I was older, and decided on an amniocentesis. We opted to know the gender of the fetus before it was born; we thought it was absurd that the lab technician should know more about our child-to-be than we did. The six weeks waiting for the results of an amnio are among the longest days in anyone's life, and when the doctor called, saying he had good news, I was elated. "Everything's fine," he said. "It's perfectly healthy. And it's a boy!"

"Oh, my God," I said. "What am I supposed to do with one of them?"

"They're very cute," the doctor said.

"Yes, but I don't know what to do with them."

He told me I'd figure it out.

I'd lived an unusually female-centered life. I am an only child, and my father died when I was seven. My mother and I then moved in with my grandmother and my aunt. I went to an all-girls' high school and a women's college, I wasn't a tomboy, and I wasn't someone who had a lot of male friends. The important relationships in my life were with women friends and male lovers—for most of my life it was in that order. Now I was (and still am) married when I learned the news that I was to have a son, so I was going to be bringing one of *them* up alongside one of *them*. You would think I needn't have been so alarmed. But I was.

I was in my early twenties in the first years of the women's movement: I came of age as a feminist. It would be pleasant if one could become a feminist without a consciousness of the injustices and abuses perpetrated on women by men. But it didn't happen to me. For those of us feminists who are heterosexual, it had been a struggle to reconcile our rage against male culture with our feelings for the men with whom we enter into what is perhaps the most intimate of human relations. The most intimate, that is, except that of giving birth.

It's one thing to be angry at a grown-up male, even unjustly, sometimes, for acting according to type, of representing the values of a gender with a history of oppressing, but what about a kid? What about one who lived inside your body for nine months, who is sustained by the milk in your breasts? This is the kind of thing I was afraid of. Would I take my generalized anger against male privilege out on this little child who was dependent upon me for his survival, physical to be sure, but mental as well?

And what would I do with him? I didn't like sports; I wasn't interested in soldiers, or cowboys, or cops, or cars. What would we talk about? If I brought him up to be interested in what I was interested in—so we could have a good time hanging out—would I be depriving him of his rightful place in the world of men, a world he had no choice but to inhabit?

In retrospect, I realize that I was thinking about what men did all day in ways that were grotesquely stereotyped. I didn't imagine that my daughter and I were going to spend the day talking about cooking or hairdos; why did I think my son would come into the world equipped with a football helmet and a six-pack?

I had to learn. Of course, the body is a great teacher. If my mind told me, occasionally, that the creature inside me was "the other," my heart leapt with joy every time I felt him move inside me. The slow grinding of his head against my belly, the undulant curve of his midnight swims wiped out the very hint of separateness. Then he was born: an easy birth, three hours. And he was David. He wasn't *him*.

From the beginning, he was less fierce than his sister; he always seemed to have more of those qualities Carol Gilligan says girls have than his sister did. He was much more interested in pleasing, in cooperating; she was interested in what was right. She could block out the world to achieve mastery of a task. I once saw her literally step over a weeping classmate in nursery school in order to get to the shelf where the books were kept. He could be distracted from his pursuits by the presence of other people, particularly if he felt they weren't happy.

Everyone told me that boys were more physically active than girls and created more domestic havoc. I was poised, but it wasn't true in my son's case. He has had, from the beginning of his life, a remarkably contemplative nature, an ability to sit quietly musing, looking, thinking; at sixteen months, he crawled away from all of us at a dark beach picnic. In a panic I shone a flashlight into the black night and saw him sitting quietly—transferring sand from one hand to another.

From the moment he noticed other people, he's had a tendency—anguishing for a mother to observe—to suffer when other people are suffering, to intuit their suffering, to turn himself into a pretzel—telling jokes, giving them toys—in order to make them happier. When he was in kindergarten, there was a child in his class who'd been born addicted, who'd had a difficult life, moving, often several times a month, from one welfare hotel to another. Each morning, he began his day sitting on David's lap, and David rocked him for a few minutes until he was ready to join the other children at their play. He always went out of his way to include difficult or isolated children. Anna, however, has never had any tolerance for bad behavior, no inclination for charity play dates. David's guilt (which he, but not Anna, took in with his mother's milk) often leads him to invite people he doesn't like and then feel trapped by their presence. Anna knows her limits, and states them clearly. When she was a kindergartner we went (God help us all) to Disney World. There, the characters walk around, and children get their autographs. Mickey, Donald, and Goofy were mobbed. But no one was around Chip and Dale. I said to my daughter, "Why don't you ask Chip and Dale for their autographs. They must feel sad that no one's asking them."

"I didn't tell that guy to be Chip," she said. "It's his choice and his problem."

My daughter could hear the unexpurgated Grimms' stories, delighting Bruno Bettelheim's heart, and not turn a hair at the most bloodthirsty myths (*Beowulf* was a favorite with her), but we quickly learned that David was very troubled by cruelty or violence in stories or on the screen. *Raiders of the Lost Ark* did him in at age eight. A friend of mine had invited him over to watch it, and David came back, pale and distraught. "He invited me to see another Indiana Jones movie tomorrow," David said. "Tell him you won't let me go. Tell him it's too violent." When my friend walked in the house the next day, David said, "She won't let me see it. I just begged her to let me see it but she said she thinks it's too upsetting." He knew what he didn't like, but he felt it unmanly to admit that he was frightened by something. So he came up with a public strategy, one that he could be confident would be a hit: bend the truth and blame Mom. Whereas Anna is Joe Friday's ideal respondent—just the facts, ma'am—David's not above a little creative storytelling to grease the world's wheels, to make people happier, to spare their feelings, to make himself well liked.

You often hear mothers of boys and girls say that their boys are more fragile than their girls, and in case of my family, it seems to hold. But thinking of your son as fragile can lead a feminist to the pitfall that my daughter insists is my chief one: overprotecting the son. Because many of us tend to characterize the world of men as predatory, aggressive, ruthlessly competitive, we fear for our sons more than do mothers who see the world of men as more benign. We may worry that, growing up in homes that stress feminist virtues, they have been underprepared for the cold, tough world that is still run on the whole by men who haven't been very susceptible to the feminist message. In addition, many feminists who have managed to be competent simultaneously in the traditionally female world of domestic life and the traditionally male world of moneymaking, and who see that most men can't even conceptualize what we think of as routine, can fall into the trap of thinking that men are the weaker sex, perennial boys we have to do end runs around in order to keep the world spinning. And since even feminists sometimes undervalue domestic work, it's easier for me to remember that I want Anna to go to law school than that I want David to learn to cook.

Do I ask less of him because I think, as a male, he's capable of less? Or do I get off on serving a son in a way I don't a daughter? There is, I have found, a romance of a surprising potency between mother and son, one that male writers have told us about—from Lawrence, to Proust, to Philip Roth. But we've heard about it from the son's point of view. I never expect to be loved again with the uncomplicated sweetness with which David loved me when he was small. I always felt that Anna and I were shoulder to shoulder in the world, but I knew she saw me clearly, warts and all. For David, I was the most beautiful, the most charming, the best cook, the most brilliant writer in the history of the world. He would look through catalogs and tell me which clothes he was going to buy for me when he grew up. I basked in this adoration—who wouldn't—and worried what I'd do when it stopped. This year, I got a clue that the romance was ending. "You know," he said, "my friend Tommy's mother is very beautiful. I think she's a lot younger than you." He asked me if I knew how much gray there was in my hair and if I'd ever considered dyeing it. A few months ago he said, "My friend Johnny said he thinks you have a big butt, and I couldn't tell him he was wrong."

This is the year he discovered basketball. Ten months ago, I coaxed him to join a team because a friend of mine was coaxing her son as well. Suddenly, he discovered he was very good at it. He practiced obsessively. He spent his money on basketball cards, hats, and posters. He watched games on TV that were broadcast from cities I'd never heard of. What was worse, he asked me to watch with him. My husband couldn't be pulled in—but I couldn't say no to my son. Also, I had to admit that it was something of a relief to me to see him involved in a traditionally male activity that wasn't horribly aggressive, that seemed like it was fun, that might be able to teach him the good side of competitiveness, and those things that women are said to lack because we didn't play team sports.

There I was, watching basketball. The very person who'd always made fun of people who talked sports and accused women interested in sports of trying to please their fathers. As a teenager, I'd invented something called "sportspeak," a skill I tried to pass on to younger women. "Sportspeak" was based on the theory that any woman could learn three sentences and convince any man that she knew a lot about sports by inserting them, in well-chosen places, into his monologue. You could do fine by saying: "Well, at this point in the season, it's hard to tell"; "Of course, it all depends what happens in the clutch"; and "Sometimes they start slow and pick up speed, and sometimes they just run out of gas." Suddenly, this year, I discovered buried in my heart a passionate, undiscovered Knicks fan. I found a new role model, Knicks coach Pat Riley. He had so many things I wanted: great hair, Armani clothes, blind obedience from those around him. When the Bulls beat the Knicks, I was inconsolable. But wait, it wasn't just me. It was me and my son.

The trouble came when he wanted me to actually play basketball with him. I told him I wasn't very good. He said he'd coach me. After a few minutes, he turned to me in near despair. "Mom," he said, "are you going to hold that ball like a baby, or are you going to hold it like a ball? Because if you're going to hold it like a baby, I'm going to grab it out of your hands." I told him I'd try to hold it like a ball. It wasn't good enough. "Mom," he said, "you're just not aggressive enough. You have to really want to get that ball away from me." I told him that our relationship had been based on my not being aggressive with him, and, rather than wanting to take things away from him, I always wanted him to have things. "Mom," he said, "don't think of me as your son. Think of me as your opponent."

For a few months, everything was basketball. He didn't want to go to museums with me anymore. Going to museums had been one of our favorite things to do; talented at drawing and painting himself, he was excellent at describing how he thought paintings had been constructed. But one day on our way to the Metropolitan Museum of Art, he asked if we couldn't just go for an ice cream instead. "I think I'm not into art anymore," he said. I took a deep breath and asked if he wanted hot fudge. A few months later, he said, "Why don't you take me to the museum anymore? You know art's one of my favorite things." We went to the museum and spent twenty minutes in front of a Hopper lighthouse, talking about the shadings of the sky. He's still obsessed with basketball. But there are other things, things that came to him partly as a result of knowing me. But maybe he needed to know he could get away from me, that he could move in a world I wasn't in charge of, that he could share a world with me, but on his terms.

As I was writing this, an incident happened that expressed for me the complexities of being a feminist mother of a son. We were all swimming in a lake—Anna and David had settled on the raft. I was off on my "long swim," a situation that puts me in a Zen-like state of calm. From far away, I could see my children on the raft. Then I saw a boy about Anna's age push her off the raft. She must know him, I said to myself, he must remember her from the day camp she went to when she was five. Then I saw the same boy wrestling with David, saw him push David off the raft, saw David get back onto the raft, only to be pushed into the water again. When I got to shore, I asked Anna what had happened. "That jerk pushed me in, and David got upset, and he told the guy he couldn't do that to his sister. So he tried to push David in. It happened twice. David was just too small for the kid; he didn't have a chance. I thought it was really nice of him to stand up for me."

I, too, was moved. But after a minute, I didn't want to buy the idea that a woman needs a man to stand up for her. "Why didn't you do it yourself?" I asked.

"Why would I waste my time on that moron?" she said. It didn't seem to mean much to her.

But I could see that David was seething. He swam away from us and headed toward the raft. I watched with trepidation as he treaded water near the raft and then swam back to us.

"What was that all about?" I asked.

"Well, I went out there, I said hi, how you doing to the guy, like I was trying to make friends. Then I gave him the finger and swam away."

He was very happy with himself.

It isn't just Huck and Jim on the raft now—if it ever was. Our boys have to contend with boys who are surrounded by people who give them enough rope to hang all of us and then excuse their behavior with a shrug, remarking that "boys will be boys." But what boys will be what boys? And what then will these boys become? As feminist mothers of sons, we have a stake in the world of men. We can't afford wholesale male-bashing, nor can we afford to see the male as the permanently unreconstructable gender. Nor can we pretend that things are right as they are. We have hints that our sons are different from us, but it may be impossible to tease out what is DNA and what is environment. The task of setting limits while allowing a child to be her- or himself is the central one for all parents, but a feminist mothering a son may find the limit/freedom tightrope a particularly vexing one to walk. We must love them as they are, often without knowing what it is that's made them that way.

Our best bet, I think, is to remember there's no perfect solution, to enjoy them, ourselves, and our relationship with them in all its paradoxical complexity, to keep our sense of humor, to provide them with excellent role models. Mel Brooks, maybe. Or Groucho Marx. Or perhaps Odysseus. Because it is a new journey we are making with our boys, one that they will eventually have to make without us. The routes are unmarked, the dangers misnamed, or named insufficiently. The vista we've dreamed of is still on the horizon, past the shoals, the whirlwinds, the distracting sirens' song.

PRISCILLA LEIGH McKINLEY

Jonathan Bing

"HERE'S THE picture of your son," my mother said, placing a photograph in my hand. "He looks like your father, don't you think?"

My son Jonathan was on a respirator in the intensive care nursery, and my doctor had left instructions that because of my high blood pressure and erratic blood sugars, I was not to move. There were doctors and nurses taking care of my child, but I wanted to see him, to touch him, to hold him in my arms. I didn't want to settle for a picture, a Polaroid taken by one of the nurses, but I was desperate.

I lifted my head off the pillow and took the picture from my mother, but with an IV in one arm and an automatic blood pressure cuff on the other, I couldn't bend either of my arms enough to see it. Even when my mother took the picture and held it up as close to my face as she could, all I could see was a square shadow, gray on gray. "It's too dark in here," I said. "Can you turn on the light?"

"The light's on," she said, pausing momentarily. "Your vision's probably just a little blurry from all the stress. I'll turn on the overhead lamp."

I heard the click of the lamp and moved my head back and

forth, trying to see the picture, trying to see Jonathan. But all I could see was that square shadow against the light. "I can't see it. I can't see anything."

I lost my sight on March 17, 1984, St. Patrick's Day, the day my son Jonathan was born. In the eyes of pregnant diabetics, the blood vessels grow rapidly and expand, causing a slight decrease in sight. During my pregnancy, I could read most things, but some magazine print was too small for my blurred vision, which made the individual letters look like fuzzy black lines moving across the pages. Also, I could drive during the day, but at night, the lights of the oncoming cars bothered my eyes. The doctors had told me that my sight would return after delivery, once the blood vessels settled. However, after developing preeclampsia six weeks before my due date, I had an emergency C-section, and the blood vessels in both eyes hemorrhaged, leaving me almost totally blind.

I remember the first time I went down to the intensive care nursery the day after Jonathan was born. Pressing my face against the incubator glass, I hoped to see something, anything. But all I could make out was a dark figure on a light blanket—a shadow, a blur, a blob. There was a torso but no details; a head but no distinguishing features. I stuck my arm through one of the holes on the side of the incubator, searching desperately for Jonathan. When my hand came in contact with his, an exhilarating feeling came over me, sending chills up and down my spine. I caressed his small, fragile hand with my fingertips. It felt so soft, so wonderful. As I felt for his little feet, the palm of my hand brushed against a plastic disposable diaper and a smooth bony leg. I counted his toes—five on the right, five on the left. Perfect!

After working my way up the entire eighteen inches of his four-pound body, I reached his head. Because Jonathan was premature, he couldn't breathe or eat on his own, and the sides of his scalp had been shaved for IV's, leaving a strip of dark hair down the middle of his head, but a miniature stocking cap covered this. I smiled, imagining my son deliberately hiding his wild hairstyle, his Mohawk. With the back of my finger, I felt his hollow cheek and his little ear—no bigger than a penny—sticking out from beneath the hat. I didn't want to disturb the various tubes hooked up to his nose and mouth, so I imagined the features that the nurse described—his thin lips, his puggy little nose, his blue eyes, and his bright red eyelashes.

For nine months, I held on to the hope that I would get my sight back, that someday I would be able to see my son. After the first eye operation, a vitrectomy to remove the contaminated vitreous and reattach the retina in my left eye, I could see a hint of color, usually a patch of Jonathan's bright clothing, especially red and yellow. Every day, the doctors grew a little more optimistic. They believed my sight would come back and I believed them. But when the scar tissue from that operation obstructed the drainage duct, I developed diabetic glaucoma and lost all that I had gained. I had three trabecolectomies to create artificial drainage ducts in my left eye, but they all failed. When Jonathan was nine months old, I had a vitrectomy in my right eye. I knew that it was the last chance to get my sight back, the last chance to see my son. I imagined seeing Jonathan for the first time, looking into his grayish-blue eyes, watching him watch me. But that never happened. The operation failed.

A huge oak with a tire swing stood just outside the back door of my mother's house, where Jonathan and I lived until he was eighteen months old. With one arm around Jonathan and the other arm straight out in front of me, I usually managed to find the tree on the first try. Other times, when I missed by a foot or so, I flung my right arm back and forth in front of me, feeling for the tree or the ropes that supported the swing. I spent hours pushing Jonathan on that swing. Almost every time the swing came back to me, it hit me in the thighs. Jonathan thought it was a game; laughed and laughed, a low-pitched chuckle, an old man's chuckle. As I pushed him on the swing, I sang the same words over and over and over, changing the tune only slightly each time. "Jonathan Bing is on the swing. Poor old Jonathan Bing. Swing, swing, swing, swing. Jonathan Bing is on the swing." Often the tears rolled down my cheeks, but I managed to keep a smile on my face, the way I did every night as I sang Jonathan to sleep.

I did not sing the typical lullabies like "Rock-a-Bye Baby" or "Hush Little Baby." Instead I sang songs I remembered from Girl Scouts, like "I'm a Little Piece of Tin" and "I Stuck My Head in a Little Skunk Hole." Sometimes I sang "Home on the Range," a song I never really liked. The songs took me back so many years, to thoughts of sitting around campfires, singing and laughing and loving life. But then, every night, I ended with "My Favorite Things" from *The Sound of Music*. I would be fine through the first and second verses, but I always broke down in tears by the last. When I started singing, "Girls in white dresses with blue satin sashes/Snowflakes that stay on my nose and eyelashes," the tears started and the singing stopped. Yet I kept that smile on my face. I would look down at Jonathan and smile, saying over and over, "I love you, Jonathan Bing." As he drifted off to sleep, I rocked back and forth, back and forth, hearing only the creaking of the hardwood floor beneath my white wicker rocker.

I loved Jonathan with all my heart, but since I didn't have experience in either blindness or motherhood, the first few years of his life were the most difficult of mine. In many ways, Jonathan protected me more than I protected him. He protected me from myself. With a new baby, I didn't have as much time to think of my own problems. Still, suicide was always on my mind. One minute I would think I should live for Jonathan; the next minute I would think I should die for him. I thought Jonathan would be better off with a sighted mother, an adoptive mother. At night, I dreamt of the various ways I could kill myself. In my dreams, I could see everything perfectly—the shimmering reflection of the moon on the lake where I drown myself, the bright red warning label on the bottle of sleeping pills I took, the curious smile on my face when I hanged myself with a rope of bread dough that I was supposed to be using for a braided bread-dough Christmas wreath. Despite the disturbing nature of the dreams, I actually started to enjoy them—the colors, the light, the beauty. The dreams helped me escape from my dark world.

The worst dream during that period of my life—the Memorial Day dream—wasn't about suicide. It was about Jonathan. In the dream, my mother, two-year-old Jonathan, and I were heading down the sidewalk on West Fourth Street, the main street in St. Ansgar, my small hometown in northern Iowa. On our right, colorful tulips, petunias, and impatiens filled the flower boxes attached to the big white houses. On our left, the American flags on the light poles stretched out over the street, creating a river of red, white, and blue. When we reached the downtown area, the entire three-block stretch, we stopped and looked for a place to sit in front of Learann's Shoe Shop. While my mother min-gled with the other spectators, Jonathan and I sat on the curb, watching the Memorial Day parade—the legion members dressed in their navy blue uniforms, twirling their rifles in front of them; the veterans from World Wars I and II, riding in the backs of big shiny Buicks and Cadillacs; the groups of Boy Scouts and Girl Scouts, a few worn-out Brownies and Cubs trail-ing behind. When the St. Ansgar High School band marched by in their red-and-white uniforms, I turned to see Jonathan's reac-tion, but he was gone. I looked around for my mother, but she was gone, too. I screamed, over and over and over, but the blar-ing trumpets and big bass drums muffled my cries. Instead of waiting for the noise to die down, I set out in search of my son.

When I reached the elementary school, I noticed the sign on the door, *St. Ansgar Meat Packing Plant*. I opened the door and saw Jonathan, dressed in his red-and-white-striped shirt and blue Osh-Kosh overalls, sitting on a conveyer belt between two chunks of bloody, raw meat, heading straight for a meat grinder.

I yelled at him to get down, but he just smiled and waved. He couldn't hear me. The machine was too loud. I ran over to the control panel, but everything melted together, transforming into a shapeless, colorless mass. I couldn't see the switches. I couldn't see anything. I ran my hands over the controls, hitting each and every button. Finally I hit the right one. The roaring and rattling of the machine stopped. I breathed a deep sigh of relief and looked up toward my son, but it was too late. He was gone.

My fears as a blind mother weren't quite as bad when Jonathan was a baby, as long as I knew where he was each and every minute. I put bells on his booties and shoes so that I could follow him when he started scooting on the floor. He did what my mother called the elephant seal hump, pulling his knees up under his chest, lunging forward, landing on blocks and other toys, laughing all the while. When I fed him, I felt his mouth with one hand while shoveling food in it with the other so I wouldn't get strained peas or carrots in his eyes or nose, something he managed to do all by himself. And as for changing? I used twenty diaper wipes at each change just to make sure he was clean, and it wasn't hard to tell when he needed a change. Yes, I managed pretty well when he was an infant. But then he started to walk, to run, to climb.

When Jonathan was eighteen months old, I married Jim, my rehabilitation counselor from the Iowa Department for the Blind, and Jonathan and I moved to Iowa City, which wasn't like St. Ansgar, where one could leave the doors unlocked at night and feel safe. To me, the absence of light meant the absence of security. I was afraid of everything, paranoid about everyone. I refused to leave the apartment alone, fearing the outside, the unlimited space, the world, fearing I would fall down a flight of stairs or get hit by a car. I would be kidnapped or mugged or molested. Even worse, something would happen to Jonathan.

We lived in a lower-level apartment, and I always kept the doors and windows locked. I opened the curtains only on the days my vision seemed a little better than others. I would open the curtains in my bedroom, make Jonathan lie down on the bed, and bend over him, trying to see what he looked like, but he usually appeared the same as he did the first time I saw his four-pound body in the hospital incubator—a shadow, a blur, a blob. I don't know what Jonathan was thinking as I knelt over him, turning his head from side to side, but he didn't like it and usually wriggled away, sliding off the side of the bed, running into the other room. Then I would quickly close the curtains again, blocking out the rest of the world.

I felt safer when Jonathan and I stayed home, especially when Jim was there, but he was often away from home. In addition to being gone from 7 A.M. until 6 P.M. Monday through Friday, Jim was usually away one or two nights a week for his job. So Jonathan and I spent the days together, just the two of us. In the morning, we watched game shows or played in Jonathan's room, often making robots and airplanes out of Legos while listening to Big Bird or Bert and Ernie or Oscar the Grouch or the Cookie Monster read books on tape. I had ordered some Braille books for children (regular children's books with clear plastic Braille inserts), but by the time I was finished saying, "Once upon a time, there was . . . ," Jonathan was off and running. He didn't have the patience to wait for the words as my fingers slid slowly along the Braille bumps. In the afternoon, Jonathan slept while I listened to TV soap operas like *As the World Turns*. I hoped that the horrible happenings on the show would make me feel better about my own life, but usually nothing seemed worse than my own situation. (There was one character who went blind, but alas he hit his head a few months later and regained his sight.)

A cedar chest stood in front of the living room window and Jonathan would crawl up on it whenever he heard something outside. Since I wouldn't let him open the curtains, he would stand between the window and the curtains, watching excitedly.

He liked seeing the garbage trucks lift the Dumpsters and empty the contents. (When he was three, he said he wanted to be a garbageman when he grew up.) He liked watching other tenants carry their baskets of clothes to and from the laundry room. Most of all, he liked watching the neighbor kids. He stood on the cedar chest for hours, watching the other children play ring-around-the-rosy or "London Bridge" or kick ball. At his age, he didn't know that he could join in the fun, that he could be one of them, which was fortunate for me.

I took him outside only when I heard another mother out with her kids. I knew that if something happened to Jonathan, the other mother would be able to see him, would be able to protect him. Cheryl, the mother of two girls, Ann and Mary, ages five and four, sat outside with her kids quite often. Mary was very quiet and liked playing with Jonathan. Ann liked playing with Jonathan, too, but for different reasons. She reminded me of Pippi Longstocking, sort of loud and obnoxious, running through the mud puddles in her sundresses and bare feet, never worrying about the dirt. For her, Jonathan, the youngest child in the apartment complex, was an easy target, someone she could bring to tears. If the kids played tag, she would make sure that Jonathan was always It. If the kids played jump rope or jacks, she told Jonathan that he was too young.

"You can't play, Jooooonnnnnn," I overheard Ann say one day as I stood just inside the apartment door, her voice ranging between mean and whiny, stretching out the last syllable so it sounded like a foghorn.

"Why?" Jonathan whined, his voice shaking as though on the verge of tears.

"'Cause I said so. I don't want you to play with us."

Jonathan started crying. "But I wanna pway."

As soon as I flung open the door and stepped out on the sidewalk, Jonathan ran over to me and hugged my legs with his little hands, wiping his eyes and nose on my jeans. I looked in the direction of Ann's shadowy figure and gave her the blind evil eye. "Come on, Jonathan. You don't want to play with *someone* mean." Then, scooping up Jonathan in my arms, I stepped back into the apartment and slammed the door as hard as I could.

As many times as I wanted to take Ann in my arms and shake her, I was actually glad that she was around. When Jonathan started begging to go out and play, this was the excuse I used: "Ann will just make you cry, so you might as well stay in." Then I would bribe him with a treat or a special video. Sometimes it worked. Other times, Jonathan still insisted on going out. I guess he thought it would be better to be around mean kids than no kids at all.

I felt guilty for not letting Jonathan be a kid, but, at the time, I didn't know what else to do. I didn't think of the parents I had seen in K Mart, frantically running through the aisles, calling out the names of their lost children. I thought I was the only mother who worried about protecting her child. After all, how could a blind person keep a child safe? How could I tell if he ran out in front of a car? How could I keep him from going down big slides, from climbing trees, from being a kid? I didn't want to smother him, but what could I do? I wanted him to have a "normal" childhood, to experiment, to learn, to grow. But how could I give him that freedom?

One blustery winter day about a month before Jonathan's second birthday, he and I went to the store to get a few groceries. The store was only about five blocks from our house, but I was afraid to walk that far, especially in the snow, so we took the bus, which was only about half a block from our apartment. Jonathan and I had been to the store with Jim several times, and I had memorized the items that were in each aisle, so I could usually tell when we were nearing the canned vegetables or the frozen pizzas. As I pulled the cart through the aisles, Jonathan picked out the items we needed. He could not talk very well, yet he could understand what I wanted when I told him to "get the one that Mommy uses." If we were in the cleaning supply section,

Jonathan would grab a bottle of Era from the shelf. If we were in the dairy section, he would grab a box of stick Parkay. If the store moved things around, Jonathan and I threw fits, mine a little quieter than his. That was usually the only problem, except for the boxes of Twinkies and Ding Dongs I would find when unpacking the groceries at home.

On this particular day, when Jonathan and I got to the front of the store to pay, there were lines at every register, and it took much longer than expected. As we were leaving the store, Jonathan let me know that the bus was pulling away from the stop. "Bsss! Bsss!" he shrieked. With my cane in one hand and Jonathan's hand in the other, the two full plastic bags of groceries hanging from my arms, we hurried outside. Jonathan pulled me through the icy parking lot, but it was too late. I could hear the bus pulling out into the heavy traffic, the sound disappearing down the street. Jonathan started screaming. I yelled at him to stop. Then I threw the bags of groceries down on the ground, sat down in a snowbank, and cried. I hated myself for being blind. I hated having to depend on buses and taxis. I hated having to depend on others to lead me around, as I did on that day at the grocery store. When I finally got up and told Jonathan that we had to walk home, he screamed even louder. He wanted me to carry him, but, with the bags of groceries and my cane, it was physically impossible. So, with Jonathan leading the way through the crusty snow, we walked home, the teardrops freezing to our faces.

I had a red corduroy vest/leash for Jonathan, sort of like a harness for a guide dog, but I only used it once. I was afraid that someone would cut the cord without my knowledge, just as another cord had been cut months before, as I lay unconscious on the operating room table, unaware of what was happening to me, unaware that at the moment the cord was being cut, the blood vessels in my eyes were hemorrhaging. No, I couldn't take the chance that someone might take Jonathan, leaving me with nothing but a bright red corduroy cord hanging limply from my hand. Instead, I depended on Jonathan to lead me around by the hand, sometimes crying because he wanted me to carry him, wanted me to do the leading, wanted me to be like the other mothers he saw in the neighborhood. I depended on him to tell me when cars were coming, when it was safe to cross the street. I depended on him to do what I was supposed to be doing—protecting.

One day when Jonathan was about two and a half, I decided to make a video of him playing in the bathtub. As I sat on a stool in the corner of the bathroom, holding the video camera on my lap, looking through the lens, seeing only light and shadows, hoping he was in the picture, Jonathan sang "Yankee Doodle" and "Mary Had a Little Lamb," over and over and over. He said his alphabet and I quizzed him on the sounds of each letter. I would say a word and Jonathan would make the sound of the first letter, say the letter, and repeat the word. "*Ba. B. Ball.*" It was a game we played almost every night before he went to bed.

For so long, I had worried, and I think my mother had worried, that because of my blindness, Jonathan would be behind the other kids, so right after his second birthday, I had started teaching him his letters and the sounds they made, using a set of magnetic letters that I could feel. I couldn't wait to show my mother how much I had taught Jonathan, and, when she was visiting a few days later, I stuck the tape in the VCR.

"Very impressive," my mother said, hearing Jonathan saying each letter and its sound.

I reached over and gave Jonathan a hug. "Yeah, he's pretty smart for a two-year-old."

My mother laughed. "But he'll never forgive you when he grows up."

I smiled. "Only if I show the video to his girlfriends."

All of a sudden, toward the end of the tape, after Jonathan's performance, my mother shrieked, "My God, Priscilla! You shouldn't let Jonathan jump off the edge of the tub like that! He could hit his head and drown!"

•   •   •

When I was little, my mother repeatedly told me not to slide down the slippery side of the old claw-foot tub. I remember how she would hold her hand on my forehead as she washed my hair, promising not to let any water get into my eyes, the eyes she said were the most beautiful brown she had ever seen. I would lie in the tub, flat on my back, submerged in the warm water, squeezing my eyes shut as tightly as I could, listening to the sound of my mother's voice through the water. "Here it comes," she would say, pouring the first glass of water over my hair. "All done," she would say, pouring the last.

When I was about three years old, I thought I was old enough to carry my chicken pot pie—a delicacy for the six kids in the McKinley household—to the table without help. I made my way from the kitchen to the dining room, balancing the hot pie on a plate, still in its tin. When I reached the table set for eight, I went over to my usual spot at the end next to my mother and lifted my arms to set the plate on the table. Before I even knew what had happened, my mother was throwing me into a tub of cold water. That's how my mother was in emergencies—fast. The moment the hot chicken gravy hit my chest, the moment I screamed, she scooped me up in her arms, turned on the cold water, and threw me in.

Another time she had to act fast in an emergency that occurred when I was ten. I was making May Day baskets for the other kids in the neighborhood, using decorated cupcakes as the baskets and pipe cleaners as the handles. I was standing over the counter, mixing the batter, making sure all the dry lumps were blended in, when all of a sudden my head was in the bowl, my long, dark hair wrapped tightly around the beaters. I screamed for my mother, who was on the phone in the dining room, and she came running through the swinging wooden door. She yanked the electric cord from the wall, even though the motor had already died.

"I'm going to have to cut it," my mother said, touching the mangled beaters, examining the situation.

"Nooooo! You can't cut it!" I screamed. "You can't cut it."

Mom pushed the eject button and the beaters hung from my hair, the batter dripping onto the counter and floor. She led me over to the kitchen sink and told me to wait there. Then she opened the basement door and disappeared. Within a few minutes, she returned, hacksaw in hand.

"Nooooo!" I screamed again. "You can't cut my hair!"

"I'm not going to cut your hair." She laughed. "I'm going to cut the beaters."

For the next hour or more, I stood over the sink as my mother hacked away at the mangled beaters, little by little, piece by piece, until all that was left in my hair was the still dripping devil's food.

"You're lucky your hair is strong," she said, helping me wash the sticky batter out of my hair. "Those beaters could have ripped out every last strand."

My mother had always protected me, and I wanted to protect my son in the same way, but she didn't make it easy. She was continuously pointing out the ways in which I couldn't protect Jonathan, which made me doubt myself. When I came up with a solution to a problem, my mother would come up with a different one. When Jonathan was about six months old, I told my mother that I was thinking about getting a playpen. "That's a terrible idea," she said. She took a book from the shelf in her library and quoted a few lines, probably from Dr. Spock, about how children should be allowed to roam around the house, free to explore. (Was he thinking of blind parents when he put these words on paper?) Instead of buying a playpen, my mother thought I should childproof the house—putting all the poisons in the cupboard above the fridge, concealing my drugs on the top shelf of the medicine cabinet, covering the electrical outlets with little plastic prongs, boxing up all the breakables. Sure, all of these things would help, but what about all the accidents I couldn't prevent? What about all the ways I couldn't protect my child in the same way my mother had protected me?

I grew angry every time my mother hinted that I wasn't a very good mother, but I thought she was right. How could I care for a child when I could barely take care of myself? When Jonathan and I were still living with my mother, she was the one who noticed the little red spots, like measles, the one who searched through the Childcraft medical guide, the one who diagnosed him with roseola. When Jonathan's arm popped out of its socket, she was the one who noticed it hanging at his side like a wilted flower, the one who rushed him to the hospital, where she learned that this was common in premature babies.

At age twenty-one, when I broke down and told my mother that I was pregnant, that I planned to keep the child, even though I wasn't married, even though there was a good chance the father would never be a part of our lives, I thought she was jealous of me. What kind of mother would react the way she did—leaving the house in a storm, going to the public library, checking out books and magazines containing articles on diabetic pregnancies ending in miscarriages and stillbirths, placing them on the nightstand beside my bed, hoping I would read them and decide to have an abortion? At the time, I believed she envied me for being the young woman that I was, for becoming what she used to be. But now I believe that she was just trying to protect me, the way she wanted me to protect Jonathan. Still her words hurt, just as the unspoken words had hurt months before, right after Jonathan was born, the silence that seemed to be saying, "I told you so. I told you so. You shouldn't have had this child. Didn't you read the articles and books? Didn't you see that I wasn't worried about a miscarriage or a stillbirth but that I was worried about you, my youngest daughter, my youngest child? Didn't you understand that I was just keeping the shampoo out of your eyes and throwing you in a tub of cold water and sawing away at the beaters, trying to save you from harm? Didn't you understand that I was only trying to protect you?"

•　　•　　•

When I was six months pregnant, my mother and I went to see the movie *Terms of Endearment* starring Shirley MacLaine and Debra Winger, a movie about the strained relationship between a mother and daughter. It was the first time my mother and I had been to a movie together, just the two of us. I laughed hysterically at the opening scene when Shirley, the mother of a newborn, jumped into the crib because she thought her child had stopped breathing. My mother laughed, too. As we drove home that night, we recalled the scenes that had made us cry and laugh. As I rested my hands on my swollen stomach, Mom told me that she remembered feeling afraid after bringing each one of her six children home from the hospital, saying that she checked us every half hour, just to make sure we were breathing. I thought this was fairly funny, until two months later when I was getting up several times every night. My room was the way it had been when I left for college over four years before, with bright yellow walls, bright orange curtains, and coordinating yellow and orange flowered bedspreads, except for the crib that sat in the corner beneath the silver dolphin mobile and the bulletin board, still plastered with miniature pictures of my classmates from kindergarten to senior high. I would stand there in the dark, my palm placed on Jonathan's back, feeling his body move up and down, hearing the sound of my own heart beating as fast as his.

Now I have experience in both blindness and motherhood, and I don't worry about Jonathan as much as I did those first few years of his life. I am a confident blind woman and he is a very responsible thirteen-year-old. But even when Jonathan was little, when I was afraid of everything, including myself, I never had any real problems protecting him because of my blindness. He never got hit by a car. He never fell off a slide or out of a tree. He never hit his head and drowned. But the fear was always there, the fear that I wouldn't be able to protect my son.

The most frightening experience I had with Jonathan

occurred one day shortly before his second birthday. When I woke up after my nap, I could see a hint of light at the end of the hall, a light gray on black. I knew the light had to be coming from Jonathan's room, but I remembered shutting his door when I put him down for his nap, as I always did. Jonathan wouldn't sleep unless his door was shut. Using the walls as my guide, I headed down the hall to his room. As I covered every inch of his crib with my hands, my heart started beating faster. He wasn't there. I stooped down and moved my arms back and forth across the thick shag carpet, but I only found his fuzzy musical teddy bear and a few wooden blocks. I called out his name, but there was no response, only a piercing silence.

After checking the locks on the windows, I hurried down the hall to the living room, calling out his name again and again. I walked around the room cautiously, stopping every few steps to scan the surface of the floor with the bottom of my outstretched foot. With my hands, I felt the cushions of the couch and chairs. I checked in the kitchen and the closets. Frantically, I ran back down the hall to the bathroom. I felt the floor with my foot. I brushed the bottom of the bathtub with my hand.

Running back to the living room, I checked the front door. It wasn't locked, but I couldn't remember if I had locked it. Could Jonathan have left the house by himself? Or could someone have come in and taken him? I grabbed my cane in the corner, opened the door, and flew out into the yard in my bare feet. I called out his name, over and over and over. I knew that if he was in the yard or at the park, he would be able to hear me. But he didn't answer.

I hurried back to the apartment and groped for the phone on the wall in the kitchen. I called Jim at his office. Sobbing, I told him I had lost Jonathan. Jim said to call 911. As I was dialing the second digit, I heard a sleepy sigh coming from the other room. I hung up the phone, ran into the living room, got down on my hands and knees, and crawled around, feeling every inch of the floor. When I reached behind the wooden rocking chair in the corner, there was Jonathan, curled up beneath his big fuzzy lion blanket, sound asleep. I wanted to smother him with hugs and kisses, tell him that I loved him over and over and over. I wanted to take him in my arms and never let him go. But I couldn't. Instead, I placed my hand on his back, feeling the blanket move up and down, feeling him breathe. For the moment, he was safe. For that afternoon, it seemed to me, we were both protected by a force I could only whisper might be hope.

JO-ANN MAPSON

9

Navigating the Channel Islands

WE HAVE TAKEN to referring to our nineteen-year-old son as "the Channel Islands." The phrase was coined by a poet friend of mine, with two sons of her own, after she'd listened to my tales of parenting woes for the better part of the last seven years. For those unfamiliar with California geography, the Channel Islands include eight separate landmasses, located just off the southern coast, adjacent to the sleepy and exclusive town of Santa Barbara, and fingering south down the coast toward San Diego. Wild and remote, they possess some of the state's most exquisite and varied landscape, yet people can't survive there without hauling in food and drinking water. The ocean crossing to reach them can be treacherous.

My son was planned, wanted, and brought into this world with love. Due to problems at birth and a misdiagnosed inherited blood condition, the first two years of his life were difficult and frightening. He was sick a lot, in and out of hospitals, with doctors performing tests on his tiny body that ranged from weekly blood draws to bone marrow biopsies. Talk of a terminal diagnosis hovered in the background. The first pediatrician I saw advised me "not to get too attached to this child." If not for my constant gleaning of information from medical libraries, standing up to renowned physicians who casually treated my son as if he were only an "interesting case," and refusing to take no for an answer, he might have lingered forever in the purgatory of misdiagnosis. He might have, as were many of the children at the teaching hospital center we frequented, been treated with tainted Factor 8 blood products, and died from HIV infection.

I tried to make the medical treatments he needed as easy to bear as possible. One affliction common to his condition was bruising easily. When he developed a huge shiner from a small bump, we painted one on his favorite doll using purple eye shadow. When he required an infusion for a prolonged bleeding episode, the doll got one, too, with my son in charge as his doctor, acting out every step of the treatment, and, hopefully, in the process, feeling some control over the situation. Despite his pediatrician's warnings, he learned to ride a bike. He fell out of trees. He rode skateboards; he got in fights. In short, he did regular kid stuff because we wanted him to believe he was a regular kid.

His illness, von Willebrand's disease, is manageable. To offer up the *Reader's Digest* condensed version, his blood clots slower than other people's. His platelets are malformed and do not aggregate properly, or form strong chains. Therefore, even when a clot forms, it has a tendency to break loose. It's nowhere near as devastating as hemophilia, but he sometimes experiences similar "bleeds" that require immobilization, medication, and infusion with blood products. If he ever has to undergo major surgery, he'll need to receive transfusions and more health care than you or I would. It's a worry I carry in the back of my mind at all times.

When he was an infant, I was a little overzealous when it came to naps and schedules, and overprotective, but like any new mother, I wanted to do everything right. As soon as he began to toddle and form sentences, I was in my element as a mother. A picture of him that resonates in my mind is around age three. This precocious conversationalist made everyone he came into contact with laugh. His head of loopy blond curls shone golden against his fair skin. He woke up laughing and fell asleep smiling. He wore the tiniest pair of blue jeans I'd ever seen in my life. He refused to go anywhere without his Donald Duck baseball cap. We watched *Sesame Street* together, visited children's museums, read stories, enrolled in a "Mommy and Me" class, took pint-sized hikes, generally had a blast.

Estranged: the sonics of the word communicate its meaning quite concisely. It sounds stranded, as in castaway on an island, far from communication, no telephones, no human interaction. Robinson Crusoe before he met Friday. Where, after a shipwreck, one might feel grateful to have a life, thrilled to discover the most unspoiled of beaches, to marvel over perfectly shaped shells. To view breaking waves and silvery fog as nature's gifts, while simultaneously experiencing the heartbreaking frustration of not being able to share such moments with a loved one, someone who understands the most primal of connections. In short, we have the Channel Islands.

I vowed that if I was lucky enough to become a mother, my child would know he was loved. There would be no beatings, no psychological undermining, no forcing him to eat when he didn't care to, none of that continual disapproval, sarcasm, and never meeting expectations that wore me down. As if to test the strength of my convictions, until he was school age, my son existed on a diet of bacon, white toast, peanut butter, scrambled eggs, cheese, sweet potatoes, apple juice, and milk. Sure, he'd veer from his list for cookies and cake, but nothing green or nutritious would pass those lips. If I insisted he take a small taste of a food, my reward was his vomiting on the table. His pediatrician said not to worry, that children left alone to select their food eventually balance their diets. I trusted her and waited.

He was read to every night, rocked when he was sad, told daily he was loved. His father, an artist, helped him build forts and a tree house. They played with dolls, read books together, sang songs, drew pictures; theirs was a strong and loving bond. His grandmother took him out to breakfast after church, just the two of them, every week. His cousins, aunts, and uncles treated him with kindness, respect, and an abundance of good-natured humor. Until he was school age, I didn't work outside the home. When financial necessity demanded I return to work, I tried to fit my hours around his, to be there when he got home from school.

When his troubles began, around age twelve, I didn't panic. Hormones, I thought, it happens to all of us. Team sports, such a defining part of a boy's world, were a source of humiliation and frustration due to the bruises they caused. School was no longer solely about learning, but popularity and male bravado, too, and my son was neither outgoing nor particularly athletic. He felt left out and sad, and, to cheer him up, every week his father drew him a cartoon. These comic adventures featured my son's dog experiencing exactly what he was going through. Somehow in a comic strip with dogs chasing soccer balls in orbit around Saturn, P.E. became a little less humiliating. And his first wood shop project, which turned out wobbly—his father rendered it as a dog dream house, complete with a special storage room strictly for baloney. We all looked forward to the cartoons, which his father thumbtacked to the inside of the front door on his way to work each Monday. I collected them in a photo album, a creative record of his difficult adolescence. From time to time, I look over those silly drawings, where love and humor were offered up as a bandage for his very real aching. It's in his school photos, too, the easy smile turned to a set, determined expression that tries to mask his bewilderment, and fails.

From age twelve on, he began to get into trouble at school. There were small acts of vandalism at home. We tried approaching his behavior problems in new ways. Conventional grounding and extra chores had no effect. If anything, our son became more steadfast in his convictions that however contrary, he would do things his way. His moods swung wildly. He told lies. There were a few instances of petty theft. All the perks of puberty, sure, but these incidents didn't go away. As his problems progressed, he underwent medical exams, psychological testing, counseling, Tough Love; we even had him attend a few Alcoholics Anonymous twelve-step meetings, but asked him to stop when we discovered he was lying to the other recoverees.

The consequence of all this earnest parenting was that our son learned that whatever boundaries the authority figures set could, if he leaned into them hard enough, always be broken. All that needed to be done to accomplish this was to maintain an iron will, and continuously invent new ways to undermine his parents' trust. If we sat him down to talk about a lie we'd caught him telling, he'd tell another. Faced with the newest lie, the original lie was forgotten. When we confronted him about not doing his homework, he argued that the teacher hated him, and no amount of discussion, pleading, or promises made him get the work finished. He'd sit at his desk with his books open in front of him for hours, doing nothing. Yet it began to be more than a battle against parents. Often it seemed that his behavior singled out me, his mother, as the target. He threw away the lunches I prepared for him. He stole money from my wallet, and when I confronted him, he repeatedly lied to my face. The transition from such an easygoing kid to troublemaker was difficult for his father to accept. Working a great deal of the time, he generally heard about the problems secondhand. An optimist, he remained steadfast that these difficulties were transitory. The picture looked much bleaker to me, but maybe I was just being pessimistic. We tried to remain united, but our son knew just where to wedge between us, the exact point to apply pressure. After a while, he could break me down emotionally in a matter of minutes, and often did. My husband would then try to comfort me, but it wasn't comfort I wanted, it was support and for our son to just follow the few simple rules the rest of the world was willing to follow. What began as a three-way discussion frequently ended with his parents fighting between themselves, as our son slipped away, forgotten.

In the spring of 1994, my second novel was being published. It's widely known that the second novel is the effort that makes or breaks a writer. Something like 40 percent of fiction writers never produce the second book. I was teaching college full-time, trying to juggle work, a wobbly marriage, and, despite being by nature a hermit, venturing out into public to promote my work. On top of all that, I was turning forty-two. My son, now teenage, was hardly neglected, but the dynamics of home life were changing for everyone. He spent a great deal of time with his friends, but sometimes I sensed that he resented that the bulk of my attention was focused on my work. It seemed that if I had a book signing or interview scheduled, or a piece about me ran in the newspaper, my son would act out in a way that forced me to set aside my obligations, or be so upset that I could barely get through them.

Coming into our lives at this time, my book advance seemed a long-awaited blessing. With it, we were finally able to accomplish much-needed improvements on our old tract home, which meant remodeling to include a family room we all could enjoy. A new oak floor was being installed in my bedroom. Everything had to be moved out, which necessitated packing up odds and ends, temporarily relocating furniture, and my jewelry, which I generally left lying on the dresser top because I'm one of those people who can't sleep wearing rings or earrings.

The night before the floor installation, I placed my wedding ring in a small box along with some other jewelry. I tucked the box into my top drawer. My wedding band is unique, old-fashioned, a piece of estate jewelry, five baguette diamonds set sideways across a narrow platinum band. The contractor installing the floor was a man I trusted with keys to my house, a friend; for a time, he had dated my sister. He performed his usual excellent work while I ran errands, taught classes, did whatever else it is one does when the house is torn apart and it's best to stay away. That night, my husband and I camped out in the living room. The next morning, I took the box with the jewelry out of the dresser to put on my wedding band and found it missing. I tried to imagine the ring falling beneath the flooring, or that I'd left it someplace other than where I was sure I'd put it for safekeeping. Only four people had been in the house: the contractor, his assistant, my husband, and my son. At once, with a sinking sensation, I knew my son had taken my wedding ring.

I confronted him point-blank, but he denied it. *Mom, you really think I would do that?* Maybe I was being paranoid. Reluctantly, I asked the contractor if he knew anything about it. He said my son had been in my room before the dresser had been moved out. I could see his conclusion in his eyes. When I told my husband what I suspected, he made an impatient face. The subtext of his expression was clear: *What kind of mother thinks her own child capable of such an act?*

By this time, Channel Islands, age sixteen, had acquired a long history of lying and petty theft. At first, they were small items, easily confused. A dollar bill from my purse—Wait, weren't there six singles in there? Then the entire contents of my wallet. I was sure I'd gone to the bank, but maybe I only imagined I had. I began taking my purse with me wherever I went, including into the bathroom while I showered. The contractor installed locks on both our bedroom door and my husband's office. Our son was furious that I "didn't trust him." My husband did, but I didn't. For every incident we confronted him with, he made up a story, sometimes convincing, sometimes absurdly transparent. All kids lie during their teenage years. I wasn't much different when I wanted to see a boy on a school night, and said I was "going to the library." But increasingly, his stories were unnecessary. He often tripped up, but showed little embarrassment at being caught. Eventually he lied even if it only bought him two seconds of freedom, if moments later his lies toppled like dominoes, and the consequences meant he was grounded from special events, such as the prom. There seemed to be no reasonable explanation for his behavior. Exasperated, we had him drug tested, and he came up negative. Was he trying to engineer his parents' divorce? If so, he was getting close. Did he hate me? It sure seemed like it. Or did he only want to drive his mother, the one person who knew him so well she could see through his lies, insane? At times, trying to understand his behavior certainly made me feel that way.

I tried to see things from his point of view. Was my writing truly at the heart of his unhappiness? It was true, my focus had shifted. But wasn't it natural for that gradual separation of mother and son to occur? He was teenage; he hardly wanted to be seen with his parents in public. Many nights I sat on the edge of his bed and begged him to tell me why he behaved the way he did, to tell me what he needed. He had no answers for my questions, only rage and lies. Once, in desperation, I asked him point-blank if he despised me because I had saved his life. No answer.

Every night as I lay in bed trying to sleep, I silently agonized. My husband, a few inches away, said nothing. This man, the one true love of my life, had joined sides against me with the other love of my life, my son. He accused me of blowing the theft incidents out of proportion, worrying needlessly, of continually harboring suspicions, and expecting the worst. I fired back that it seemed like he never supported me, that he believed our son over me, even when the evidence stared him in the face. Our son sensed the rift and played us against each other like a game of checkers: *Dad's my buddy, but Mom? She's unreasonable.* Nothing ever got settled. The money just kept disappearing. I felt so alone and conflicted that sometimes I thought we would all be better off apart. In the still hours before the alarm sounded and neither of us was sleeping, my husband and I whispered to each other about getting divorced. It felt as if my life was dismantling, yet at the same time, my books were being published, a goal I had worked toward my whole life. I had a job I loved, teaching college. Film people were interested in my books. I should have been happy, but all I could think was *This is my fault*. As a mother, how had I failed to impart to my only child the basic moral tenets? Shame filled me up. The feelings of failure overflowed every facet of my life until I was certain everyone could see how close I was to the breaking point. In the classroom, I'd stand at the board patiently explaining the art of writing the process essay to thirty curious faces, but inside I was shaking. I'd smile at photographers, be interviewed by journalists, carefully steering their questions away from my fragile personal life. On weekends, I'd travel to distant cities, read my work in public, autograph books, return to the hotel to messages from my husband that things at home were unraveling. There were more lies, there was more theft, now what should we do? We'd run out of alternatives. I'd lie there in some anonymous king-sized bed, sobbing into my pillow because things made so little sense. Then the next morning, I'd fly to the next city, smile, and pretend I was fine so as not to let down my publisher.

Even in the bleakest hours of my marriage, and we've experienced our share over the last twenty-three years, that ring was more than a symbol to me. I came of age in the sixties, when diamonds were considered bourgeois, and monogamy a "cop-out." But I knew when I met this man that he was the one I wanted to share my life. So we got married, with half my friends in the pews snickering at my white dress and church wedding. In 1974, we hadn't been able to afford more than plain bands. My husband bought me the ring after we'd been married ten years. When he gave it to me, he said, "You never get anything nice. Let me do this." The ring was worth maybe five hundred bucks. Long ago, it had belonged to someone else. Often, as I twisted it on my finger, I wondered if the woman who'd worn it before me had done any better with her life, or her children. Had her marriage stayed happy and strong? Diamonds are forever, but love can easily get lost. As I turned the house upside down searching for my ring, my birthday loomed, birthdays with their unique ability to make one take stock. My son said, "I'll help you look for it, Mom."

On the morning of my forty-second birthday, I was at the computer pounding out a chapter on my third novel, *Shadow Ranch*. Between wiping my eyes and feeling hopeless, I crafted a story about three generations of a family. These flawed, very human people had so loved a child in their midst that in spite of the pain of losing him, they were finding a way to knit themselves back together as a family. I was also in the middle of promoting my previous novel, *Blue Rodeo*. At book signings, people asked me how much of my book was taken from real life. *Blue Rodeo*'s basic plot involves a newly divorced mother, estranged from her newly deaf teenage son. I delivered my stock answer: *A writer makes the leap into fiction when she can leave the truth behind to embrace a larger possibility.* The hubris of these words caught in my throat. Almost from the moment it was published, *Blue Rodeo* had been optioned to television as a movie-of-the-week. Soon it would go into production, slated to air in the fall of 1996. Up there on the screen for millions of people to witness would be the metaphoric elements of my life, my painful relationship with my son. I popped Tagamet like it was candy. I developed high blood pressure.

The evening of my birthday, my husband and I sat down to dinner at the kitchen table. He'd offered dinner out, but I was weary of pretending in public. He lavished me with an abundance of carefully wrapped gifts. The week before, we'd gone to the mall to escape the stresses of home, and here now, in front of me, was every little thing I had admired: a handmade box from the art museum gift shop, a silver pin, a box of imported chocolates, a pink silk blouse. I knew that he was attempting to heal some of the wounds inflicted by our son, so I thanked him and tried not to let my discomfort at all this generosity show. While we were in the middle of dinner, our son showed up. At his father's prompting, he mumbled, "Oh yeah, happy birthday," then fled with friends. There was no birthday card for me, no good wishes, not even a hug, just the echo of the slamming door. My husband and I ended the evening arguing over the missing ring. He insisted our son couldn't have taken it.

I thought about checking into the hospital, I was that depressed. My feisty, childless younger sister had a better idea, and took me to La Costa for two days of "spa therapy." While I had my muscles pounded and sat in saunas breathing in the healing scent of eucalyptus, at a Tough Love meeting, my husband discovered that our son's girlfriend—both attended the youth group—was wearing a platinum band with five baguette diamonds. My son told her that his grandmother had instructed him to give this ring to the first girl he loved. Chagrined, my husband apologized to me, but coming that late, after such a long siege of disbelief, his words couldn't fix the unfixable.

Eventually, my ring was returned, but not until we learned he'd also given this girl two blown-glass perfume bottles from my collection. At first, she resisted the truth, but soon became overwhelmed by the web of lies my son had spun. She gave him the gate, and for the first time in many years, I saw my son cry. I felt sorry for him, but relieved. I thought that the moment had arrived, "bottoming out," they call it in twelve-step programs, that painful, necessary pit everyone must hit before things can begin to get better. I was wrong.

If anything, his hostility increased. Only at my repeated urging did the doctor put my son on medication for depression. At first it seemed to make a huge difference, and to fill us with hope. Then one by one, the behaviors resumed. We swallowed our pride and borrowed money from my mother and my father-in-law so that our son could spend the summer at an expensive, beachfront camp renowned for reaching troubled teens. He had a good time there, made friends. My husband and I enjoyed a respite, and I finished another book. But when the school year started, things fell to pieces. We spoke to his teachers, the school psychologist, guidance counselors, anyone who might offer a possible new avenue. Our son was bringing home straight F's, but marks for "Outstanding in Citizenship." Nobody but us saw anything wrong with this. "It's not like he's carrying a weapon," the principal told me. It became clear that they were willing to flush our son down the academic toilet, so we pulled him out of public school and spent the money we'd set aside for his college on private school tuition.

Finally, after many long talks with the psychologist and his medical doctor, we decided to do an "intervention." While our son was at his part-time job, we emptied his room. All that remained of his well-stocked nest was a mattress on the floor and five changes of clothing. The idea was that he could earn back items with good behavior. My brother and sister came over to help; we would take turns confronting him. At first my son physically lunged at me, then at his father. When his father's warnings to stop didn't have any effect, my brother and sister stepped in. For five hours, we took turns explaining to him how his behavior had hurt each of us, had devastated our family. Steadfastly, he denied any wrongdoing. Then, suddenly, he changed tacks and was all apologies. I wondered why I was the only one who could see that this was a momentary acquiescence; he'd say whatever he thought we wanted to hear if we would just go away. His father and I continued family therapy ourselves, but all the talk didn't seem to make much difference.

At the private school, where the student-teacher ratio was four to one, our son was led by the hand through homework, forced to complete his courses. I knew deep down we were basically paying for his grades, but I no longer cared. His last year and a half he actually pulled decent marks, and won several awards for academic improvement. At his graduation, tears streamed down my face. I was certain we'd turned the corner. Despite his previous horrendous academic record, my son was accepted at a state college in northern California. There, on his own, I was sure he'd find a better way to live his life. We saw him off to school and breathed surely one of the largest sighs of relief two parents have ever exhaled. The only string we'd tied to paying for his education was that he had to maintain passing grades in all classes. This would always be his home, we told him, but if he were to come back here to live, he'd have to get a job and contribute to expenses.

A little more than one year later, every class he enrolled in was either dropped or failed. He's overdrawn his checking account so often that his returned-check fees exceed his balance. The five-hundred-dollar-limit credit card for emergencies was maxed out within two months. His gasoline credit card showed balances twice the amount of what my husband and I regularly spent. He had an accident with the car, but we didn't take it back until we learned he'd spent his summer tuition money and once again lied about his grades. Then, united, we made good on our word, and stopped paying for everything. He finally got his wish, which was life on his own terms. He is on his own, somewhere in the Bay area.

We gave him a phone card that works with the telephone numbers of home, his father's work, his grandmother, his uncle and his aunt. Because he and I still can't seem to hold a civil conversation, he's been instructed not to phone here unless it is a life-or-death emergency, to first call his father at work. When the phone rings, I look at the Caller ID display, and if it is his area code, I do not allow myself to be tempted to answer. Sometimes, not often, he leaves a message: *Hey, Mom, it's your son, just calling to say hi . . .* I listen to his voice, so deceptively friendly. I ache to pick up the receiver and tell him how much his dog misses him, and that in the garden, the sage is in furious, purple bloom. I imagine asking him what movie he's seen lately or if he's met somebody special. I envision easy conversations that end with both of us saying, "I love you." But usually what happens is that I walk out the front door and shut it behind me. I get in the car and drive to the nearby bluffs that overlook the Pacific Ocean. On a clear day, the spine of Catalina Island stands out, twenty-six miles away. It's a part of the Channel Islands chain, too, but entirely different in nature, populated by families, easy to get to, commemorated in a song that makes it sound unbearably romantic.

Several months ago, I took down my son's pictures and tucked them away in a drawer. His bedroom has been made anonymous with redecorating, but I still rarely go in there. Every morning I awaken with pain in my chest, a solid weight I've learned to carry. I get up and go to the computer, where I sit alone and write stories about hope and the power of love, trying not to collapse under the irony of such claims. Some days it's harder than others to locate that thread of possibility. I picture the broken pieces of my heart inside me like the shrapnel of a war, such as Vietnam, where no clear victors emerged, where in retrospect all that fighting seems so senseless.

On those days, I don't try to write fiction. I take long walks, cry, watch a movie, look at books of other places, study photographs that illustrate to me that this planet is much larger than any pain in my heart. I think about the nature of islands, some of which are born from volcanic eruptions that leave devastation in their wake. On those same islands, however, life eventually returns. In the lava trails, plants spring up, and lush, tropical flowers bloom from dormant seeds. No matter what happens, it seems the earth knows how to recover. Eventually people make their way to these islands and explore, sure they've found paradise.

The day my son was born I awoke, in labor, before dawn, to discover a storm had blown down several huge old pine trees, blocking our street. My husband had to drive up on the sidewalk in places so we could make our way to the hospital. Protracted and sluggish, my labor lasted long into the evening hours, and finally required medical intervention. In retrospect, I can't imagine why the obstetrician let it drag on. My son was born with a hematoma on his skull from having been lodged so long in the birth canal. When the doctor pulled him from my body with forceps, I became just like every other mother in the world. The long hours of struggling, the blood and pain were all forgotten. My heart overflowed with the miracle of this child my body and my husband's love had created. This astonishing wild creature was ours, yet wholly his own self, too, independent, his own island. He did not cry at birth. Instead, he looked around the room soberly, as if unsure he'd arrived at the proper destination. But his father cried, and so did I, with hearts so full of love and hope they spilled over, unashamed.

People tell me that after a few years getting knocked around in the real world, my son will return home with a new appreciation of his parents. They insist that mother and son will one day be so close, all this history will seem distant and unimportant. I hope that's true. Driving down the coast from a book signing in Santa Barbara recently, I pulled my car over to the side of the road and stood looking out at the Channel Islands. As it has for millions of years, the Pacific broke over the rugged spine of rock, slowly, patiently reshaping it. For an hour or so, I watched, transfixed by one of those rare, distilled California scenes of such beauty that make it easy to forget smog and traffic. The sky was painfully clear, the scent of ocean felt as healing as it was bracing. Before the familiar fog moved back in—to me, anyway— those islands looked almost close enough to reach out and touch.

ROBB FORMAN DEW

♪

Safe as Houses

FOR YEARS I envisioned the passage of time as a sort of steady trudge, not necessarily dreary, just relentless. It seemed to me that the slipping by of the hours was an intangible certainty within which one must accommodate all the events of a life-time. But it isn't so. For one thing, time accumulates from the first moments of sensibility. The minutes accrue imperceptibly into a stretch of history, and you turn around to recognize, with amazement, your own past.

But also, some days have long legs. Now and then an ordinary bit of time takes a yawning scissors step, leaving you to scuttle along behind, scrabbling to cling to ongoing events. I learned this late, when my children were nearly full grown, because it was exactly such an ordinary moment that enlarged and enlarged upon itself almost three years ago when my son told me he was gay.

It was early spring in New England, a soft day in May, and Stephen was home from his sophomore year at Yale until the first week of June, when he, my husband, Charles, and I would drive to Virginia to see his brother, Jack, graduate from Wood-berry Forest School. When the phone rang, Stephen came around the corner from the TV room to answer it, and he stood at the far end of the kitchen, lounging against the long glass door to chat with Chloe. He was talking, and pausing to listen, and also keeping part of this attention on the CBS *Evening News* in the next room.

Earlier that day we had taken the paned-glass storm windows down and put up the screens on the two porches enclosing the kitchen. When I had come downstairs from my study to start dinner, I opened the kitchen windows for the first time that season and settled at the table to work the Jumble from the morning paper while occasionally tending the chicken I was roasting for dinner.

I'm not sure why I was suddenly alert to Stephen's end of the phone conversation. My attention was caught, I think, by some tone in his voice, or simply by the realization that his phone calls to or from Chloe were never particularly private; he never took the trouble to take the calls out of earshot of anyone else in the house. Chloe is a beautiful girl, sensuous and angelic-looking at the same time, and she is funny and bright and endearing as well.

It might be that my ear was caught by what I didn't hear: there was no sense of the kind of tension that is inevitably there between two people as attractive and sexual as Chloe and Stephen. And by "sexual" I only mean the kind of magnetism that emanates from some people, especially older adolescents. Chloe and Stephen both possessed it, and, although I couldn't hear Chloe, Stephen's voice was nothing but friendly. He was completely at ease; there was a certain edginess missing.

For a long time Chloe has been in our lives. We have even acquired a scattering of "Chloe" stories that are now and then retold at gatherings of mutual friends, just as we have acquired stories of various other of our children's friends. The tales themselves aren't what is important about the retelling of them; it is the connectedness they demonstrate.

Chloe had been at school with Stephen since they were fourteen, and, in fact, two years earlier Chloe's parents and various of her siblings had settled next to us on the temporary bleachers set up at St. Paul's School in Concord, New Hampshire, to watch Stephen and Chloe's class graduate. Whatever failings St. Paul's School may have, it is a beautiful place, and the pageantry of graduation is dazzling. The girls are all in white dresses with ribbons or flowers in their hair, and the boys are in blazers and ties. The graduating seniors sit together, on a green sward that gently slopes to a lake, surrounded by parents and friends and a scattering of students from other classes. It is a glorious sight in good weather.

Chloe was sitting near us, wearing a wide-brimmed white hat with ribbons trailing down her back, and she and Stephen were not far apart in being called forward to receive awards and then diplomas. They were beautiful to see, smiling, healthy, and with the wind from the lake ruffling Chloe's long hair and lifting the rim of her hat so that she reached up to hold it to her head as she approached the podium. Stephen was not far behind her, his own hair brushed back by the breeze, and congratulatory calls from friends in the group of students making him grin with his startling smile.

Chloe's mother leaned over to me and said, "Oh, don't you wish this were just their *wedding?*" And I knew exactly what she meant: their lives seemed perfect and uncomplicated and filled with amazing possibilities in that gorgeous afternoon; perhaps they could go on that way forever. I believe I simply began at that moment to think of Chloe as the probable romantic interest in Stephen's life. There were always friends of Stephen's around, male and female, but, at a certain point, both our sons made it clear that they wouldn't answer questions about their social lives. So, in lieu of any information about Stephen's personal life, I jumped to a conclusion. I made one of many assumptions that parents should learn not to make about their children.

Two years later, though, in the kitchen on that afternoon in May, I only remember suddenly being aware—and being surprised by—the odd lack of interest in Stephen's voice. He was amiable—he is almost always amiable—but he wasn't reluctant to get off the phone, and Chloe was calling Massachusetts from the West Coast during prime time.

He hung up and turned away, heading around the corner to watch the end of the news, but I stopped him. "Steve?" He paused in the doorway and turned toward me, and I continued, "Have you been involved with anyone at all? I mean romantically? Since St. Paul's?" Off and on, he had mentioned various girls in passing, and at St. Paul's there was always an assortment of girls lagging against the car and chatting with him whenever I was parked in front of his dorm while he loaded our station wagon. Girls phoned him often at our house, and he was invited for weekends away from school at the houses of girls who lived in wonderful places. But I hadn't heard him talk about any particular girl since he had been at Yale, although many phoned him when he was home.

For an instant he was surprised, and then he frowned, and I thought he was going to walk away in anger. There was a peculiar feeling of urgency and expectation in the room that I can only recall now; I can't re-create the sensation. But it was as if both of us had an intention to which we hadn't put a name—as hard to decipher as those scrambled words in the Jumble— although our intentions were loose from us and afloat in the air.

"There's something I've been meaning to tell you," he said finally.

We both fell silent, and then he moved forward a few paces toward me and was backlit by the gauzy light filtering from the screened porch through the glass-paned door. I couldn't read his face because of the shadow, but I know my children in all their moods; I am fairly good at deciphering the nuances of their postures—vulnerable or defensive or joyous. I may well know their very scent. Probably I could find them if I were blindfolded in a room full of people. I remember when they were little boys, and I would suddenly catch sight of one of my sons precariously balanced on a chair, or racing up or down the stairs, and I would experience the sensation of a fall he didn't take. It was a similar sensation I felt watching Stephen standing in the kitchen with his thumbs looped in the waistband of his jeans, his shoulders canted toward me, his head dipped slightly forward in determination. At once I wanted to raise my hands and gesture for him to stop what he was going to say, and I also wanted to urge him on and hear whatever it was. In fact, I sat as still as a stone. I didn't move at all.

"Of course I've been involved with someone since St. Paul's," he said. He wasn't frowning any longer; in fact, he had a slight smile that I knew from years of being connected to him. It was a smile that sought to protect me and Charles from any worry or irritation on his behalf. It's easy for me to classify it now, but looking at him then, as he stood in the shadowy room, I only perceived danger.

His tone and phrasing rang down the ranks of all the days I could remember and landed me resoundingly in the distant past, where I was sitting in my bedroom in Baton Rouge in the twilight of a long-ago Louisiana evening, as the chameleons darted through the vines climbing up my window screens. My mother leaned into my room around the door frame, her heavy hair swinging forward in a parenthesis around her face. "By the way," she said, "after dinner I want to have a talk with you. There's something we need to discuss."

What my mother *did* eventually say to me, or why these two events should link themselves in my mind, I can't tell you. In both instances, however, I instinctively and immediately knew that I would never be eager to hear anything someone else had been considering so carefully. So three years ago in May, my son and I regarded each other warily.

"I think I might be gay," Stephen said.

In the instant before he spoke I'm convinced I knew what he was going to say, but at the same time I was uncertain that I understood. "Ah . . . well . . . you *think* you're gay?"

He looked perplexed, and anxious, too. "No, that's not what I mean. I mean I *am* gay."

This is such a difficult moment to remember, because the two of us had suddenly moved straight ahead into uncharted territory. I got up from the table and hugged him, and he held on to me, too, in a fierce embrace, lowering his chin to the top of my head. I felt light-headed, and my stomach clenched with dread. I had no idea what to do. "It doesn't make any difference to us," I said. "We love you no matter what."

We moved away from each other, both of us strangely embarrassed and without any rules of etiquette to cover this situation. Stephen seemed lost in his own house; he stood in the kitchen with a tentative air that more than anything in that elongated moment filled me with sorrow. His expression was precisely the curious gaze of assessment he had cast my way thirty minutes after he was born. He looked as though he wasn't at all sure that he could trust me.

Because I'm always on the lookout for misdirected impulsiveness—spontaneity that gets out of hand, that gets me into trouble—I rarely say anything entirely off the cuff. It's almost as if I *see* the words before they come out of my mouth, but I was baffled by what came out of my mouth next in my desperation to alleviate the uneasiness between me and this person I had loved for all his life. "Well, damn it, Stephen! I wish you'd told me years ago so I wouldn't have been stuck decorating the Christmas tree all by myself every year!" Since my children became teenagers, this has been my recurrent after-Christmas lament—tedious, now, to everyone who knows me, because I'm the only one who cares much if, or how, the Christmas tree is decorated at all.

He was as surprised as I by this peculiar outburst, and he merely looked at me blankly, and then he laughed. "Yeah. But I didn't think you'd want it decorated all in mauve." And then we both laughed; we were back on sure footing. We had humor between us again, but only fleetingly, because I had brushed off our discomfort with a sophistication and an attempted jauntiness I didn't yet possess, and I have no idea where such glibness came from.

This was one of those events in my life that, as I conjure it up in retrospect, appears to me like a pointillist painting, coming into focus hazily, at first, and slowly gathering the form of a whole experience. "Do you want to tell Dad and Jack?"

"I think it would be better if you told Dad. Do you mind doing that?"

"You know he won't care, Steve. He loves you."

"I know. But I just think it would be easier."

I don't know if he meant easier on him or easier on his father, and I suspect that it was a little bit of both, but mostly I think he yearned to avoid open embarrassment between the two of them.

"I don't think I should tell Jack yet," he said.

"Well, Stephen . . . " But he moved back into the other room and sat down in front of the television, although I thought he was as astounded as I was by the revelation of so much truth in the space of, perhaps, five or ten minutes. An atmosphere of unrelenting honesty is not hospitable, really, to domestic life. It is exhausting, since it bars the possibility of tactfulness or diplomacy.

Charles had dashed home from a history department meeting and gone upstairs to shower and change clothes before heading back to meet a prospective faculty member and introduce her to several other members of the department, who would join them for drinks. He had been harried all semester, reluctantly chairing the department and teaching two courses. It seemed imperative that I tell him before he came face-to-face with Stephen, who would assume his father knew, but Charles was obviously in a hurry. He had scarcely noticed that I was standing next to him while he put on his tie in front of the vanity mirror. I put my hand on his arm to draw his attention, and then without taking the time to consider what I was doing, I simply said what I was determined to tell him.

"Listen, Stephen just told me he's gay, and he wanted me to tell you. I know it won't—"

"What? What did you say?" His words fell on top of my own,

although he spoke slowly and softly, and he stopped still in the middle of adjusting his tie.

"Steve is gay. He wants you to know, but . . ."

He was moving away from me and out of the room as I spoke, and I followed him downstairs. Charles reacted exactly as I had to Stephen's news. In fact, he used almost the same words. "We love you, Steve. Nothing could ever change that." And he hugged Stephen and held on to him for a long moment. Both of us had the feeling that somehow Stephen was slipping away from us, as though he were being swept off by a strong current, and we wanted desperately to catch hold of him and pull him back to shore.

During several weeks that May following Stephen's sophomore year at college, the rooms of my house seemed to me, each one, a foreign country. The three of us ranged around that newly strange place in a paralysis of politeness, afraid that we would blunder into some area of hurtfulness of the other two.

I know now that Charles and I—even in our manner of acceptance—were unwittingly cruel, but either Stephen was so shocked by his act of revelation that he didn't notice, or he took us at our intention. We were doing the best we could with information that filled us with fear and sorrow and confusion.

My husband and I were well brought up; we are excellent products of middle-class Anglo-American behavior. We kept our sorrow to ourselves. I found myself, at one point, standing under the hot water from the shower, cradling my head against the tiled wall and weeping and weeping, struggling with a thought that wouldn't come clear. "It would be easier if he were . . ." I had no idea how I meant to finish that sentence, nor did I know in what direction it was leading, until finally it occurred to me that I thought it would be easier for Stephen to have discovered he was black than to have realized that he was gay. When I had to admit to myself that I had had that thought—an idea so fraught with my own conveniently repressed knowledge of the hatred and inequity still extant in this country—I stood all alone under the running water and covered my face with my hands in embarrassment.

Stephen must not have known what to do next. Charles and I were relentlessly chipper and incurious over the few days following the day he told us he was gay. We didn't ask any questions at all, apparently less interested than if he had told us he had read a good book, and I don't remember that Charles and I even discussed these new circumstances with each other.

In the evenings we sat with books before us, but we didn't read; it requires reflection. We watched any sports we could find on television. There was no refuge in anything else on TV, because we discovered right away that, in 1991, the most innocent of sitcoms almost invariably had a passive but definite anti-gay agenda. Trotting out a stereotypical gay man—although rarely ever a lesbian—was apparently always good for a laugh. Or at least it filled a little time in those generally mindless scripts. How had we not noticed and been offended by it before? We watched a lot of baseball.

The second night I had a dream of dreaming. Even in my sleep I had to sneak up on myself, I think, because I love my children very much, and I couldn't bear to think that I had put either one of them in harm's way. I dreamed that I was asleep and having a dream in which I got out of bed and went into Stephen's room, where he, too, was sound asleep and only eight years old.

My dream of my dream-self began to speak to him. "I forgot to tell you something," the me of my dream's dream said, while my immediate dream-self looked on disapprovingly. "I think I forgot to tell you about sex." But Stephen didn't wake up; it was clear in the dream that he didn't need to know what I was saying, and the dream's me wandered slowly back to my own bed and—in the manner of an animated cartoon—merged with the me who I was dreaming was lying there next to my husband. I remember the feeling in the dream of absolute peacefulness.

The next morning, however, I awoke to a solid wall of speculation. Had I done this to my son? Had I tempted fate? After
nearly seven years of struggling, I had just finished the manuscript of a novel, *Fortunate Lives*, which had been a difficult
book to work on while my children were young, because in part
it is about the death of a child. I had had to wait until my children were past the age of the child in the novel before I could
conclude it. At last, though, I had completed it, and I was in
that early stage of being done in which I was still in love with
what I had created. Now it seemed to me that my euphoria
about my own work had endangered my son, although the idea
of what that danger might be was still amorphous; I hadn't
named it yet.

I had managed to repress my acknowledgment that Stephen
was somehow now imperiled until that peculiar dream the night
before. And if Stephen was imperiled, then there must be some
way in which it was my fault. The following morning I wandered
around the house and looked out the windows while trying to
fend off an overwhelming sense of impending doom and an
image of my own family's sudden isolation within our own town.

From the upstairs front hall window I gazed out at the street,
at my neighbors' houses. Our road rises at a moderate incline to
an ancient forest owned and protected by the college. The
Williams College ski team roller-skis our hill; ambitious joggers
pass by. At the top of the street, out of sight of our house, live
the Michaelsons, an elegant couple with children grown and
gone. Bill Michaelson walks a brisk route past our property every
day, walking stick in hand, tweed hat handsomely canted, his
step purposeful. It was he who had stopped, though, to study the
sign Jack and Stephen had nailed to our failing maple tree at the
front gate when they were six and seven years old, respectively.

Dew Detective Agency
Steve Dew . . . Detective
Jack Dew . . . Associate
(No case too small)

My friend Gail Godwin was fond of my children and had sent them three splendid books on detecting, and Stephen and Jack were fascinated, reading all the detective stories they could find. Having read their way through mysteries written for children, such as the Encyclopedia Brown series, they had decided to try their own hand at sleuthing.

I saw Bill pause to read the sign with care, and I went to the door when he turned down our drive. As he approached I smiled in acknowledgment of what I knew was a sort of conspiracy, but he remained quite serious.

"I have a matter of importance to discuss with Detective Steve Dew and his associate, Jack Dew," he said. "I wonder if they're at home this afternoon." Of course, he could see that they were home, because they were sitting behind me at the kitchen table having lunch. I left the three of them alone, and Stephen and Jack eventually solved the "Case of the Barking Dog" for the Michaelsons.

And farther down the hill, on our side, live the Hendriks. A large cannon resides on their front lawn, aimed, in fact, at the side of our house. I still have a copy of *The Slade Road Sentinel*, First Ed., Vol. 1, Steve Dew, editor; Jack F. Dew, editor. By the time they took up journalism, Jack was eight years old and far too canny to be persuaded by his nine-year-old brother to take second billing when the two of them decided to start a neighborhood newspaper. In their first and last edition, Stephen interviewed Mr. Hendriks for this story:

The people of Slade Road might want to know the history of the cannon that sits on the Hendriks' lawn. The cannon was actually made from two wagon wheels, an axle, and a porch column all bought at an antique show in Greenfield. It is a replica of the Dahl Gren gun. The famous revolutionary Dahl Gren gun was used for naval and artillery purposes. Mr. Hendriks designed the replica, and he had to carve the porch column to resemble the barrel of the gun.

Charles decided out loud at dinner, after reading the article, that he would fashion a missile silo out of our barbecue grill and some leftover aluminum duct pipe in a Slade Road version of arms escalation. The boys were amused and simultaneously defensive of Mr. Hendriks's cannon, which is, indeed, impressive.

Almost a decade later, though, as I looked out at the street where we had lived for seventeen years, where my children had grown up, where we were when we heard the ongoing news of our far-flung families, and where we resided while incorporating into our perspective the evolution of world events, I was not feeling the loss of a sort of saccharine, Norman Rockwell exis- tence. For one thing, that's never what we had on Slade Road or in the larger community of Williamstown. Life is always more complicated than that. I was contemplating the possible loss of approval, of communal acceptance on behalf of my son and the rest of us, too. I saw that we might plummet like stones if we were cast out of the familiar embrace of the community we were so accustomed to.

I wandered up and down the stairs, in and out of the rooms, trying to reconcile all the disparate parts of our new situation. Finally I made coffee and sat down in the kitchen. I had man- aged to conclude only one thing; I had decided we should move to San Francisco. So unwittingly caught up in stereotypes was I, our options seemed remarkably narrow.

Most of what I had read about homosexuality—and I hadn't read much, but since I read all the time I found that I had come across more than I realized—was in contemporary literature that had generally dealt with homosexuality as a tragic consequence of having a suffocating mother and a weak, indifferent, or absent father. I considered this for about twenty minutes. Had I been a suffocating mother? I don't know; I had meant to be a good mother, the best parent in the world. I had thought our family was a happy family, whatever that actually is. If I had smothered Stephen, then I had equally smothered my younger son, because, for better or worse, I love them equally. Was Charles weak, indifferent, or absent? Charles is probably the kindest man I've ever known, and he is certainly not indifferent to his sons, whom he loves deeply, nor has he been absent from their lives—literally or figuratively. My attempt at revisionist family history was agonizing; it was getting me nowhere, and my fear for my son didn't bear investigation. So I put my reflections on hold and got up and went about my day in a state of limbo.

Charles and I pretended an ease with the new status quo that we didn't feel. We had each quickly and independently fashioned a sort of ludicrous etiquette of feigned heartiness, because we couldn't have stood to have Stephen know he had thrown us into a state of grief. His revelation had shattered our expectations of who he was. We pretended that his sudden emergence as a gay man in what we had considered our conventional family was a matter of no consequence, something that had slipped from our minds completely.

The three of us spent several days occupying the rooms in a state of careful good cheer. Charles and I were busy all the time; we never settled very long in one place, and I don't know what Stephen must have thought, but eventually he approached us in the late afternoon where we were sitting on the screened porch in the balmy air.

"Steve!" Charles said. "Would you like some iced tea? Or a beer?" His voice was warm, perhaps overly exuberant.

"Yeah. Thanks. I'll get some iced tea. Do you want anything?"

"I'd love some tea, Stephen, if it's not too much trouble," I said, beaming at him. I was so nervous that my mouth went dry. Stephen has my father's family's brown eyes—an orange brown, the iris rimmed with black—and arched brows, and his expression caught my attention that afternoon because it was filled with compassion. I think now that it struck me so forcefully because he was only nineteen years old, but his expression held far more empathy than anyone that age usually possesses.

He brought our glasses of tea from the kitchen and sat down, too, not saying anything for a few moments, and then he looked directly at us, still with an expression of gentle tactfulness. He gazed at Charles and me steadily while he spoke, probably afraid we would find some chore to take us off if he didn't say what he wanted us to hear. "Listen, I know this must be really hard for you. I just want you to know how much it means to me to know that it doesn't change the way you feel about me."

"Nothing could ever change the way we feel about you, Steve," Charles said. "We love you more than you know."

"We do, sweetie," I said.

"I *do* know. But it must be hard for you," he said, "because I know you didn't expect this. I just wanted to tell you that you can ask me anything you want to know. I mean, you must won-der about a lot of things. I don't want to have any secrets. I don't want you to feel uncomfortable around me." This was a terrible admission—a plea—from my own son, and I tried not to let myself start crying. "I'll be glad to answer any questions you want to ask," he said.

All around the porch the lilac bushes were in bud, with just a few blooms among the branches, so that their delicate scent reached us only when a breeze picked up, but I remember the smell of lilacs in conjunction with Stephen's words, and the combination was such a generous offering in the mild weather that it was very nearly heartbreaking.

PATRICIA J. WILLIAMS

9

On Throwing Like a Girl

THE DAY BEGINS at the subway station. My five-year-old drops his pocket change in the paper cup of a homeless man. "God bless you," says the man, "and stay in school." The day ends with a lovely dinner party at which four different lawyer friends of mine independently demand an accounting of what I am doing to ensure that my son is properly instructed in sports.

The two ends of the day feel worlds apart, as far apart as the world in which I grew up from the world in which my son must find his place. I grew up in Boston, in a sumptuously tree-lined, ethnically mixed, mostly lower-middle-class neighborhood. The classes at my public school were large by today's consensus— thirty or so with one teacher. Nevertheless, I received a solid, unimaginative, but thorough education from dedicated teachers, abetted by my ambitious mother, who read us stuff like the whole of *Pilgrim's Progress* before we got to kindergarten. There were no organized sports for either boys or girls where I grew up. We just went out and played, in backyards, in vacant lots, or in the middle of the street. We children fought and played and confided in one another and grew close, grew apart, grew up, and then moved on.

Decades later, my son is growing up in a high-rise in New York

City. Every last moment of his life is scheduled. I shepherd him from class to class to class, for everything in New York, even sports, is taught rather than played, in "structured learning environments." Children not only don't play on the streets where we live, they are surveyed, measured up, all but given IQ tests for the pleasure of a play date at each other's house. They are like little lemmings, all rushing to their great reward, small legs buckling beneath the weight of parental anxiety. I try to maintain a quantum of leisure in my son's life, but it's hard in Manhattan. The dreamy, quiet moment for one's thought to blossom is constantly besieged by the anxiety of needing-to-attain-perfection no later than the age of three.

I do not know whether to attribute this breathless push to self-advancement to the vagaries of time and place—the whole world has changed so much since I was a child, and no place has ever beat New York for panic-as-a-lifestyle. Nonetheless, it does seem to me that in the recent push to what some are openly embracing as "global dominance," a highly specialized metaphoric order seems to be emerging, organized a little like a corporate beehive. The queen bees are on top, all brain and genetic endowment, but with soft, impractical bodies. Below are the worker bees, who enjoy buff bodies but no brains.

Zoological accuracy notwithstanding, this much of the image is limited enough, but then it's overlaid with race. The Brains are white, the Bodies are black. Everyone wants to be a Brain. No one wants to be a black Body—at least in this Manichean sense—even blacks, so much of whose political energy has been thus siphoned into the great yes-and-no-quagmire question of all time: Am I only and always this Body? Similarly, working-class and middle-class whites fight to place themselves in this dualism, and they twist back and forth—from envying and fetishizing black physique (particularly in the realms of crime and sports) to proving that they themselves are really-and-truly-deserving white Brains.

Whole industries have cropped up to cater to these self-dividing anxieties. The designated Brains spend lots of money trying to figure out how to reproduce themselves. Under the illusion that they have no bodies, they seem convinced that reproduction is best done with drugs and dishes and needles and incubators. The designated Bodies, on the other hand, spend a lot of time repenting and apologizing for the simply astounding rate at which they are presumed to be spreading. And with such ease! And from each and every orifice! Lots of money is spent devising potions to make them stop.

The Brains subsist on air kisses, black coffee, and toast points. Scientists with Ph.D.'s work hard at packing a six-course meal into a pill with no calories. Meanwhile, the always-insatiable Bodies devour oxen and babies and boulders, indiscriminately consuming all the resources of the earth. Technicians labor to wire their jaws shut.

The Brains work so hard for everything they have that they are tense, depressed, and on the verge of nervous breakdowns. The Bodies never, ever suffer depression or mental illness because they are built for industry, although being brainless they have a propensity toward idleness that must be patrolled in order to smack those hands back from straying into the devil's workshops.

For leisure, the Brains need lots of toys from Sharper Image. Assuming all the chores are done, the Bodies are best engaged in games, games, and more sport until they tire themselves out and lie their restless carcasses down for a nice, safe nap.

My son and I exist at a fascinating crossroads in all this. He is a preschool Young Black Male; I am a perimenopausal Black Single Mother. Like my mother, I read ambitious and improbable texts to him so that his brain, like mine, may be haunted by the rhythms of literature as much as by its meaning. We play the piano together. We have the great luxury of being able to travel to interesting places in conjunction with my work. In deference to the gentleman on the subway platform, we plan to commit him to school for a good, long time. And best of all, we visit my parents frequently so that he may play ball in the backyard.

It's as well balanced and comfortable a life as the world has to offer, I think. Yet for all this, I find myself facing a curiously consistent pressure in one area. I am not exaggerating when I say that scarcely a day goes by without the worried chiding of one male friend or another that I am blessed with the care and feeding of a little boy who is conspicuously large for his age, who can hit a home run, play goalie, who has a nice forehand slice. Now, it's not as though my son is sports-deprived: he plays soccer and T-ball and swims. Rather, the pressure seems to deploy sport as a cipher for anxiety about his fatherlessness. I have had men actually ask me why I adopted a boy and not a girl. Wouldn't I be happier with a girl . . . that is, um, particularly as a single parent? And so the men my son encounters are singularly absorbed with imbuing him with sporty "guy" mannerisms, from adjusting the precise angle of the baseball cap to high- and low-fiving—everything but how to spit a wad of tobacco. Furthermore, since many of my friends are white, and since so many of the gestures of hypermasculinity are coded as "black," there's an almost comic aspect of triangulated projection about it all. "Basketbaaawwl!" says my preternaturally husky-voiced little black son, sounding exactly like a white person imitating a black person who has absorbed the message that heterosexual identity and social acceptance are tied up with the ability to say that word in just that way and so ends up imitating a white person imitating . . .

This is such a touchy thing to talk about, I know. On the one hand, I am genuinely grateful for the intervention of my friends. Many of these men are doing their best to fill a perceived void with a generosity and attentiveness that is kinder than anything I knew back in the Dick and Jane mist of my freewheeling youth.

Then too, it's certainly true that, raised in a family of girls, sport is a culture I never quite fathomed—the gladiatorial politics, the body-envy somehow vaguely related to women's anxieties about weight and hair, the pressure to do Little League a bit like the pressure for little girls to enter beauty pageants. "It'll be good for him," one coach told me, and then, while eyeing his height: "We *need* him on our team." It mystifies me, this stuff about the pain, the pathos, the glory, the contradiction. I have a friend who is a fiftyish former triathlete who is always limping off to Toys 'Я' Us to buy my son an assortment of footballs, bats, and shin guards. He's had four knee operations and can hardly walk. "Sports are the most satisfying part of a man's life," he tells me, gritting his manly teeth against the pain.

On the other hand, there is an undercurrent to it that seems to assume that I will be the ruination of my son, that I will crush the fledgling male instinct with the unchecked voodoo of single-mother sissification. *Sports will keep him out of trouble.* He's a happy, normal five-year-old. Why the assumption of trouble? *Organized sports will teach him discipline, cooperation, and fair play.* Quite possibly, although the same might be said for homework, music, and the tutelage of kind adults. *Your son has the hands of a great athlete—look at that spread!* Yup, he'll be able to play Rachmaninoff *too*, I say. That part about Rachmaninoff always seems to send them over the top, as though I had said, "I plan to dress him in lace collars and velvet pantaloons," and so they gallop right along to the heart of the matter. *Sports are where the secrets of manhood are lodged. Guys'll make fun of him if he doesn't know the rules of the game.* Aha.

Again, please understand that my son is deprived neither of schooling nor of sport. But the preposterous polarizing of these as paths to success occasionally leads some people to act as though every other aspect of his brain and being was insignificant beside the prowess promised by the width of those five-year-old shoulders. *Why are you bothering with piano lessons? He's got basketball scholarship stamped across his forehead,* says a friend of mine who went to school on a chemistry scholarship. It's not just that my son's bursting physicality seems to bring out the thwarted athlete in not a few of my bookish, tweedy, bespectacled male friends—it's as though some people are upset because I'm trying to expand my son's life opportunities. *How can you get a good hoop dream going when he's living in a home* with all those silly distractions! No, it's not that in so many words. They don't resent education itself, surely, but repeatedly they seem to resent the allocation of time to things other than sports; persistently they seem to resent my offering him anything that isn't a game.

If my son becomes an athlete, I will be very proud of him. But his size, his body shape, can hardly be his exclusive destiny, and the gnawing anxiety that pushes him to that end betrays everything that is best about America. It may help to remember that in the United States, only about one person in every one hundred thousand, who participated in sports in high schoool, ends up playing on a professional team. One's odds, in other words, of getting a paying job as an engineer are much better any day than of landing a job in basketball. This invites speculation, I would hope, about what kinds of resources we spend preparing our children for the one career as opposed to the other. Yet the analysis of how many young lives are being wastefully directed, tracked so as to make sure they tumble into the yawning chasm of educational disparity, is lost on those who scramble in sheer panic over the fine distinctions in offerings between independent schools on the Upper East Side as opposed to the Upper West Side as opposed to East Village as opposed to the West.

A friend of mine teaches in a decaying public high school where almost all the students are working class or poor. He speaks despairingly about his students, the smartest of whom qualify for all sorts of colleges but who simply don't have the money, who will go to junior college instead and have it held against them, as though it were a matter of merit. "You know," he says, "those junior, supposedly lesser, 'imitation' colleges unpeopled by 'elites.'" He talks about "all these smart, smart kids" who sleep their way through school. His supervisor requires that he write "sl" beside their names, but he always tries to wake them first. "Try to keep your eyes open," he says, but he knows that they have been looking after younger siblings, cleaning house, doing laundry, working extra jobs, helping their families make ends meet. He fumes about policies that would make it harder for such students to complete both high school and now public colleges. "Homework!" he says. "Some of these kids don't have homes; and as for work, they work harder than most middle-class adults, if not always on school assignments. I'll give you merit," he says glumly.

But however variously divided along lines of black and white, rich and poor, rational and irrational, deserving or not—sooner or later, the brain must be able to abide in the physical realm, and the body will survive only as a thinking being. Not only for the sake of ourselves but for our collective future, these two conceptual halves must be joined—this is what needs most to be married in the world—for without that reunion I think we stray farther and farther from the path to our salvation.

My son has got the knack. He says, "I can jump backwards into bed. Want to see me? I can do it just like an astronaut coming back to earth. Pretend this is the earth's atmosphere," he says, patting the bed. "Here I go. No. Pretend I'm half astronaut and half a whale. I can balance a basketball on my nose. Watch this. I'm going to leap into earth's atmosphere, leave a trail of sparks across the sky, and land backwards in the sea with a basketball on my nose. Pretend this is the basketball." He puts his finger to his nose. "Here I go."

He runs, runs, runs across the room, leaps, does a miraculously age-inappropriate half-twist in the air, lands backward with a crash on the rickety bed. He looks a little like an astronaut; he looks somewhat like a breaching baby whale; he looks exactly like my little boy. When he resurfaces, the basketball is still balanced perfectly upon his nose.

PATRICIA STEVENS

$$9$$

Auto Mechanics

HE'S BEEN working on the 1964 Mustang, his first car, for several months now, rebuilding the engine, repairing the clutch,
putting on new belts, new hoses, reconnecting loose wires.
There are car parts everywhere. In the garage, in the driveway,
in the yard, on the front porch, on the back porch, in his bedroom, in the living room. Spark plugs lie dead and partially
buried in the grass; the original left fender, dented beyond repair
by one of the three previous owners, sits in the middle of the
driveway; four hubcabs have become metal shrubs on both sides
of the sidewalk. Inside, while watching TV, he's rubbing down
rusted metal car parts with sandpaper. The air cleaner that goes
over the carburetor, which he plans to spray-paint, is now a
sculpture sitting on a bed of newspaper in front of the couch.

His fingers look dirty all the time now, even though I've
bought both Lava soap and a half-pound tub of Goop. When
he's off at his part-time job at Econofoods, where he cashiers or
works behind the service desk, the customers can see his oil-
stained fingers when he's counting out their change or checking
their IDs. When I remind him of this, he rolls his eyes at me. His
younger brother, Jordan, who's also in the room and has no
interest in cars but does have an established interest in sibling

conflict, says, "Yeah, Michael Panic is in my history class and asked me if you ever take showers."

"Dirty fingernails. It's a turnoff for the girls." I can't help myself either.

Jeremy shrugs. "It doesn't come off," he says. Sometimes he says, "Would you get off my back?" He's heard about the fingernails before. I'm on him again. I'm always on him, it seems, for something.

He's blowing off his senior year, and I'm on him for that, even though he earned most all of his credits for graduation in his freshman, sophomore, and junior years, plus he's going to the university in the fall, has been accepted into the College of Engineering, and has earned a grant that will pay his tuition. He's not affected by peer pressure; he isn't obsessed with his hair or clothes; he works hard, earned $5,000 last year, has friends I approve of, doesn't drink or do drugs, knows how to fix things, loves the outdoors, can take care of himself. I'm proud of him. Still I'm on him: for not studying, for not cleaning his room, for working too many hours at Econofoods, for having dirty fingernails, for not getting a haircut (but when he does, for getting it cut too short), for not having enough social life (Don't you like girls?). He can't win. "It won't stop," he tells me.

He's right. When I wake up in the middle of the night (which is when I have the most time to think), I say to myself, *You're on him too much*. Why are you doing this? I'm cramming, I tell myself. There's a last-minute desperation to turn him into everything I expect him to become before he leaves home in a couple of months.

But if I'm honest, I have a second motive: in my relationship with Jeremy, I'm often run by guilt. For years now, I have tried to amend for all I took from his childhood. I'm on him all the time because I think that if I can just make him more daring in social situations, more confident in intellectual pursuits, and less tight with his feelings, then I will no longer be guilty of having wrecked his life.

From behind the kitchen window, I can see him out there on the oil-blotched driveway, leaning his lanky six-foot-two-inch-plus frame over the innards of the Mustang. Next year he'll grow another half inch. He towers over me. His brother will just reach six feet. When I walk with the two of them, I am a dwarf. I'm just over five-four. Their father is a hair over five-ten. All four grandparents are shrimps. Jeremy's height, we believe, is a throwback to his maternal great-great-grandfather, who was six-foot-four back in the mid-1800s.

He's got his shirt off, revealing a long, smooth back, which is smudged with grease and curved over the car's engine. He has a project. He's happy when he has a project. When he was two and three, it was the bright orange Fisher-Price bulldozer or the bright yellow backhoe. Instead of his stuffed rabbit, he sometimes took the box that once housed the backhoe to bed with him, so he could fall asleep dreaming of owning all the other Fisher-Price equipment that was pictured on the back—the steamroller, the dump truck, the crane. Then there were his Legos, which occupied him for hours at a time, and each year the structures grew more and more elaborate. There was also a lot of digging in the backyard—the squirrel trap that was never really meant to catch a squirrel but was a pit so well camouflaged with twigs, clippings, and leaves that it accidentally trapped the housepainter's left leg. Sometime after that there was the wood phase: the tree house in the backyard, the cat feeder, and much later the book holder, the chessboard, and the oak plant stand he gave me as a birthday gift. There were trains—HO- then N-scale—the work on his bicycle, the repairs around the house. Why wouldn't cars be next?

He knows how things work, and all this time that I've been a single parent—nearly twelve years now—I've relied on him. *Have I depended on him too much?* I hate machines and he's never been afraid of them. Once, soon after the divorce, when the electricity went out in the living room, he took me down into the basement, pointed the flashlight into the metal box, and showed me how to tell which fuse it was. Amazing! How did he know such things when he was only seven years old?

When he was in the second grade and I moved him and his younger brother halfway across the country, from the central coast of California to sixty miles short of the Mississippi River, he was our navigator, poring over the maps each time we were about to cross into another state. He's put in storm windows, fixed the lawn mower, replaced the torn front-door screen, stopped the running toilet, and taken the U-joint off the sink to clean out the trap. Whenever we camped, he was the one who put up the tent and built the fire.

Jeremy tells me he wants to take a trip in the Mustang, though he's not sure just where yet, and that he plans to leave a few days after he's awarded his high school diploma. He tells me this just after he announces that he won't be attending his high school graduation. Except for auto mechanics, where he is the only university-bound student, he's hated this last year of high school.

Because I've learned to choose my battles, I decide not to engage in a bout over graduation. Yet, in the middle of the night my eyelids suddenly snap open and I'm staring up at the dark ceiling wondering why he's alienated. This obsessive worrying at 3 A.M. has been my plight for years now—the plight of the guilty single parent. I believe I am responsible for everything.

Instead of involving himself in school activities, he's spent his senior year working, earning money. Surely this is my fault. "I'm not going to end up like you," he says, meaning he doesn't want to worry about money. He's becoming a workaholic and skinflint. We argue about this constantly. "Would you rather I spent my time drinking beer and doing drugs?" he asks. The question, I later realize, is a veiled reference to his parents' unfortunate history.

A few days later he tells me he's going to drive the '64 Mustang to Alaska and hike. "By yourself? You can't go into the Alaskan

wilderness all by yourself!" I'm shouting. "Even the most experienced backpackers don't go *alone.*"

"You can't tell me what to do. Try 'n' stop me."

Because he's just turned eighteen, I know I must tread lightly.
He's ready to be sent out into the world and he wants to be sure
he isn't dragging a protective mother behind him. To my good
fortune, this skirmish doesn't turn into a full-blown war. (After
so many wars over the years, we have both finally learned that
all combat has a price.) A friend gives me a copy of the *Outside*
magazine that includes the story of the twenty-three-year-old
who went into the Alaskan wilderness alone, couldn't find a way
to get back out, and was eventually found dead, literally a sack of
bones, starved to death in his sleeping bag. I know I can zip my
mouth shut about Alaska when I come home from work one day
and find Jeremy lying on the couch reading the article.

Eventually, the Mustang motor trip to Alaska turns into a Mustang motor trip to California to visit his father.

I know I have to let him go. Isn't that what parenting is? The
long, slow, anxious process of getting your child ready to be
launched into the world to be whoever he will be? But in addition to being a guilty parent, I've also been a protective, and
often controlling, parent. Not controlling in the way that I have
seen some parents do by choosing every class their son will take
in high school, deciding what he will write his English papers
on, determining which sports he will play and who his friends
will be. My particular brand of controlling takes two forms: I
want to be certain I can keep my sons physically safe, and I want
to protect them from any more emotional torture.

Of course, I know I don't have control over either of these,
but I cannot seem to give up trying. With Jeremy, if I can keep
him from driving across the country, he can't be injured in a car
accident, get lost hiking in the mountains, fall off a cliff, starve
to death, or be axed in his tent by a serial killer. If I can just get
him to be more conscious of the physical dangers out there and
more able to take some risks in social situations, maybe I can let

him go next year—as long as he promises to take a friend along to help with the driving, stay in motels along the way, and not go off hiking alone. After that, it's only a matter of time before I'll make him more gregarious, less tight with money, more emotionally forthcoming, and so on.

Though graduation passes (without our being there), for another week and a half high school is still in session for freshmen, sophomores, and juniors, which is fortunate for Jeremy because the Mustang still needs some work and he can still attend auto mechanics. Bit by bit he's putting back all the parts he'd taken out. And of course he has the rebuilt engine. But the car is a 1964—many years older than he is—and I'm worried. Is it safe to drive? When I ask him if I can call his auto mechanics' teacher, he shrugs and says, "I don't care," which means he's curious about what Mr. Hillery will say about him and the Mustang.

What he says is that there's a lot of rust on the body, including underneath the car, but it's perfectly safe. "Will it make it all the way out there and back?" I ask. "He's going alone, did he tell you?"

"I wish I'd done something like that when I was eighteen," Mr. Hillery says, clearly giving the thumbs-up for Jeremy to go. Then he tells me he has two daughters, one in college, one just out of college. "I know," he says, "as a parent you're gonna worry."

"This is my baby," I say.

"He's a good kid."

"It's hard to let them go."

When I hang up the phone I feel a little better. Somehow I trust him. He loves his daughters, he likes Jeremy, he wouldn't tell me the car was safe if it weren't. And he's looking out for Jeremy to get to do a guy thing. I start to see the trip a little differently—as a male rite of passage, something I know little about. And then I take a few minutes to grieve over not having had a Mr. Hillery as the father of my sons.

•   •   •

What is this thing I'm about to let him do? And why does he want to be out there alone?—proving something. It's true that I admire what he's done with the car, rebuilding the engine and all. I have never even changed the oil in any car I've owned. To me, a flat tire means a call to the Triple A. In a strange way, I'm envious that he's taking this leap at age eighteen. A huge part of me really wants him to do this, but I am overcome with fear, and it's the uncontrollable terror that's making me want to harness him. If anything happened to him, I would not get over it.

I call him in from the driveway, where once again he's working on the Mustang. It's his turn to help with dishes, which is also a time when we have some of our best talks. As usual, his conversation begins with cars—Mustangs, Challengers, Cobras, old Corvettes, engine sizes—but by the time the table is cleared and we're through the glasses and on to the plates, he's suddenly talking about the divorce. Out of nowhere, he says, "No judge should have let someone who didn't have a job take two kids halfway across the country."

That old guilt falls over me, mingled with some anger and sadness. "So," I say, "the person who assumed the nonpaying position of caring for the children should not get to have them?"

"Not if a person doesn't have a job," he says.

"What if the person who took care of the children offered many times to be the one to support the family because the other person hated his job but wouldn't give up the job he hated?"

He's staring at me.

I don't mean to, but I start to cry. Ten years we've been living outside California. For ten years twice each year, at Christmas and summer vacation, my children have had to get on an airplane and go halfway across the country, and the grief over all of this still comes in tsunami-sized waves. I'm crying, crying. "You could have gone to school somewhere closer," he says.

"I did what I could do at the time," I say, a weak plea for understanding. I've already accepted that I may never be forgiven for turning his childhood into a long series of long-distance house-and-identity switching. He has always let me know how much he hates commercial airplanes.

"I know, I know," I say. "You've had a raw deal with this divorce, but I have to tell you that I probably would have done it all over the same way."

Like most women, I thought I wanted at least one daughter, but after giving birth to two sons, I have never grieved not having had a female child. The mother-daughter relationship is presumed to be the most difficult (as my mother and I will both attest to), and if I'd had a daughter, the poor girl wouldn't have stood a chance. I have always felt that my sons were placed in my custody to teach me something: if you want to learn what makes a man, watch a boy grow up. Even so, the conflicts between my sons and me have often run long and deep, and as the older of the two, Jeremy got the worst of it. He once told me that his life was happy until he was four. When he was four and his brother was two, the chasm in his parents' marriage was already Hell's Canyon. A couple of casualties from the sixties, his father and I were regular marijuana users who'd begun to dabble in cocaine. Whether the drug use escalated because we were so profoundly disappointed in each other and so unhappy living together, or whether the escalating drug use took away any semblance of decency we might have once had is unlikely ever to be determined. My guess is that had we been healthier people at the time, we never would have married. And had we not married, we would not have had our two sons. And had I not had my two sons, I don't know what would have kept me getting up every morning, and if I keep on this road, I'll go batty.

What happened happened, and the aftermath has been years of shame and guilt. I took a curious, innocent, sweet child and allowed him to watch me and his father scream at each other and then, in the desperation that was my life back then, I screamed at him, too, just for being a kid. There is a photograph of him, taken by the school photographer when he was five and barely in kindergarten. Every few years when I go through the photos and come across that one, it is always a reminder of how much I wish I could have those years back to do over again. In this photo I can see that his usually stunning, lively hazel eyes, which can go from green to blue depending on the shirt he is wearing, are dulled and sad. His upper lip is red and chapped from running his tongue up and back, over and over it, in a year-long obsession that is the most obvious symptom of his anxiety. But the worst part is that he is alone with the huge pain because he's got two parents who are so involved in their own war that they seldom get a glimpse of how he has been caught in the cross fire.

After the family disintegrated and I moved to Iowa to attend the writers' workshop, I started growing up. I was already into the second half of my thirties, but for years I'd been stuck on the marijuana, which I continued to smoke post-divorce until my sources dried up. For me, the cocaine didn't last long, only that last, terrible year we were married. One morning at 5 A.M., with my heart racing out of control, I lay there praying (and I am not a religious person), "Please, God, don't let me die. I promise I'll *never* do this again." Then I got up and dumped what remained of the white powder down the toilet and watched it swirl away.

The regret, though, was harder to flush, which was tough on Jeremy because, like all kids, he had his antennae working over-time, picking up all those guilty vibes. I felt so bad for him: he'd suffered so much; he was so vulnerable; he didn't deserve what had happened to him; and on and on. I was tentative with him, which helped turn him into a monster: he began to terrorize his brother, which was also his way of getting at me. Not that his brother was an innocent victim, but with Jeremy there was no negotiating. The boys shared a bedroom for a number of years, and if Jeremy wanted the light turned out, the music turned off, the window shades pulled down, it happened. If his brother objected, too bad. My first child was a despot and I was powerless to stop him. A kid was running my house. And yet, the more he acted out, the more guilty I felt, the more he thought there was something wrong with him, the more I thought everything was all my fault, the more he bullied.

This little dance went on for years, really—that's how long it took me to figure out that I was crippling him. This thought occurred to me one night when I was watching a newsmagazine show about a family that had fourteen kids, most adopted and with physical problems. When a girl with no arms—who refused to learn to walk because every time she fell she landed face first—joined the family, the parents refused to feed her unless she got herself to the table. It took only a couple of missed meals and she was walking. After that, she learned to take out the garbage and change the baby's diapers with her feet.

When I saw that girl, dragging the trash bags with her clenched toes, the light went on. I took us off to family counseling, found us some help from a man who got Jeremy to agree to stop the terrorism and me to admit to Jeremy that he hadn't deserved what I'd once handed out to him. I also learned to hold firm: "You may *not* do this anymore. I will *not* live this way one minute longer." It took several years to get us turned around. Even then, he continued to be angry with me, and that didn't really change until he spent the first half of his sophomore year back in California with Brad. I cried and cried when he left, but by the time he'd decided to return six months later, his rage had burned down to a heap of smoldering embers. Maybe I wasn't Mommie Dearest after all.

Every June, just before the boys went off to be with Brad for the summer, we all got weird and started picking fights with one another. It was a pattern, our way of coping with the anxiety over having to once again shift gears from our school-year lives into our summer lives. By June, I was usually so tired from having done the year's parenting single-handedly—the soccer games, the parent-teacher conferences, the sibling rivalry, the birthday parties, the overnights with friends, the food shopping, the cooking, the clothes shopping, the carpooling, the everyday worries—that I was more than ready for a break. But I would be overcome with a great sadness, too. And fear. I knew from the boys that Brad not only still had his hunting rifles, but he'd acquired at least one handgun, and when he took the boys camping deep into the Ventana Wilderness, he took the weapon with him.

Though Brad had remarried a year after the divorce and had stayed married, he lived in a house he and Marianne had built in Cachagua on a piece of property he and I had bought. Because of its isolation, I had never been able to imagine actually living there, but the place was fine for Brad and Marianne, whose lives seemed to be centered on the land and their five dogs. But what about the boys? They were isolated all summer long with no other kids to play with, no organized summer activities, and guns in the house.

It was with this stark terror (along with my fear of airplane disasters) that I stuck my children on the United flight out of Cedar Rapids every summer, and after I'd watched the tail disappear into the clouds, I got back in the car and bawled all the way back to Iowa City. I was sending them off into the unknown, into a part of their childhood that was a mystery to me, that I would never understand, that I would never share, and that I could only hope they'd return from.

They'd be gone nine weeks, June 15 to August 15. By July 1, I was usually fine, basking in my freedom until about August 1, when I began to worry again. But even the one month I had during which my emotions were fairly temperate, my mood would sometimes turn on a dime.

One of these mornings on my way to the community center, where I was about to swim laps, I sat in the car in the parking lot and watched a mother with two boys who were about the same ages as Jeremy and Jordan at the time. She opened her car door, got out, let the boys out of the backseat, and ushered them up to the front door of the center, where the city had a summer day care program. Squatting to their level, she wrapped her arms tightly around each boy and kissed him on the cheek. I broke into racking sobs that continued for several minutes, and when I recovered I went home to the empty house and cried some more.

I saw Brad once, after many years. I drove to California to visit friends and picked up the boys on August 15 so we three could camp through Idaho, Montana, Wyoming, and South Dakota on the way back to Iowa. I didn't think Brad would want me on the Cachagua property—I wasn't anxious to be there myself—but the boys told me to pick them up there. Later, I found out that it had been Marianne's idea; she's the other one who once had dreams of putting the last surgical stitch in the whole mess.

I was nervous as I drove past Garland Ranch, where Brad and I used to hike with the boys up to the rock grotto with the narrow waterfall; the Chatterbox, where we all went for breakfast on Sunday mornings; the walnut orchard, where the boys and I lived for six months after we sold the house; and past Esquiline, the road that leads up to Calle de la Paloma—"Street of the Dove"—the little house carved into the hillside where Brad and I first lived. This had been Jeremy's first house, the place where he and his father used to garden on Sunday mornings. Several miles from Carmel Valley village, I saw the gate to the property Brad and I had bought together. It was open, and I drove back the packed-dirt road while five dogs chased alongside the car. The boys were waiting. As was Marianne. Brad was inside. It was an awkward moment for all of us.

Marianne told the boys to show me their room, which they did. Brad was standing in the living room in front of a huge window that looked out across the valley. I saw that his hair was thinner and his mustache was gone; his clean-shaven upper lip looked odd to me, as though I'd never seen his mouth before.

Several feet away from him I stood and searched through the glass for the cattle that had once grazed the distant hillside. "You got what you wanted here," I said. I'm not sure, but I think I was trying to say that *he* belonged on the property but *I* didn't.

When he looked at me I saw the fear in his eyes, the vulnerability. It made me feel sad and scared all at the same time. "You have no idea who I am," he said.

That was it. Ten, maybe fifteen minutes. The boys and I packed the car and drove off and I thought: Every night for years I climbed into bed with you; together we created these children.

When I dreamed of having children, when I planned my pregnancies, when the children were born, at no time did I intend to raise my sons the way they were raised. In single-parent families the dynamic is askew. Situations are sometimes blown sky-high out of proportion. There are no days off, and there's no one to tell you at night when your children have been arguing incessantly all day long that it's normal behavior. Everything is your responsibility, everything is your fault. The boundaries start to blur. You're not quite sure where you end and they begin. Everything they do, good and bad, reflects on you, or so you imagine. You gave them their good grades in school, you gave them their shyness, their propensity for junk food, their industriousness, their quick tempers. You gave them everything, except for the few moments when you're sure they're going to be just like their father.

Their father. He loves his boys—in his own way. He and I are, I suppose, still slogging through and out of the mess we made.

Now we are battling over car insurance. Like Mr. Hillery says, Jeremy is a good kid. He's responsible. Most of the time. But he's eighteen and thinks he's invincible. He's also a tightwad (my fault because in the midst of the divorce, when I was always anxious about where the money was coming from, I was oblivious to his listening in on my desperate phone calls to friends, banks, lawyers), which is why he doesn't see any reason to spend money on anything, including insurance. "I'm a good driver," he says.

"You *are* a good driver, but things can happen. You can hit black ice, you can swerve to avoid a deer."

"Nothing's going to happen."

"You are not leaving here without insurance."

The battle goes on for days, and at some point I phone Brad. What possesses me to do this? Do I think that suddenly we will begin to work together as parents? It's more a measure of my desperation. I have convinced myself that this would not be happening if we were a two-parent family. We would be aligned, gang up on our son, give him no choice.

But instead of forming an alliance, our old patterns resurface: I get frustrated and Brad gets pissed off and hangs up. At first I feel the rage surging through my veins again, but within a minute or two I'm just sad. When there are children involved, divorce is a huge dark mountain of sorrow that is always in the background. Sometimes the boys bring snapshots of Brad back from their summers in California, and when they're left lying around on the dining room table I sneak a look. They are nothing like our New Year's Eve wedding pictures, where Brad is grinning with life. Now his eyes are glass eyes, all humor sucked out of them. I can vaguely remember him doing comedic monologues for me; I can vaguely remember us laughing together, though surely we were stoned. Once, a year or two after we were divorced, when I'd finally regained my own sense of humor, I bought a card to send him. Then, knowing he wouldn't laugh, I never mailed it. It was a plain card, all text, no graphics. On the front in big block letters was printed, WAS IT REALLY LOVE? And when you opened it up inside, it said, OR WAS IT JUST DRUG ABUSE?

Finally Jeremy agrees to go with me to the insurance agency, where I've already predisposed the agent to set him straight. But when we get there he slouches in the chair and scowls. I see on his face that he's thinking these women don't know for shit. I'm the standard he judges women by, and when it comes to cars, I know next to nothing. Using a deductive method, he thinks he knows everything about cars, including car insurance. Linda, the agent, explains that in Iowa, even though insurance isn't required by law, he must present at the scene of an accident proof of his ability to pay. "Or you could be sent off to jail," she says.

His head is bent; still, I can see his eyes rolling up toward the ceiling. She could go on for an hour and nothing would convince him.

I pay for the first three months, and he agrees to pay after that. I'm not thinking about the battle we'll have over this same issue three months hence.

He asks to borrow my Triple A card to get maps and tour books. He brings them home and at night he spreads them out on the dining room table. He gets a baby-blue highlighter and marks his route from Iowa City to Carmel Valley. I'm trying not to think about it too much, but then I notice that as early as Nebraska, he's planning to get off the interstate and take the scenic. Reality stings me: he's going to drive a rusted 1964 Mustang halfway across the country. Then, when he informs me that he's certain he's going to camp his way to California, I panic. He'll be out there and I won't know where. If he doesn't arrive in California, how will I know where to begin looking for him? He hasn't lived long enough to know all the dangers yet. He's eighteen and he doesn't believe anything will ever happen to him because the worst that he can imagine happened long ago when the family exploded apart. I didn't protect him back then, but now I want to make him the boy in the bubble.

To quell my panic I start buying things. At Sears, I get him a two-man dome tent and a flashlight with Duracell batteries. At the grocery store, I buy cans (ravioli, soup, pears, applesauce, beans); boxes (juice, cereal, granola bars); paper (plates, bowls, towels); and plastic (forks, knives, spoons). I go up in the attic and find our camping utensils: a blackened skillet, an aluminum pot, a couple of bent serving spoons. I go to Triple A and get him an auxiliary card so he can be towed if he needs to. I co-sign for a Visa card so he can't run out of money, and I bring home an updated Motel 6 directory so he can call ahead and get a cheap room. He takes it all, but of course lets me know that he would never consider phoning Triple A or sleeping in a motel room.

True to his workaholism, he's doing the madman shift at Econo-foods, and with the leftover hours, he's finishing up work on what his brother now refers to as the Rust Bucket. The car parts have disappeared from the living room, the front porch, the back porch, the garage, the yard, the driveway. He has repaired the clutch. He has attached the new front right panel. He has the brake lights working. He's supposed to set out for the trip on Saturday, but on Friday the car doesn't sound right. He says he's worried and decides to wait until Tuesday morning to leave so he can drive the car back up to school on Monday and have Mr. Hillery listen to it. "Have the timing checked," he adds.

This is when I see a narrow window of opportunity. "Maybe you'd rather take the train to California."

Surprisingly, he doesn't object to this. The window is larger than I thought, so I call Amtrak, find out that indeed he could depart on Tuesday, arrive Thursday. But by Monday afternoon when I get home from work, I see he has the sleeping bag out, that he's packing the camping gear. Mr. Hillery must have assured him that the Rust Bucket will make it.

Very gently I try to persuade him once more to take the train. When he says no, that he's driving and leaving early in the morning, I hug him and say, "If you're a little nervous, that's per-fectly normal. I always get nervous before every trip. You'll do fine." I know I'll worry until he gets there, but I'm proud of him. He has to do this for himself. He has to overcome me.

•   •   •

I make him smoked turkey with Swiss sandwiches, pack apples and cookies, give him my AT&T credit card number, and insist that he call me once a day. I find out that Brad has requested the same thing. *Ah, for once in all these years we are a united front.*

I hug him and tell him I love him. He gets into the car. "You'll do fine," I say again. It's 6:15 A.M. and 65 degrees, and as he backs the Mustang out of the driveway, I choke up, but he doesn't see this. I go back into the house, where it's now just me and the cat since Jordan took the United flight out of Cedar Rapids several days earlier.

He calls that night. He's already in Colorado but doesn't tell me that he's not ready to stop driving yet so I don't know until the next night that he breaks down a half hour after we've talked on the phone. He pushes the car in the dark and somehow coasts down the hill and into a campground in Rocky Mountain National Park. He sets up the tent, but it's cold and he didn't take the heaviest sleeping bag, so he sleeps fitfully because his toes are icy and he's worried about the car. His worst nightmare has come true. But early the next morning, he diagnoses the problem as the fuel pump, about the only part he didn't replace, and phones into the nearest town, Granby, twenty-five miles away, and orders the thing. Then he goes off hiking alone (there's still snow on the ground) in his new Red Wings. The following day (by this time I know what's going on and I'm freaked), he hitches into Granby, starting out before six, gets the fuel pump, hitches back, installs it, and drives off. That next night he calls and says proudly, "I'm in Scofield." Scofield, I discover after I hang up and check the road atlas, is somewhere in the Utah outback.

It's a harrowing trip. For me.

The fourth night, it's very late, eleven, and I haven't heard from him. I'm frantic, and in my desperation, I phone Brad. Marianne answers the phone. "Jeremy!" she shouts. "Is it you?" I can hear that she's upset, too. We talk for a minute and she promises to phone me the minute she hears anything; I agree to do the same.

But I don't hear and though I fall asleep around one, I'm awake at two, three, and four. It's not until hours later that I hear that he arrived at Brad's only forty-five minutes after I'd talked to Marianne *and no one there suggested that he call me!* So much for the united front.

But he made his passage, and I sing his praises to all my friends, to my coworkers, to my parents, my sister, my brother. What a kid.

I'm cleaning the house. Finally. I've let it go for months, except for the basics—the dishes, the laundry, the bathroom—so there's dust everywhere, and papers stacked all over the dining room table. I'm going through everything—making decisions on what to save and what to toss. I'm also giving things away—clothes no one will wear, old coats, boots, books, including the Hardy Boyses and the Laura Ingalls Wilderes. I always know when it's the end of another era because I have the uncontrollable urge to be organized, to scale down my possessions, to prepare for what the new era will bring, to grieve what I'll never recover from the past. I'm approaching another turning point: I am finally launching one child.

After I finish in the kitchen and the dining room, I go into Jeremy's room, which is downstairs, off the living room; it's the room I put him in when I realized I had to separate the boys. The place is a pit: everything lands on the floor—clean clothes, dirty clothes, mail, books, pens, his RollerBlades, his racquetball racquet, an empty Mountain Dew bottle, a crumpled corn chip bag. Why couldn't I have done a better job teaching him to keep his room clean? "You can't do this with a college roommate," I hear myself telling him. "It's inconsiderate. Who wants to live in someone else's trash?"

Despite the mess, the room is stark. (Must be my fault.) He's not been one to cover the walls. It's a small room with a single bed, a desk, a chest of drawers, and a long plywood table covered with an old cotton Indian bedspread. His train is underneath—the N-scale. He hasn't worked on it for a few years now, never finished the elaborate mountains and tunnels he'd once spent months planning. When he returns from California in the Mustang, we'll have to decide how we're going to store it.

He's leaving home. Is he ready? He's eighteen and I couldn't do it all. I've made lots of progress, traveled billions of miles from where I'd once been—maybe if I had just one more year with him. The grief is always there, at the back of my throat.

With Jeremy in the dorm, the house will be a bit more quiet— just Jordan and me and the cat. Jordan, who despite his very good grades, watches too much TV, is a procrastinator, doesn't clean his room either, leaves banana peels and dirty socks on the living room floor, plays his music too loudly. I'm sure I'll be on him for something. I'm sure I'll still wake up at 3 A.M. worrying.

The dust is making me sneeze. I decide to go out for a walk, but before I do, I go into the bathroom to wash the dirt from my hands, to splash cold water on my face. As I reach for the towel, I catch my reflection in the mirror. My face is changing, there is no getting around it. Suddenly I'm staring at this woman in the glass, this woman who is twenty years older than when she married Brad. All of it is right there in her face. It's all a part of her now—the jobs, the drugs, the moves, the travel, the worries, the laughs, the marriage that didn't work out, the years spent raising two sons alone—it's who she is. She can't go back. She made some terrible mistakes, but hey, she did some things right, too. So she should drop the guilt. Start forgiving herself. After all, she's got a couple of great kids. They don't drink, they don't do drugs, they think, they're adventurous, when they set their minds on something, they go after it.

He is going after it—I can see it on his face. It's 6:15 A.M. He's already loaded the car and given his mother the obligatory hug. There are no dull eyes in this picture, no chapped lips. We are standing outside the front door. He towers over me. He says good-bye and I say don't forget to call. A smile forms on his mouth, around his eyes, just before he takes a joyous leap off the porch, bounding over three steps in one graceful, long-legged stride.

He is off. Behind the wheel of the rebuilt Mustang, he is as happy as I have seen him. He is free. I can't help smiling too.

He has released us both.

VALERIE MONROE

9)

Feet

I WAKE UP one Saturday morning to seven guys in boxer shorts wandering around my living room: my son is celebrating his twelfth birthday with a sleepover party.

Soon after, I stand at the stove making pancakes, for an hour, nonstop. The boys, in their boxers, and shirtless, crowd around the kitchen table, shouting compliments and encouragement at me as they eat: "Great cooking! Best pancakes I ever had! More where these came from!" One large box of Bisquick, two quarts of milk, and a half-gallon of orange juice later, they're full.

They're only twelve, a couple of them not even, and yet most are as tall or just a bit taller than I. In some ways they're peculiarly feminine: at my height, their shoulders not yet broadened with the promise of manhood, their voices almost exactly the same timbre as mine. A dark down graces an upper lip or two, but it doesn't look at all manly; rather it makes them look like changelings, like little boys taking on the soft, fleecy characteristics of baby animals. Their faces are still round; some of them—my son among them—don't even have real noses yet, only those puggy little protuberances with the round nostrils. But they all have feet. Real feet.

One of the boys—one of the large ones, nearly as tall as I, but still showing the sweet, padded cheeks of childhood—trails a foot-long shoelace wherever he goes. Why is that shoelace so long? I wonder. When I begin to feel sure that he will trip on it, I offer to tie it for him. Tying a child's shoelaces is something a mother gets used to; I haven't done it in a while, but as I kneel down, I recall that familiar feeling of parental servitude and competence I so much enjoyed when my son was smaller. No matter how many mistakes, big or small, I might have made in raising him, both he and I knew that tying shoelaces was one thing that I could do unfailingly well. This large boy, my son's friend, sticks out his foot in the comfortable way children do when they're submitting to the shoelace-tying procedure; on the face of it, everything seems normal. But when I gather the laces in my hands and look down at the boy's foot, I see not a child-sized sneaker, but a mammoth, black-and-white leather production of edificial proportion.

"My god, D., what size shoe do you wear?" The boy seems surprised by my question, or at least by my awestruck tone; he seems concerned that he supply me with the correct answer, as if I were giving him a pop quiz.

"Ten," he says quickly, and then, probably remembering his last trip to the shoe store, "No, no, I'm wrong, eleven." I look at the giant shoe from where I kneel, then up at the boy's delicate prepubescent face, and back down at the shoe again. It might as well be a hoof I kneel at, goatish, coarse, and bony, or the rubbery, webbed, splayed-toed foot of a duck, for all it seems to have to do with the boy above.

My son's feet are not yet quite as big as my own size nines. He has his father's feet, beautiful, long, and perfectly shaped. But he hates them. He says he thinks they're ugly, though he doesn't know why.

"They're lovely," I tell him, rubbing his feet as we sit on the living room couch. I cradle one of them, brushing my hand over the sole, remembering the infant soles, pink and silky, I held in my hand twelve years ago. Remembering how I used to hold his feet and nibble his toes, one foot, then the other. Suddenly I lift his foot and kiss it. A light kiss, not tentative, but discreet. Did I think he wouldn't notice?

"Oh, God, Mom, disgusting!" my son cries, pulling his foot away. "How can you do that?"

"It's *your* foot, honey," I tell him, as if that explains everything. For me, it does.

It's Christmas Eve, about a month before my due date, and my husband has somewhat reluctantly agreed to celebrate the way I want to: we'll dine on rib roast, roasted potatoes, and a special bottle of red, while watching Alastair Sim in my favorite movie rendition of *A Christmas Carol*. We've set up a makeshift table in front of the TV, and I, especially, huge as I am, try to pretend that we are a happy couple, joyfully anticipating the arrival of our firstborn. But facts are facts. Though my husband and I lived together for nearly two years before we conceived, we don't really know each other very well. Worse, *we know* we don't know each other. This pregnancy came as a delightful surprise to me; to him, an alarming one. He doesn't feel ready to have a baby, he says, he wishes we could have waited a little longer. Though as my belly expands, he seems to grow more used to the idea, the knowledge that there will be three of us very soon is disquieting. It seems surreal, as we sit here eating roast beef and watching TV, that there is actually another person—very present, but unseen—in the room with us.

Finished eating, I lean back to allow my food to move from my throat to my chest, which is about as far down as it seems to go. The scratchy black-and-white picture flickers in the darkened room. Alastair flies through the night sky, snowy hair and dressing gown streaming, his face frozen in abject petrifaction.

"I love this part," I murmur, taking a sip of wine. I balance the glass, holding it lightly by the stem, on my mountainous stomach. My husband doesn't get it, doesn't feel the terrifying sense of impending doom or revelation. He glances at me sideways. At that very moment, the moment of his glance, something phenomenal rises up out of me, out of my deepest insides, and, with a mighty jolt, kicks the wineglass off my belly.

Doom or revelation, I'm not sure which, but my husband suddenly gets it.

"What was *that?*" he says.

I'm mopping up the spilled wine with a paper napkin. "I think it was a foot," I say.

My husband's clothes hang in his closet like a dead man's, undisturbed, a rebuke against the life I thought we were going to have. His shoes, suede oxfords, elegant leather lace-up boots, unoccupied, seem to belong to someone else, some other man who had shopped for them and admired them, and wore them confidently.

Our son is a year and a half, and my husband's identical twin brother has committed suicide. He has been addicted to drugs, has tried, unsuccessfully, to stop. One night in a terrible, ragged despair, he runs into the path of an eighteen-wheeler. Soon afterward, I discover that my husband is addicted, too. It becomes clear that he wants to join his brother, that the lure of drugs has become far more powerful to him than his wife and son. He leaves us for days at a time, getting high, baiting death. While he's gone, I imagine the phone call—"Hello, Mrs. —? We've found your husband. . . ."—try to imagine what it would be like to raise our son without a father.

On one of the dreary winter evenings my husband is out, I prepare dinner for Reid—nursery food, a lamb chop, boiled potato, broccoli—my thoughts always spinning into the future, what am I going to do next, what next? Reid has just disappeared into my bedroom and it is suspiciously quiet.

"Honey?" I call. "Baby? What are you doing?" I leave the stove and head toward my room. Down the long, shadowy hallway he slowly comes, dragging his feet in his father's big black shoes. Moving along requires a lot of work: he clutches a large, padded ski glove in one hand, a folded umbrella in the other. It is one of those Kodak moments, and it brings me to my knees. Every happy thing it might have symbolized is subsumed by the nightmarish haze of the circumstances of my marriage.

"Oh, honey," I say, evenly at first, trying not to show my son what I feel, "not your daddy's shoes." Then, I can't help it, I'm crying, "Please, baby, don't wear your daddy's shoes."

We are standing on the beach in Spring Lake, New Jersey. Even at the water's edge, with the cool, silvery sea foam washing over our toes, popping and sparkling as it recedes, it's hot; the damp seaside air feels thick and heavy. Reid is not quite three, and round, round all over. He wears a tight, stretchy blue-and-white-striped bathing suit with square, boy-cut legs that grab the rolls of fat around his thighs. His solid little belly balloons over the suit's drawstring waist. He's struggling to maintain his balance in the sand, which floods and shifts as the water licks our feet. Holding his hand to keep him up, I can feel the powerful pull of the sea tugging us toward the water. Another little boy, no more than five, skitters up to us, a sandpiper in neon bathing trunks, and takes a stand beside me.

"Hi, sweetie," I say. "Having fun?" The boy glances all around, at the crowded beach behind us, the huge, gray ocean floating ahead, down the long stretch of sand, left, right, as if he's plotting where to hurry to next. But his quick eye falls on my son, the most interesting thing, at this moment, on the beach. He points excitedly at Reid.

"Why his feeder surround?" he asks. I glance down to where he points.

"Why his feeder surround?" I repeat, looking hard, trying to make sense of his question.

"Yes!" says the boy, pointing emphatically. And then his words break through, with the sudden clarity of an image in a find-the-hidden-picture game.

"Oh!" I say, laughing. "Why his feet are so round!"

Only partly buried in the wet sand, perfectly round indeed, are Reid's chubby feet, toes clenched so tightly that they look like two little fists. I turn back to the five-year-old, but he's gone.

"Well, he's still really just a baby," I say, half defensively, grasping Reid's hand a little tighter. "All babies have round feet."

One recent afternoon while Reid is at school, I steal into his room and sit on the side of his bed. Furtively, I slip my narrow foot into one of his sneakers. Aha! Just as I'd hoped! Too small! I clomp across the room and back, happy to be the ugly stepsister, relishing the feel of my toes curled hard against the shoe's front end. Its unyielding smallness seems to defend my son's innocent, magnificent youth. I pry my foot out of the sneaker, sit back on the bed, pluck absentmindedly at his blanket. All at once, for no reason I can put a name to, my eyes sting and hot tears slip down my cheeks.

Why should I care how big his feet are? What do the size of his feet have to do with who he is, or who I am in relation to him?

After the initial shock of delivering a creature with a penis attached, my son became to me just a baby, an uneroticized, delicious, milky human confection. I would not have called him a boy baby any more than I would have ordered a male crème brûlée. The particulars of his boyness, aside from the aforementioned attachment, were never especially striking or remarkable to me. What was remarkable, and is still, is the size of him, from the dainty, pale and puckered, slightly underripe newborn with a head the size of a grapefruit to the gangly creature, bangs falling into his eyes, who takes up the whole length of the bed he once was too little for. But now his increasing size begins to suggest something else: a change in aspect, a transformation for which I have no template.

Since he was very small, my son and I have sat on the sofa

and measured our feet against each other's, sole to sole. At first, his feet came up only to my instep. Could I imagine, no matter how old Reid got, that his feet would one day be larger than my own? It seemed he would have to be an entirely different person—some version of my son, but not one I could conjure up. What voice would go with his size 10's? What legs?

Keeping apace with his feet, his sneakers grow larger and larger. They bode a striking metamorphosis—every six months now, he sheds them like a pupa.

Opening the door into the darkness of his bedroom as I go to wake him early one morning, I trip over them; he has left them in the doorway, where he'd kicked them off the night before. The path to his bed—once clear enough that I could sleepily make my midnight way to his side to comfort him after a bad dream—is now cluttered and unsafe. His sneakers are land mines, dangerous, unpredictable.

"Don't leave your shoes there, honey," I tell him, scuttling them to the wall as I leave his room. But he doesn't care. He doesn't know that I come into his room after he's asleep, lean over him still, the way I did when he was an infant, breathing in the dense, sweet, humid odor of the back of his neck, trying to guarantee that sense-memory forever.

Reid's first sneakers, bought the day he heaved himself up off his diapered behind at ten months and started walking in a kind of drunken lockstep: blue canvas with white rubber half-moon tips. They fit in the palm of my hand. No bigger than doll's shoes, and no more worn-looking. The pebbled soles never lost their clean, beige patina. But how those sneakers emphasized his new mobility! He had been wearing little corduroy booties with plastic nonskid feet; even when he was fully dressed, his slippers—like a smoking jacket over trousers and a dress shirt—seemed to root him to home. The finished, sturdy look of his Keds suggested that he would soon be moving on to more rugged terrain, and soon he was: the lobby of our building, the street, eventually the playground. In his first pair of sneakers, he had officially entered the society of the upright.

I saved those navy sneakers, and only one other pair, the last that were no bigger than my hand. They were canvas high-tops, multicolored orange, yellow, and blue, and very beat-up and decrepit-looking by the time my son grew out of them. The puffy tongues lolled to the side, like some worn-out dog's, and the laces, broken and frayed, were knotted only halfway up. They were clownish, these shoes, whimsical, goofy, and Reid played hard in them the year he was three. He wore them to preschool, scuffed them on the slide and the playground's rough rubber matting; he painted in them, learned how to square dance, and even got married in them to his favorite preschool friend, the bright-eyed and vivacious Nicolette. Their wedding photograph, a hastily taken three-by-five, radiates the ebullience of their special moment as they sit side by side on small wood chairs, Nic resplendent in a pink tutu, paint-spattered T-shirt, and a bright plastic lei, Reid, appropriately formal in a dark turtleneck, jeans, and plaid snap-on bow tie. Oh, and those sneakers. They're holding hands and smiling to beat the band. What have they discovered? The deep, serious pleasure of a good joke.

"Mom," Reid says casually, as I'm walking him home from school, late in his sixth-grade term. "My feet hurt."

I have heard this many times when the prospect of walking a couple of city blocks sounds to him like the most daunting task, when the fact that I decline to hail a cab to carry us from Twenty-third to Twenty-ninth seems like a cruel refusal. The way I deal with the painful-feet complaint is by exploring it, rather than denying it. This makes me feel like a creative, competent mother.

"So, where do they hurt?" I ask, buying time and ground. "Is it like an ache, or a pain? Is it in your instep? Do you know where your instep is?"

Reid doesn't especially care. "No," he tells me, "my toes hurt. My toes hurt because they're crammed up against the end of my shoes. Ma," he says, "I think my sneakers are too small." I notice that he seems to be limping. Hasn't he been limping, slightly, for weeks? Why didn't I ask him about it? My mind races, trying to remember when I last bought him shoes. I can't recall. I flip through the seasons, picturing us at the shoe store first in T-shirts—no—then sweaters—no—then our heavy, winter down parkas. No! How long has it been?

Standing at the curb, arm in a stiff salute, I promise to buy him new shoes as soon as possible, maybe even tonight, after supper. His sneakers look pathetic to me now, grazed and bald at the front where the dark fabric's worn away, the heels run-down where the sidewalk's taken a bite out of them. He's obviously a poorly cared for child—just look at his hair! When was the last time *that* boy saw the inside of a barbershop? The dentist's office? His pediatrician's?

Back home, Reid kicks off the pinching, offending sneakers and, sighing loudly, vigorously rubs his toes. As I mark the calendar to make appointments for his haircut and a dental checkup, I wonder what it would have been like to have had two children, three, or more. How would I keep track of who was ready for the next size? Would I even try? With a swarm of children, would it matter to me that one, in shoes too small, was limping his way out of childhood?

I see them in a crowded shop window, in a forest of toys: baby dolls luxuriously swathed in pink and blue flannel buntings, stacks of wooden handcrafted puzzles, candy-colored rubber balls in pastel-painted wire baskets, alphabet board games, yellow rubber duckies of every size, hand-knit ski sweaters for people no bigger than a ski boot. The old wood floorboards creak as I make my way into the store, through the maze of caps and bright little slickers and other adorable pint-sized paraphernalia. A lone salesgirl, sitting near the old-fashioned cash register and carefully sorting zebra- and leopard-print infant socks, looks up at me serenely.

"Those green wellies in the window?" I say, gesturing back toward the door. "Do you have them in a size three?"

She slips off her high stool. "I'll see."

A moment later she is back, carrying a white shoe box. "Here we are," she says, handing it to me. "Have a look."

I take the boots out of the box and set them on the counter. Two pairs of bulging froggy eyes stare at me with a curiously smug expression, as if they know they're too cute to resist. They are.

"Wow! Cool!" Reid says, pulling them on when I bring them home. He sits on the floor and tucks his jeans into them carefully. Then he strides around, looking down. I think it is maybe the cutest thing I have ever seen. But the more Reid looks at them, it seems, the more conscious he becomes of how they look on him.

He stops striding. "Mom," he says, "why do these boots have eyes?"

I feel something slipping away. "Well . . . because . . . because they're supposed to look like frogs. And they're rain boots, and frogs live in the water, so there's that frog and water connection. . . ." Wanting to remain upbeat, I suggest Reid remove the boots since it isn't raining, and he can wear them on the next wet day. "They're even waterproof!" I tell him cheerfully. But I can see, as he pulls them off, that he's skeptical.

He wears the boots for a couple of months, uncomplaining. On a first-grade class trip that requires tramping through some soggy woods, he rests happily on a large rock, eating a bagel and swinging his froggy feet. After that, we have a long spate of fine weather. The boots seem to migrate to the back of the closet. Then one rainy day when I pull them out—"Hey, look, honey! Your froggy boots!"—he puts his foot down.

"*No way*," he says.

•   •   •

My husband's recovery from addiction and depression is slow, and marked by setbacks. But he is coming to life, and he is beginning to enjoy his son. In the spring and fall he likes to take Reid to a seaside retreat in South Carolina. My husband goes there to relax and meditate, to remind himself of a powerful spiritual connection he once felt before his brother died. He has taken our son there a couple of times before I join them. It's curious to think about what they do together; my husband is not, was never a playful man, and I find it difficult to imagine how they pass the time. But once there, my son shows me around the pristine, lovingly tended grounds.

"Here's the game room, Mom, where Dad and I played Ping-Pong," he says, opening the creaky screen door and pointing inside. Coming in from the bright afternoon sun, the room is dark and musty, but I can make out the shape of a Ping-Pong table and a couple of armchairs. Reid pulls me back outside, down a couple of steps, and leads me, trotting after him, toward a grassy play area. "And over there's the basketball court," he says, "and the jungle gym, and this is the way," he says, pointing ahead to a sandy path, "to the beach. . . ." It's a wonder to me that my son, at five, is familiar with a place I'm not, familiar enough to lead me around. The staff at the retreat know him, greet him by name, and he, with a mature, easy wave, greets them back.

One afternoon, returning from a solitary walk, I find a note taped to the porch door of our bungalow. *We're at the lagoon cabin*, it says, so I make my way down a wooded path to the lake. My husband has spoken about meditating in this cabin, about how he has found a measure of serenity there, and why it has become, for him, a special place at the retreat. I have tried to imagine the pain he felt over his twin brother's death, tried to understand his anger, his isolation, and to accept the fact that I could neither save him from it or even help him through it. He had to find his own way. That is what the cabin represents to me: it is one of the places where my husband began to find his way.

The shingled roof of the small cabin and the screen door are dappled golden with late afternoon sun. As I approach, I can see that inside the cabin it's already dusk, though a pale light glows around the windows. Two silhouetted figures, an adult and a child, sit on the floor, cross-legged, facing away from the door, side by side and very still. I recognize them, of course, as my husband and son. They are just sitting together, unmoving. Then my husband silently reaches over and puts his arm around our son. I think he is whispering something. Reid leans in closer to him, and they remain like that while I stand watching from the path.

On the doorstep are two pairs of shoes, carefully placed side by side: two pairs of slightly worn sneakers, large and small. I stand outside the cabin, looking at the figures within, thinking about the past, daring to entertain expectations for the future. Gradually it becomes too dark to see inside the cabin, but a weak yellow light continues to bathe the front step. No shadow falls on those sneakers yet, an emblem of sad history and hope. I turn from the cabin and walk toward the beach, almost sure, for the first time, that my son will have a father.

"Hey, Mom, Dad, listen to this," Reid says, emerging from his room. He is reading a book I gave him about puberty. "Some people think if a man has big feet, he's also got, like, a big penis. Or big thumbs, big penis, or big ears . . ."

"Pretty silly, huh?" I say. "You know you inherit your body type from your parents, don't you? What does the book say about size? Does it say anything about how unimportant it really is? Because men sometimes make a big deal about it, honey, but for women it's not that, you know, big a thing. In fact, for a woman—"

"Big a thing, ha-ha and thank you very much!" interrupts my son. "I'll just be leaving now." Reading, he walks back into his room. The door shuts behind him with a heavy thud.

A couple of evenings later, as we're getting ready for bed, my husband says that Reid has asked him a peculiar question.

"Oh?"

"He wanted to know how big my feet are."

"What did you tell him?"

"Big enough."

My son's slippers rest on a wool hooked rug by the side of his bed. They have sat there for a week, untouched, like everything else in his room. I try not to go in there much; the sense of emptiness I feel, of something missing, grieves me. It'll be three weeks till Reid returns; I force myself to imagine him having a wonderful time at sleepaway camp, but his letters don't reveal anything. *Dear Mom and Dad,* he writes, *They make us write a letter before we can have lunch. I'm hungry. Love, Reid (your son).*

I wanted him to take his slippers, but he was adamantly particular about footwear. He wore his favorite sneakers and brought along only a pair of blue mesh water shoes, despite my exaggerated warnings about frosty Adirondack mornings and potential mud slides. In a convincing, rather macho display, he insisted he would make do.

I thought of him mornings at camp, gingerly walking barefoot across the cold, splintery plywood floor. Telling myself he'd be glad in the end, I'd considered packing his slippers at the last moment, tucking them into his canvas duffel, where he might find them while he was putting away his things. I had wrapped the slippers in a plastic bag, was about to slide them in, when I was overcome by a strong and remarkably discomfiting feeling. Betrayal.

As I unwrapped the slippers and carefully placed them on his rug, I thought, they're his feet, after all. And step by step, they will take him away from me.

PERMISSIONS

the Michener Foundation, the Rona Jaffe Foundation, and the Massachusetts Council for the Arts. At present, she directs the undergraduate creative writing program at the University of Michigan.

Jewell Parker Rhodes is the author of two novels, *Voodoo Dreams* and *Magic City*, and a nonfiction work, *Writing the Funk: Lessons for Black Authors*. Her essays and short fiction have appeared in *Ms.*, *Seattle Review,* and *Callaloo*, among others. She is the recipient of a National Endowment of the Arts Fellowship in Fiction.

Patricia Stevens is a graduate of Bowling Green State University and the Iowa Writers' Workshop. Her essays appear in both *Minding the Body: Women Writers on Body and Soul* as well as in *The Healing Circle: Authors Writing of Recovery*. She has received the James Michener Fellowship, the Nelson Algren Short Story Award, and has been in residence both at the Virginia Center for Creative Arts and at the Ragdale Foundation. She is the mother of two sons.

Sallie Tisdale is just finishing her sixth book, *Pigs in Blankets: The Problem with Food* (Riverhead Press, 1999). She is a contributing editor at *Harper's*.

Kris Vervaecke is a recent graduate of the Iowa Writers' Workshop in fiction. Her essays have appeared in the Graywolf anthology *Body Language* and in *The Healing Circle*.

Patricia J. Williams is a columnist ("Diary of a Mad Law Professor," *The Nation*), and a Professor of Law at Columbia University. She is the author of three books, *Seeing a Color-Blind Future: The Paradox of Race*, *The Rooster's Egg*, and *The Alchemy of Race and Rights*. She also contributes regularly to *Ms.* and *The Village Voice*.

ACKNOWLEDGMENTS

I wish to acknowledge a special group of supportive guides: Diana Allen, Jo Ann Beard, Marian Clark, Patricia Foster, Jim Kaufmann, Cynthia Miller, Corbin Sexton, and Dan Vitale. I would also like to thank Jane Rosenman, my editor, and Gail Hochman, my agent, for their enthusiasm, patience, and thoughtful comments. I am indebted to the mothers and sons whose stories make up this collection.

Printed in the United States
By Bookmasters